I0222738

CHINA'S GRAND STRATEGY

China's Grand Strategy

A Roadmap to Global Power?

Edited by
David B. H. Denoon

NEW YORK UNIVERSITY PRESS
New York

NEW YORK UNIVERSITY PRESS
New York
www.nyupress.org

© 2021 by New York University
All rights reserved

References to Internet websites (URLs) were accurate at the time of writing. Neither the author nor New York University Press is responsible for URLs that may have expired or changed since the manuscript was prepared.

Library of Congress Cataloging-in-Publication Data
Names: Denoon, David, editor.
Title: China's grand strategy : a roadmap to global power? / edited by David B. H. Denoon.
Description: New York : New York University Press, [2021] | Includes bibliographical references and index.
Identifiers: LCCN 2020035210 (print) | LCCN 2020035211 (ebook) | ISBN 9781479804085 (cloth) | ISBN 9781479804092 (paperback) | ISBN 9781479804115 (ebook other) | ISBN 9781479804108 (ebook)
Subjects: LCSH: Geopolitics—China. | China—Foreign relations—21st century. | China—Foreign economic relations. | China—Politics and government—2002– | South China Sea—Strategic aspects. | China—Relations.
Classification: LCC DS779.47 .C476 2021 (print) | LCC DS779.47 (ebook) | DDC 327.51—dc23
LC record available at https://lccn.loc.gov/2020035210
LC ebook record available at https://lccn.loc.gov/2020035211

New York University Press books are printed on acid-free paper, and their binding materials are chosen for strength and durability. We strive to use environmentally responsible suppliers and materials to the greatest extent possible in publishing our books.

Manufactured in the United States of America

10 9 8 7 6 5 4 3 2 1

Also available as an ebook

CONTENTS

PREFACE

DAVID B. H. DENOON

Over the last three decades, no country has received more attention from academics, journalists, and policy analysts than China. The "Rise of China," debates over trade, investment, and technology flows, and China's role in the COVID-19 pandemic have become a staple of international commentary.

In the period from 1990 to 2010, the commentary on China was overwhelmingly positive, noting its rapid growth and transformation into a modern society. The massive fiscal stimulus China undertook in 2008 played a key role in stimulating the world economy, and China gained respect as a manufacturer and assembler of an increasingly diverse range of exports.

Yet, after 2010, international sentiment began to shift. Attention began to focus on China's trade surpluses with the United States, its theft of intellectual property, and its aggressive occupation of atolls in the South China Sea. By 2016 the entire scene had changed: the International Tribunal on the Law of the Sea had ruled that China had no right to occupy territory in the South China Sea, and many of China's trade practices were being viewed as predatory and in clear violation of World Trade Organization rules.

China went from being a savior of international economic growth to being a problem. This has led many analysts to start asking more fundamental questions: What are China's long-term intentions? Will China's economic success be used to fund an expansionist foreign policy? Does China have a grand strategy? If so, what are the key features of that strategy?

We don't know if China has an explicit grand strategy statement like the US *National Security Strategy Report*. As shown in the Appendix to Chapter 1 of this volume, however, China does have an elaborate set of sector strategies, including: detailed social goals; foreign policy objectives spelled out in the rationale for the Belt and Road Initiative; a manufacturing strategy laid out in "Made in China 2025"; an education modernization plan; a cyber security strategy; and a rural revitalization strategy.

Rather than speculate on what might be in China's grand strategy statement, if it existed, we have decided to approach the subject by offering chapters on three functional areas (national security, economic and technological development, and diplomacy) and six regions (Northeast Asia, Southeast Asia, South Asia, Central Asia and the Middle East, Europe, and North America). Also, to give the reader a sense of the variety of perspectives that exist within the spectrum of Chinese policy scholarship, we have chosen authors with a broad range of views.

An additional issue to be aware of is the rapidly changing circumstances surrounding the COVID-19 epidemic. Each of the authors has tried to make their chapters current, as of April 2020, but we are well aware that major changes in the situation could occur between the time of writing and when the book is published. We have thus tried to stick to basic trends that we think will shape Chinese strategic thinking regardless of how a particular policy topic develops.

* * *

Just as this manuscript was going to press, there were two important new developments in US-China relations: the White House published a new *US Strategic Approach to the PRC* and the Chinese National People's Congress decided to change the wording of its security law, tightening control over Hong Kong and the protesters there.

The new White House policy statement indicates a sharp break with the positions of the previous three administrations. The new policy rejects "engagement" as a tool for the US to encourage the People's Republic of China to behave cooperatively. It also endorses direct "competition" as the preferred way to proceed. For its part, China's new policy toward Hong Kong is likely to antagonize Hong Kong residents and all outside powers who had hoped that Beijing would honor its prior commitments to implement the "one country, two systems" policy.

It is too soon to know whether either of these policy changes will create a strong counter-reaction, but the American statement is clearly meant to show that the US is no longer willing to make a series of concessions to preserve amicable relations. Conversely, the Chinese guidelines for security policy in Hong Kong demonstrate that authorities in Beijing are more concerned about maintaining order than they are about preserving the open, market environment.

The hardening of positions on both the Chinese and American sides increases the chances that policy differences could escalate into either confrontation or conflict.

Introduction

DAVID B. H. DENOON

In the past two decades, China became the world's second largest economy, built up the world's largest foreign exchange reserves, established new development banks, created institutions for political cooperation in Asia, became an active member of the United Nations Security Council, and became an important member of the World Bank, the International Monetary Fund, and the World Trade Organization. In addition, China has committed over $1 trillion in loans and grants to over one hundred countries through its infrastructure development program, the Belt and Road Initiative. No other nation-state in the history of the world has increased its profile so quickly and made such a rapid climb on the international stage.

Yet observers are also aware that China has frequently undercut majority views in international organizations, has set up new organizations that it can control when it doesn't agree with prevalent norms in existing organizations, has funded the fastest-growing military budget of the major states, and has frequently chosen to ignore international law when it disagrees with rulings against its behavior (as in the Law of the Sea Tribunal's decision on the South China Sea dispute). Moreover, the Chinese government has facilitated the theft of a massive amount of intellectual property from Western governments and corporations, and has set up a harshly authoritarian monitoring system to follow its citizens and many organizations and individuals at home and abroad.

We thus have a very mixed picture of China's rise. On the one hand, China has dramatically improved the livelihood of hundreds of millions of its citizens and has stimulated economic growth throughout the world. On the other hand, China clearly rejects democratic principles, undercuts many conventions in international commerce, and uses coercive technologies to impose its will on other states.

Given the strength and influence of this brash new actor on the world scene, it is clearly important that other governments and specialists in foreign and national security policy understand China's motivations, operating style, and objectives.

To help us understand this phenomenon, we could assemble a massive data set cataloging Beijing's recent actions; we could analyze several key case studies; or we might try to extract interpretations of Chinese behavior from interviews with Chinese government officials and specialists. Instead, what this volume attempts to do is to assemble leading specialists in the field and have them present competing views of Chinese actions. We have tried to use chiaroscuro, that is, shining a light on the topic from different angles. This uses the resulting light and shadows as a way to illustrate the key features of Chinese behavior.

China's current president, Xi Jinping (2012 to the present) is the strongest leader since Deng Xiaoping (1978–89) and has done more to centralize power in his own hands than any Chinese leader since Mao Zedong. Hence, it is reasonable to assume that Chinese policy initiatives reflect elite decision making but are led by Xi and approved by the small circle of those around him.

The goal of this volume is thus to identify the major policy directions that China has undertaken and to see whether they fit together into a coherent overall or grand strategy.[1] To do that, we have divided the book into two parts: a functional section that analyzes Chinese policy into its national security, diplomatic, and economic components, and then a section that examines six regions of the globe (Northeast Asia, Southeast Asia, the Middle East and Central Asia, Europe and Russia, and North America).

To provide the setting for these chapters, the remainder of this introductory chapter presents a summary of the current debate about China's motivations to give the reader a broad context in which to place this volume. It should be noted that the volume's authors have been selected to represent a wide variety of viewpoints. Chapter 1 and the concluding chapter therefore seek to compare these competing views.

In the decades between 1979 and 2008, China's foreign policy followed the dictum "proceed cautiously and hide your capabilities." This meant that China concentrated overwhelmingly on its internal economic growth and took few actions that threatened its neighbors or directly challenged the major powers.

In 2008, however, three important changes occurred: (1) Xi Jinping became vice president and thus the heir apparent positioned to move into the top leadership role in 2012; (2) the US entered a major recession that reduced its international leadership role; and (3) China was able to avoid most of the 2008–09 global recession by implementing a highly stimulative economic policy. This enabled China to maintain a rapid economic growth rate while most of the rest of the world suffered a major setback.

This combination of events had a profound effect on the Chinese leadership. They no longer saw the US as invincible and recognized that Washington would be preoccupied with the Iraq War and recovering from the recession. This gave leaders in Beijing an opportunity to be more assertive with their neighbors and to challenge the US in select arenas. After 1988, China began occupying atolls in the South China Sea. Then, in 2013, despite President Xi having promised President Obama that China would not militarize its newly acquired atolls in the South China Sea, China began arming seven of them in the Spratly region. In addition to runways for military aircraft, China installed ground-to-air missiles and radars to increase the accuracy of its systems and has harassed Japanese shipping in and around disputed areas in the East China Sea. It also launched the Belt and Road Initiative to extend Beijing's economic and military power into Central Asia, Africa, and the Middle East.

These measures China has taken in the last decade clearly represent a change in tactics on its part. But do they represent a change in strategy? That is the question we explore in this volume. The view being advanced here is that China's actions since 2008 represent a change in both tactics and strategy.

China's Strategic Setting

China has two distinctive and highly advantageous assets: (1) its enormous size, and (2) its land borders with fourteen states. Because of its size, no rational government would currently consider a land invasion of the Chinese homeland. And because it borders so many other countries, China can threaten, or potentially coerce, fourteen other governments simply by moving troops or military assets inside its own territory.

Given these advantages, today, as China considers how to increase its power and influence around the globe, it can focus primarily on raising its profile in regions away from its borders.

This circumstance has led to China's first major strategic decision in the twenty-first century: to recognize that it will be extremely difficult to extend its power eastward into the Pacific Ocean. Although China has rented the island Tulagi from the Solomon Islands to build a port and airfield, and has recently gotten diplomatic recognition from Kiribati and Vanuatu, most of the Pacific still has close ties to the US.[2] Not only do the US alliances with South Korea, Japan, and the Philippines present an obstacle to China, but there is the additional question of how to deal with Taiwan. US territories in the mid-Pacific, as well as the US state of Hawaii pose an additional set of barriers to Chinese expansion. It is thus not surprising that Beijing's early focus in the Belt and Road Initiative was in the areas south and west of China. Most of the states in Central and Southeast Asia are small and ideal candidates for inducements or coercion.

If China's geographic position has fortuitous features, it also has one big disadvantage: four of the countries it borders on are nuclear-weapon states: North Korea, Russia, India, and Pakistan. North Korea has mostly been an ambivalent ally of China, but while India and Russia have been explicit allies at various times, at other times they have been antagonists. Although many Chinese analysts express frustration at dealing with North Korea, and China would face a major dilemma if Pyongyang were to reach a direct rapprochement with the US, there is no question that Russia and India pose more fundamental strategic problems for China. That is why China's military cooperation with Pakistan is so important: it increases the range of Chinese influence and counterbalances India.

At present, Russia and China are on good terms, but neither side considers the current congeniality to be a long-term situation. As for India—the only Asian state that could plausibly counterbalance China—both sides recognize that the present diplomatic niceties are fragile. The Indian government, for its part, does not trust China and in November 2019 decided not to join ASEAN's major trade initiative, the Regional Cooperation and Economic Partnership.

As we proceed through this volume, we keep these very basic Chinese strategic assets in mind and recognize that most of China's military expenditures and energy are likely to go to its south and west.

The Current Situation

The three major issues that dominate China's foreign policy now are: (1) the protests in Hong Kong, (2) trade negotiations with the US, and (3) the coronavirus pandemic.

Although Hong Kong is officially part of China, the 1984 agreement to transfer sovereignty from the United Kingdom to the People's Republic of China guaranteed Hong Kong fifty years as an autonomous region. China's violations of that agreement have precipitated two major protest movements: 2014's Occupy Hong Kong movement and the massive riots of 2019. The recent protests have been more widespread and violent than any in the past. At the time this volume was being written, in the spring of 2020, the COVID-19 pandemic had caused a sharp reduction in the scale of the protests. It is unclear how the standoff between the protesters and the Chinese authorities will end. Nevertheless, the size of the protests, involving millions of Hong Kong residents, and the escalating violence, certainly mean that China cannot dismiss the challenge as minor dissatisfaction with Beijing.

The results of the Hong Kong District Council elections on November 24, 2019 were also stunning. Twice the normal number of voters turned out in those elections, and the pro-democracy candidates won over three fourths of the seats. The pro-Beijing candidates were trounced; the public sent a clear electoral as well as protest signal to Beijing. Legislative Council elections originally planned for September 6, 2020, were postponed because public sentiment would have been hostile to the pro-Beijing candidates.

In certain ways, the current China-US trade negotiations are similar to the 2019 Hong Kong protests. The trade negotiations are meant to address long-standing grievances about unequal market access and Chinese pilfering of Western intellectual property. Despite repeated efforts, the US has been unable to get China to change its behavior. China needs to change its trading practices if it wants to avoid deep ruptures in its commercial relations with the US.

The scale of the current trade imbalances is staggering. In 2018, the US trade deficit with China was $419 billion. Although in 2019 the deficit decreased slightly, to $346 billion, this was clearly because of US-imposed tariffs and China has done little to address the underlying structural reasons for the trade imbalances.[3] (The Phase I US-China Trade Agreement, signed on January 15, 2020, is discussed in Chapter 2).

At this time, it is uncertain whether President Trump can persist in pressing for major change in China's trade policies after the effort taken to get the Phase I Agreement. Many in the American business community, virtually all of the key players and groups in China, and many third countries would prefer to continue with present trade policies. Yet the current direction will further the de-industrialization of the US and allow China the opportunity to dominate global manufacturing for the foreseeable future.

In addition to bargaining with the Chinese, President Trump faced the uncertainty of the impeachment effort in the Congress. Although the Senate did not remove the president, the wrangling over this process may have led China to conclude that President Trump was in a weaker position than he actually was.

Themes of this Volume

Although the authors of this volume were selected to provide differing perspectives on China, there are four basic themes (below) that run through all of the chapters.

1) Because China's rise on the international stage has been so rapid and has affected so many different sectors, many non-Chinese observers have failed to realize the breadth of China's transformation. China is no longer behind the West, for example, in many scientific and military areas. China is actually equal to or ahead of the West in aspects of space exploration, computing speed, and in 5G communication technology.

2) Above all, the Chinese Communist Party seeks to maintain its dominance of the domestic levers of power. However, in the past decade, as the party leadership has become relatively confident of its internal political base, it is now willing to embark on an extensive effort to spread its power internationally.

3) The Chinese leadership would like to absorb Taiwan and spread its influence into East Asia and the Western Pacific region, but US military power in the Pacific and US alliances there prevent it. China

continues a relentless policy of intimidation toward Taiwan and seeks to undermine US links in the Pacific as well. Yet it is still much easier for China to focus its efforts on expanding influence to the south and west in South Asia, Central Asia, and the Middle East.

4) In Northeast Asia, China must confront the complications of dealing with Russia, North Korea, South Korea, and Japan, whereas it faces far less resistance to spreading its power in other regions.

Hence, in this volume, we first analyze how China intends to maximize its strength predominantly through internal policies in the economic, scientific, military and domestic political arenas. We then turn to six specific regions where China has active programs for expanding its sway.

Recent Literature on China's Grand Strategy

Since its founding seventy years ago, the People's Republic of China has had two fundamental strategic objectives: the preservation of its territorial integrity and the maintenance of Communist Party rule. To achieve these aims, China has pursued a grand strategy that has had several distinct variants:

1) Under Mao Zedong (1949–76), China emphasized consolidating its hold on the non-Han areas of the state (Manchuria, Inner Mongolia, Xinjiang, and Tibet) and relied on "People's War" (i.e., guerilla tactics) as its defense doctrine if the country were to be attacked. Mao was willing to pursue radical, autarchic economic policies combined with support for Marxist regimes overseas to reinforce the creation of a revolutionary state. Although China survived a war in Korea and the Great Leap Forward, the Cultural Revolution (1966–76) left the country's economy in tatters.

2) Under Deng Xiaoping, Jiang Zemin, and Hu Jintao (1978–2012), there was a continuing focus on territorial integrity but an emphasis on cooperative relations with the outside world to facilitate economic development. This economically oriented strategy was a phenomenal success, producing the longest and most rapid surge in economic growth ever recorded in human history.

To start, we need to define "grand strategy." A country's grand strategy is its over-arching set of objectives and the means to achieve those aims. This usually entails linking national security objectives with economic and territorial goals. Although most countries have short and medium-term objectives, like economic growth targets and the formation of alliances, grand strategy requires an explicit identification of long-term goals and a linked set of measures to integrate efforts in various fields.[4]

Democracies frequently have difficulty formulating grand strategies because disparate groups within a country cannot agree on priorities. It is usually argued that authoritarian countries, like China, can more easily make such choices. However, most important policy decisions in China are the result of an elaborate brokerage of positions taken by the various ministries and party officials involved.[5]

Nevertheless, in China, when an issue is of particular significance to the political leadership, a "Central Leading Group" is often formed to resolve details of a new policy. For example, in 2012, when hard-liners in the Chinese leadership were dissatisfied with President Hu Jintao's policy on the South China Sea, a Central Leading Group was set up to develop a new policy. The group was led by Xi Jinping who was then vice president. The new hard line developed by the group led to Chinese dominance and occupation in the South China Sea despite frequent protests from the US and many of China's Southeast Asian neighbors.

John Fairbank has ably described China's grand strategy during the dynastic period from 1500 BC to 1911 AD.[6] Protecting the royal court, the capital, and the Han heartland were the central goals. Limiting damage and attacks from the periphery (Manchuria, Mongolia, Xinjiang, and Tibet) were important but secondary. Obviously, during the periods when the Mongols and Manchus conquered China, the strategy was unsuccessful at keeping the non-Han at bay. Yet, for more than four hundred years, the basic strategy worked, and it still has a strong impact on the thinking of the Chinese leaders today.

Given the focus of this volume, it is reasonable for us to start at about the year 2000. This was when the success of Deng Xiaoping's economic reforms was sufficiently obvious that analysts began recognizing that China's extraordinary economic growth would have a significant effect on China's military and strategic choices.[7]

In 2000, the RAND corporation completed a wide-ranging review of China's strategic developments. The co-authors argued that rapid economic growth would lead to a "redefinition of Beijing's strategic interests" and that this could challenge the US in four areas: (1) freedom of action for the US military, (2) limiting economic access in East Asia, (3) limiting US political influence, and (4) reducing the ability of the US to maintain alliances in the region.[8] Although the general tone of the RAND volume was optimistic, the four areas it identified as particularly fraught with challenges have proved remarkably prescient.

Nevertheless, on balance, in the first decade of the twenty-first century, US-China relations were predominantly non-confrontational. The moment of highest tension surrounded the collision of a US reconnaissance plane and a Chinese jet fighter in April 2001. Subsequently, the George W. Bush administration was primarily concerned with its wars in Afghanistan and Iraq, and the Jiang and Hu administrations in China were willing to concentrate on economic growth and on taking the nascent steps toward building a first-tier military. Western analysts of China focused on economic issues and did not, in general, emphasize Chinese military capabilities.[9] In that period, China was following Deng Xiaoping's cautious guidance.

Significant changes in the behavior of the Chinese leadership began to occur, however, after the financial crisis of 2008 in the US. Chinese authorities began to refer more frequently to weaknesses in the US economic system and China began to challenge it neighbors on territorial questions.[10] China seemed more willing to offend South Korea over the Koryo historical controversy, and went even further in harassing Japanese shipping in the East China Sea and Diaoyu (Senkaku) Islands dispute. Some portrayed this as the Chinese seeking a new role on the global stage when the US was no longer leading.[11] Yet, in retrospect, there is substantial evidence that this period was a key turning point in Chinese policy making. Although Hu Jintao was still president, with Xi Jinping as the number two, Chinese policy began to take a harsher line.

It is thus not surprising that Western commentary on Chinese actions began to take a more critical stance. David Shambaugh's *China Goes Global* was one of the first studies to spell out the change in Chinese aspirations.[12] He noted that China no longer saw itself as just a regional power but as a budding global presence.

Nonetheless, Shambaugh stressed that China had limited capability to project power and that it would be at least a decade before Beijing could challenge other major powers with a blue-water navy. Interestingly, it was only four years later that China formally announced that its goal was to be a true global power by 2049.

In the last half-decade, Western perspectives on Chinese intentions have fundamentally shifted. Most Western observers now see China as planning to vie with the US for global leadership. One variant of this view sees strategic competition between China and the US as a result of impersonal forces that arise when a "rising power" confronts a "leading power."[13] Rising powers don't need to directly confront established powers and leaders can accommodate upstarts if they want. Yet it is hard for challengers to wait patiently and accept the lead of others; and leading states, not surprisingly, find rising states deeply threatening.[14]

Another variant of the "changing perspective on China" view is that the Chinese leadership has consciously misled the West about its intentions. Michael Pillsbury makes this argument in *The Hundred-Year Marathon*, and Kurt Campbell and Ely Ratner make a similar claim in their article "The China Reckoning—How Beijing Defied American Expectations."[15]

The chapters in this volume explore these arguments in depth in an effort to assess China's current grand strategy. To allow readers to make their own judgments about the intentions of the Chinese leadership, we approach the subject from both functional and regional perspectives. The three functional chapters are designed to show how different interest groups and individuals shape policy to deal with their viewpoints. Those three chapters attempt to assess what China's current programs reveal about its long-term objectives. Six regional chapters then analyze Beijing's policies toward specific areas: Northeast Asia, Southeast Asia, South Asia, Central Asia and the Middle East, Europe and Russia, and North America. Hopefully, the combination of functional and regional viewpoints allows us to make balanced judgments about China's grand strategy.

Military

In 2000, no prominent military analyst publicly stated that China had the ability to directly challenge the US. China was seen as being several decades behind the US. A leading specialist at RAND, for example, remarked that "the US could convince the Chinese leadership that a challenge would be difficult to prepare and extremely risky to pursue."[16] In the past two decades, however, China has made massive investments in its military and has implemented an "asymmetric strategy" of concentrating on its strengths and US weaknesses—hoping, in a potential conflict situation, to be able to disrupt American deployments, especially in the Western Pacific.

For much of the past two to three decades, commentary on Chinese military upgrading has focused on Beijing's plans to coerce or invade Taiwan. More recently, however, military assessments of Chinese capabilities have concluded that the Chinese leadership is trying to develop a broad-based military able to directly challenge the US in many theaters, not just in the Western Pacific.[17] Paul Bracken's chapter on the military thus evaluates China's current capabilities and attempts to explain what China's present "order of battle" could do in open warfare with the US. Bracken's chapter also analyzes what current Chinese procurement plans mean for medium-term future capabilities.

Economic and Scientific

The literature on China's current economic policies is vast. Since 2014's Third Plenum of the Communist Party of China, China has had an official set of economic guidelines that call for liberalizing the economy. The stated goals are to increase the use of market forces, reduce central control, and favor the development of the private sector over state-owned enterprises.[18] Those policies, however, have clearly not been implemented, and there is substantial evidence that President Xi Jinping is tightening central control over the Chinese economy. Import protection, programs to extract technology from foreign investors, and subsidies for key sectors (as in the China 2025 program), are all aiding the Chinese government in its push to support key sectors (such as high-tech manufacturing and artificial intelligence).

Moreover, many of China's scientific developments are for dual-use technology. Intelligent machines may be able to transform future warfare, and China has already demonstrated significant technological capability for spaceflight by landing a spacecraft on the far side of the moon.[19] Since many of these scientific advances have immediate commercial applications, the US government has become much more protective of advanced technology developed in the US and is putting restrictions on Chinese firms like Huawei and ZTE.[20]

He Li's chapter on the economic and scientific aspects of Chinese strategy thus links those two fields and shows why they are more closely interrelated than in the past. Although it was not possible, at the time this book went to press, to forecast how the current trade tensions between the US and China will evolve, He Li comments on the outlook for the Phase II trade negotiations, as well.

Diplomatic

During the Deng, Jiang, and Hu periods, China followed a low-keyed diplomatic strategy, often voting against the Western governments in the United Nations but rarely directly challenging them politically. Instead, China repeatedly claimed that it favored "nonintervention in the affairs of other states." This stance was generally explained as Beijing's way of telling others not to interfere in China's internal affairs. As with its military, economic, and scientific policies, the Xi administration has chosen a more challenging diplomatic approach.[21]

Several aspects of Xi's policies are notable. China has actively presented its authoritarian style of government as an effective model for other countries. Recently China has been willing to support Russia and North Korea even when they pursue policies that are anathema to most Western governments. And Chinese diplomats have frequently used their Confucius Institutes for intelligence collection and monitoring Chinese nationals studying overseas. It appears that the Chinese leadership is sufficiently confident of its global position that it is willing to incur criticism while actively pursuing a controversial mix of policies.

* * *

In sum, China has several key assets that make it the only state that can directly challenge American power: physical size, the scale of its economy, the talents of its human capital, high levels of national savings, the sophistication of its IT and artificial intelligence sectors, the breadth of its manufacturing capabilities, and its location bordering on fourteen other states. Despite all of these extraordinary assets, however, China still has a number of key vulnerabilities: poor quality control in manufacturing, high levels of political discontent among minority groups, an oppressive national leadership that spends more on internal policing and control than it does on its armed forces, and a history of coercing its neighbors that has created deep suspicions about its foreign policy.

Our purpose in this volume is first to identify the principal features of China's current grand strategy and then to sketch out how that strategy will affect its policies in key regions of the world. As co-authors, we have different perspectives on Chinese policies, but the overall themes are clear: (1) China aims to be as dominant as possible; (2) Beijing's focus in the next several decades will be on projecting power to the south and west; and (3) China will maintain control of its political and economic system and use its levers of power to maximize its global influence.

NOTES

1 Wang Jisi, a professor at Peking University and someone who often reflects Chinese government official positions, has stated that "anyone who claims China has a strategy is mistaken." See Wang, "China's Search for a Grand Strategy."

2 Cave, "China Is Leasing an Entire Pacific Island."

3 Mutikani, "US Trade Deficit Shrinks Sharply; Labor Market Tight."

4 For a detailed discussion of grand strategy, see Gaddis, *On Grand Strategy*; Kennedy, *Grand Strategy in War and Peace*.

5 Lieberthal and Oksenberg, *Policy-Making in China*. See chap. 2 for an analysis of patterns in decision making.

6 Fairbank, *The Chinese World Order*. See chap. 1 for a summary of common features of China's strategy across different dynasties.

7 Some earlier outside observers saw China's economic dynamism and recognized that it would have a profound effect on the country's strategic posture. See, for example, Overholt, *The Rise of China*.

8 Swaine, and Tellis, "Interpreting China's Grand Strategy—Past, Present, and Future."

9 A mainstream view at the time was evident in Goldstein's *Rising to the Challenge*.

10 One of the more nationalistic Chinese analysts is Yan Xuetong, dean of the Institute of International Relations at Tsinghua University. Yan led the way in criticizing US policies after the 2008 financial crisis. For an example of his recent work, see Xuetong, "The Age of Uneasy Peace: Chinese Power in a Divided World."

11 The World Bank and the Development Research Center of the PRC State Council, *China 2030*.

12 Shambaugh, *China Goes Global*.

13 Allison, *Destined for War*.

14 Of the sixteen cases of rising powers challenging established powers analyzed by G. Allison's Thucydides's Trap Project, twelve led to war. Allison, *Destined for War*, chap. 3.

15 Pillsbury, *Hundred Year Marathon*; Campbell and Ratner, "The China Reckoning."

16 Khalilzad, *The US and Asia*.

17 Harold, *Defeat Not Merely Compete*.

18 For a summary of the debate about central control versus using the private sector, see Kroeber, *China's Economy*.

19 Giles, "The US and China Are in a Quantum Arms Race that Will Transform Warfare"; Dejevsky, "The Space Race is Back On—and is China in the Lead?"

20 Segal, "Year in Review."

21 For a detailed review of China's diplomatic policies, see Sutter, *Foreign Relations of the PRC*.

BIBLIOGRAPHY

Allison, Graham T. *Destined for War: Can America and China Escape Thucydides's Trap?* Boston, MA: Houghton Mifflin Harcourt, 2017.

Campbell, Kurt M., and Ely Ratner. "The China Reckoning: How Beijing Defied American Expectations." *Foreign Affairs* 97, no. 2 (March/April 2018): 60–70.

Cave, Damien. "China Is Leasing An Entire South Pacific Island. Its Residents Are Shocked." *New York Times*, October 16, 2019. www.nytimes.com.

Dejevsky, Mary. "The Space Race is Back On—and is China in the Lead?" *Guardian*, January 3, 2019. www.theguardian.com.

Fairbank, John King. *The Chinese World Order: Traditional China's Foreign Relations*. Cambridge, MA: Harvard University Press, 1968.

Gaddis, John Lewis. *On Grand Strategy*. New York: Penguin Press, 2018.

Giles, Martin. "The US and China Are in a Quantum Arms Race That Will Transform Warfare." *MIT Technology Review*, January 3, 2019. www.technologyreview.com.

Goldstein, Avery. *Rising to the Challenge: China's Grand Strategy and International Security*. Stanford, CA: Stanford University Press, 2005.

Harold, Scott W. *Defeat Not Merely Compete: China's View of Its Military Aerospace Goals and Requirements in Relation to the United States*. Santa Monica, CA: RAND Corporation, 2018. www.rand.org.

Kennedy, Paul M. *Grand Strategy in War and Peace*. New Haven, CT: Yale University Press, 1992.

Khalilzad, Zalmay. *The US and Asia: Toward a New Strategy and Force Posture*. Santa Monica, CA: RAND Corporation, 2001. www.rand.org.

Kroeber, Arthur. *China's Economy: What Everyone Needs to Know*. New York: Oxford University Press, 2016.

Lieberthal, Kenneth, and Michel Oksenberg. *Policy Making in China: Leaders, Structures, and Processes*. Princeton, NJ: Princeton University Press, 1988.

Mutikani, Lucia. "US Trade Deficit Shrinks Sharply; Labor Market Tight." Reuters. December 5, 2019. www.reuters.com.

Overholt, William H. *The Rise of China: How Economic Reform is Creating a New Superpower*. New York: Norton, 1993.

Pillsbury, Michael. *The Hundred Year Marathon: China's Secret Strategy to Replace America as the Global Superpower*. New York: Henry Holt, 2015.

Segal, Adam. "Year in Review: Huawei and the Technology Cold War." Council on Foreign Relations, December 26, 2018. www.cfr.org.

Shambaugh, David, L. *China Goes Global: The Partial Power*. Oxford: Oxford University Press, 2013.

Sutter, Robert, G. *Foreign Relations of the PRC: The Legacies and Constraints of China's International Politics Since 1949*. Lanham, MD: Rowman & Littlefield, 2018.

Swaine, Michael D., and Ashley J. Tellis. "Interpreting China's Grand Strategy: Past, Present, and Future." Santa Monica, CA: RAND Corporation, 2000. www.rand.org.

Wang, Jisi. "China's Search for a Grand Strategy: A Rising Great Power Finds Its Way." *Foreign Affairs* 90, no. 2 (March/April 2011): 68–79.

World Bank and the Development Research Center of the PRC State Council. *China 2030: Building a Modern, Harmonious, and Creative Society* (Washington, DC: The World Bank, 2013).

Yan, Xuetong. "The Age of Uneasy Peace: Chinese Power in a Divided World." *Foreign Affairs* 98, no. 1 (January/February 2019): 40–46.

1

How New Technologies Are Shaping China's Military Strategy

PAUL BRACKEN

China is in a rapidly changing and unfamiliar national security position. Its greatly expanded role in the global economy and its modernized military have produced a sharp backlash. The COVID-19 pandemic has significantly accelerated this response and has led to even tougher reactions to China's policies.

This is most obvious in the United States, where the whole tone of discussion about China has shifted. The whole tenor of views on China in the American Congress, academia, and public has changed dramatically from what it was even three years ago. This shift has driven the formation of new US policies toward China in defense, foreign policy, and business. Other countries around the globe, from the EU to Southeast Asia, are also reevaluating how they deal with China.

Many foreign affairs experts have analyzed this strong reaction to China's policies, and it is the subject of a great deal of reassessment in the world of business as well. These reappraisals are the subject of a number of chapters in this volume.

But there is another aspect to this change. Technology has its own dynamics, independent of international relations or business. The focus of this chapter is on the evolution of technology and what it means for China's military strategy in the context of the more assertive reaction to Beijing that now predominates.

It is useful to say at the outset that this chapter does not debate whether it is politics or technology that is the more important factor in thinking our way through the complex problem of dealing with a more powerful China. In my view, this debate over which is more important is a mug's game that is invariably decided by the disciplinary specialty of the author describing it. Scientists focus on technology. Political scientists focus on politics and international relations. If anything, this debate may reflect the two-cultures split in the US, but it sheds little new light on China's military strategy.

What is more interesting is to analyze how each of these—technology and politics—impacts the other. The interactions between technology and politics are especially important now, because the chance of conflict between China and the US has increased. The strategic environment has become more dangerous in some important ways, and not only because of China's actions. The character of advanced technology itself has contributed its share of the increased danger.

It should be noted that the concern here isn't only with war. It's with the whole array of issues associated with the use of force in peace and war: crisis management, arms races, and nuclear stability. All of these have a new salience in a world order in which tensions between the two biggest powers are openly acknowledged. Moreover, how other major powers (Japan, Russia, India, EU) react to this strategic development with their own technology choices is likely to be a key factor of stability in this second nuclear age.[1]

Advanced Technology and China's Military Strategy

Advanced technology is now the foundation of Beijing's military power. In the Maoist era, it was ideology. Over the decades, China acquired some technology for its armed forces. But they were still based on peasant mobilization. By the late twentieth century, one could speak of a force that was transforming away from this. The focus was on what was left behind, because it wasn't clear what kind of army China was building.

There is now enough clarity to see that China has built a military, and continues to build a military, on technological foundations. It is far more capable of acting outside of its borders, and it is a more effective professional force. Yet this technological revolution has itself become a key source of uncertainty and vulnerability. It raises issues much like those raised in the early nuclear age. There are new uncertainties and vulnerabilities: surprise attack, readiness, and reliance on error-prone warning systems. Add to this crisis management, nuclear arms races, institutional issues, command and control, among many others. These are "new" because the technology is new, and this is the key point. The character of today's military technology is so different from the conventional and nuclear weapons of the Cold War rivalry that they bear as much resemblance to today's situation did as the tanks and planes of the Second World War did to Napoleonic warfare.

One parallel with the early Cold War does remain useful, however, even if the technologies are so different. In the Soviet-American case, it took over a decade to comprehend the new problems the technologies brought with them. In the late 1940s and early 1950s, Soviet and US leaders and their staffs, military and political, did not possess an adequate set of distinctions or a vocabulary to analyze the problems they faced. I would go even further. The two superpowers in the early Cold War didn't understand their own forces. The dangers of an arms race, crisis management, institutional issues, command and control, accidental war—none of these were understood. And that's why this period was especially dangerous.

It took a decade for restraints, tacit understandings, mutual agreements, and organizational changes to develop. Not until the mid-1960s did this happen enough to lower the danger level.

Something akin to this is taking place today, as China and the US deploy new, different kinds of technology. Today's technology is especially dynamic, so the consequences of relying on it are leading to many unfamiliar issues for which no one in Beijing or anywhere else has answers. By advanced technology, I mean AI, cyber, hypersonic missiles, 5G, precision strike, cloud computing, robot weapons, anti-satellite weapons, big data analytics, and so on. China has led the way in these technologies, enabling it to rapidly catch up to the US in business— and in defense. They are foundational elements of Beijing's military strategy—and are thus the central focus of this chapter. How will a military built on advanced technology really behave? Will it actually work? What does it imply for crises and escalation? And, perhaps most importantly, how will China manage a technological arms race so that the arms race itself doesn't become a larger problem than the security it is meant to provide?

These questions define the rapidly changing and unfamiliar situation that China now faces. In part because of China's initiatives in these areas, the US is pursuing a military modernization that also uses these technologies. Russia, India, and others are following suit. Even the EU is taking this road, and is a source for selling advanced technologies, something that raises many concerns.

But the changes and unfamiliar terrain facing China don't end with these questions. This must be emphasized, because China's advanced technologies are not replacing nuclear weapons. China is set to double the size of its nuclear forces over the next decade.[2] If advanced technologies did substitute for nuclear weapons it would simplify the situation for Beijing, and for the rest of the world. The military balance could be calculated by comparing only conventional arms, complemented by the new, advanced technologies.

This chapter argues, however, that any such perspective is extremely short sighted and dangerous. It's an example of wishful thinking, like the widespread belief after the end of the Cold War that nuclear weapons would fade into history. Like it or not, we are living in a *second* nuclear age, one that has almost nothing to do with the first nuclear age, the Cold War. Consider the following. China is deploying entirely new kinds of nuclear weapons: on submarines (ship, submersible, ballistic, nuclear—SSBNs), new intercontinental ballistic missiles (ICBMs), nuclear bombers, mobile and hypersonic missiles, and multiple warhead systems (multiple independently targeted re-entry vehicles). This all necessitates a radically different command and control structure than their old deterrent system of a score of unarmed missiles.

Raising the stakes, China is now surrounded by *five* nuclear-weapon states: Russia, North Korea, the US, India, and Pakistan. A nuclear context encases China's Asian security space. Some of these states are "allies," it is true. But they are allies only in a formal, "correct" use of the term. China's nuclear allies may indeed be more dangerous than its enemies. They must be viewed in Beijing as a source of tremendous uncertainty. *Their* crises could become *China's* crises. An all-azimuth nuclear context brings entirely new kinds of uncertainty into China's national security decision making. I see little evidence that it is being analyzed in a sophisticated, serious way in any Chinese doctrinal writings or by think tanks in Beijing.

Washington has declared that it is in a long-term competition with China. And so the US has begun its own nuclear modernization, driven by China's buildup, and this adds another source of uncertainty. Beijing has to assess how its military posture will shape the reactions of the US, and of Japan and nuclear India. Just as it took more than a decade for the basics of a stable relationship to develop in the early Cold War, it could take at least as much time for this to develop in the twenty-first century. Because the technologies are now so much more complex, and because there are multiple nuclear powers now, it could take much longer for a stable system to develop. A more intense arms race in Asia is not un-likely. Crises could take on a completely different character. Clearly, the US will respond. This makes arms control much more important for Beijing than it has been in the past, as a way to slow the arms race, or—at least—to slow down its rivals.

To see technology only through a narrow military lens, for improved outcomes in war, misses the most difficult strategy choices Beijing faces. This is what I mean by saying that China is in a rapidly changing and unfamiliar situation. The current US backlash against China is quite im-portant for shaping policy in Beijing. But there's more going on.

Historically, China's national security was shaped by great power ri-valry in a nuclear context. Now, it is shaped by a very different kind of great power rivalry, once again in a nuclear context, but in an entirely new advanced technology context as well.

Where We've Been: A Brief Historical Review

China has changed its military strategy over the years in relation to political and technological factors.[3] Yet two overarching realities frame these changes. First, China has always been the object of attention and pressure from the major powers. Japan, the Soviet Union/Russia and the US have tried to conquer it, keep it down, build it up for their own purposes, or overawe it militarily. China played in the big leagues, so to speak, even when it was weak. It played a skilled hand, wielding a giant army and diplomatic guile, but not much else.

Now, China has substantial economic and technological capability. The major power game continues, but China has a significant ability to shape the rules, and to make others pay if they press too hard against Beijing.

A second reality is that the entire history of the People's Republic, from 1949 to the present, played out in a nuclear context. China could have been—literally—destroyed by Washington or Moscow if it hadn't played the game shrewdly. There is a tendency in nuclear history, as it is written in the West, to overlook this obvious point. The nuclear dangers in Europe and in crises like Berlin and Cuba dominate historical memory, but the view from China was different. The nuclear threats Beijing felt from the two superpowers were up close and personal. In the 1958 Taiwan crisis, for example, Moscow's refusal to promise to back China with nuclear weapons forced China to break off the confrontation with the US. It was a key factor in China's decision to develop its own nuclear force.

At the time, Beijing feared that the US would attack China with nuclear weapons. Top secret studies, now declassified, show that the Chinese were right to feel this way. A nuclear strike actually was considered quite seriously in Washington. Positioning of US nuclear weapons around the Pacific for use against China dominated Pentagon thinking.[4] Unlike in NATO Europe, when it came to dealing with China, there was no such thing as flexible response. Daniel Ellsberg worked on nuclear command and control in the early 1960s. He describes the US strategic intent as—in essence—a devastating nuclear attack on China.[5]

Let me stress something about this nuclear context. China never got into the hypervigilant, hair-trigger, "fail-safe" nuclear alerting that characterized the US-Soviet rivalry. Nor did China have the kind of "mad" arms race like the two superpowers did, with tens of thousands of nuclear weapons.[6] China's nuclear posture was very different.

But the nuclear context that framed China's decision making still played a powerful role. It meant that even low-level crises, and the stability of deterrence during such crises, involved estimates of "where things might go" should the crisis intensify to higher levels of escalation. This is the key point about a nuclear context. It makes decision makers consider what will happen if events don't go according to plan, if the other side makes a surprise move—and makes rocking the boat itself a risky threshold. Crossing it changes the game in a way that goes beyond the immediate issue in dispute. This makes it very different from the picture painted by classical studies of international rivalry in the pre-nuclear era.

For China, this nuclear context also had a multipolar aspect. Beijing was threatened first by Washington, then by Moscow. This is relevant to China's current situation, surrounded by five nuclear-weapon states.

It introduces a very different kind of risk management than in classic military strategy. This is an important point. However complex the Cold War was, as experienced in Beijing, now there are *five* nuclear powers. Rocking the boat is altogether more complicated.

Because technology is so central to China's situation, encompassing nuclear weapons as well as advanced technologies like artificial intelligence (AI), hypersonic missiles, and cloud computing, it's useful to briefly describe China's historical experience from this perspective.

1995 to 2005

In this period, China was transforming its military, modernizing and professionalizing its armed forces. The giant People's Liberation Army (PLA) was downsized, and the freed-up resources were invested in modern warfare. At the same time, China attracted Western investment and technology. Its economic strategy complemented its defense strategy. China was so far behind that a do-it-yourself approach was impossible. It would never catch up without outside technology, education, and business know-how.

Another change China made in this period was a buildup of short-range and medium-range missiles facing Taiwan and along the coast capable of hitting targets in South Korea, Japan, and Guam. One feature of this was the development of mobile missiles. These are very difficult to track, as the first Gulf War of 1991 had shown. China shifted over to mobile missiles very quickly, using Russian technology for its missile TELs (transporter erector launchers).

The "third Taiwan crisis" took place in 1996.[7] Looking back, the political aspects of the crisis, while important, were less significant than the technological ones. China fired four missiles without explosive warheads on them into a sea area southwest of Taipei. These shots were meant to intimidate Taiwan—and failed miserably in this regard.

But the technology told another story. The US Navy analyzed the launches and found that China had dramatically improved the accuracy of its missiles.[8] To the Pentagon's surprise, the missiles had pinpoint accuracy. Somehow, China had figured out how to achieve superior missile precision. This realization sent shock waves through the American defense community.

Later developments in the 1996 crisis were also interesting. China was unable to track the US aircraft carriers sent to reinforce Taiwan's defense. Beijing was in the humiliating position of having improved its missiles, but having no idea where their targets were located. This was an impetus to improve tracking capabilities against mobile targets like ships, which became a high Chinese priority.

Developments on the business front, to attract technology and get it into China, picked up in this period. Broadly speaking, this was successful in that the Chinese got their hands on world-class technologies. But integrating the technology into government, business, and defense was another story. This proved more difficult to achieve, entailing many wasted investments in integrated circuits (computer chips), automobiles, and aerospace. New technologies were successfully brought to China. Getting them into products that could compete in global industries was an altogether stiffer challenge.

2006 to 2016

The most significant strategic development over the 2006–16 period was that China had to be taken seriously as an opponent. Its twenty-year program of military modernization and professionalization started to pay off. It paid off in a way that needs to be spelled out in detail. The underdeveloped military China inherited from the Maoist era was essentially a mass army of peasants. Training was poor, and equipment was restricted to rifles and old aircraft. China lacked the kind of command and control needed to take on a modern enemy like Russia or the US.

By the 2000s, this was no longer the case. In a war with the US, China would have lost. But this wasn't the real issue because, in terms of US and Russian foreign policy, China now had enough military in place to respond to provocations in ways that would have punished an aggressor. China's growing industrial might and its past experience also meant that Beijing could launch an enormous mobilization and engage in a long-term war. China was the proverbial "sleeping giant" the US didn't want to provoke. This reinforced those in Washington who wished to placate China, and to overlook its slow-motion seizure and construction of offshore islands in the South China Sea, a missile buildup that dwarfed anything the Soviets had against Europe in the Cold War, and aggressive probes and "hugging" of US warships in the western Pacific. Few in Washington wanted a confrontation, even one that in some narrow military terms the US likely would have "won."

China's military modernization in this period was, in a strategic sense, beginning to come into focus. It wasn't simply a case of China getting richer and putting more money into the military. The Chinese weren't building more and better tanks and artillery. Rather, they were building a different kind of military, one designed to keep the US out of the western Pacific through the use of advanced technologies to track US ships and aircraft. By the 2010s, it looked like this strategy could actually work, or at least allow China to make things difficult for the US in the region.

China's DF-21 missile came to receive a great deal of attention in the US. It became an iconic symbol of military modernization and was labeled the "carrier killer." Even with no warhead on it—that is, just a nose cone without explosives—it could do immense damage against the big carriers of the American fleet. With its high velocity and angle of attack it could drill through the multiple decks of a carrier and cripple it. On top of those, China was building a network of drones, sensors, satellites, and radars to locate and track these ships.

To be sure, China's military still had many weaknesses in this period.[9] But the growth of its capabilities in so many areas was influencing US policy. Two related national security issues were affecting China's military in these years. First, there was significant increase in nationalism. The term national security is, in fact, two terms. It is national, and it involves security. The effect of nationalism was to create support for a stronger security policy, something that would be useful in foreign policy by presenting an enemy, the US, with a "strong nation, strong army." This, in theory, would intensify Washington's reluctance to contest whatever moves China may make, such as its takeover of islands in the South China Sea in defiance of international law. The nationalism stoked in China was a latent threat—and wasn't something to challenge lightly.

Second, China greatly accelerated technology espionage. Activities here included intellectual property theft, stealing secrets, and the collection of intelligence on US personnel, processes, and other activities.[10] Between 2009 and 2013, a Chinese spy ring penetrated the network of Boeing Aircraft Corporation's computers. The "take" from this collection was immense. It included almost all of the designs and manuals for the C-17 cargo aircraft and the F-22 and F-35 fighters.[11] The full implications of this are not generally appreciated. It gave China extraordinary insight into the operation of America's frontline fighter, the F-35. The F-35 is a joint fighter, meaning it is used by the Air Force, Navy, and Marines. This aircraft is also used by US allies like Japan, South Korea, and Australia. What is often overlooked is how this level of detail exploits America's baroque defense acquisition system. It took fifteen years to produce the F-35, from concept to takeoff. The US is by no stretch of the imagination an agile player when it comes to defense acquisition. In just *two* years, China was able to capture the details for defeating a *fifteen-year* program.

Some Chinese efforts, it must be noted, were legal and open. China's companies, both "private" and state-owned, directed an enormous effort at penetrating Silicon Valley by investing in private equity and venture capital deals. This provided a ringside seat on US technological innovation for the commercial and military sectors.[12] In this period, the Department of Defense and US intelligence services were making their own investments in Silicon Valley. That China could watch this process at close hand from the perspective of the investment committee of a US venture fund is extraordinary and is a credit to Beijing's cleverness.

China also had major business successes in these years. This is an important point because, at the time, many people in the US argued that China was like Russia. Moscow had a vast espionage program and put huge resources into it. But it never really "took." The Soviet and Russian economy, and its military, never modernized. The institutional impediments crippling Russia were too great to absorb the technical information being collected, and quite incapable of establishing a Russian Silicon Valley.

This just isn't the case with China. There are many successes. Two examples demonstrate this crucial point. First, China has now developed the largest and in many respects the most sophisticated automobile market in the world. The Chinese are world leaders in electric and autonomous vehicles, for example.[13] Not only is this a huge global industry, but the competitive factors in automobiles have shifted to advanced technologies like 5G, AI, and machine learning. These same factors go into advanced military systems, as well.

A second area of success has been that China's technology companies are today among the best in the world. China Mobile, Tencent, Alibaba, Baidu, Xiaomi, Huawei, DiDi, and others now have global recognition. They all have enormous research and development budgets in the fields listed above. And they have access to the world's largest market, China, to test their systems, which may the most important advantage in AI. Chinese testing of autonomous vehicles has no restrictions on data privacy, individual protections, and transparency.

In 2016, an AI computer program called AlphaGo, owned by Google, defeated the world's best human player at Go.[14] It is difficult for laypeople to appreciate the significance of this victory of machine over man. It was like a Sputnik shock for China. This is because Go is much more complex than Chess. The AI victory was thus more significant than IBM's Deep Blue defeat of Gary Kasparov in 1997. AlphaGo used an altogether different approach to AI than Deep Blue. It demonstrated that AI could be used to handle extraordinarily complex problems.

For China, this new AI had an especially important potential. It offered a different way to compete with the US. In military terms, it was less a way to improve the performance of existing approaches than it was a strategy that could disrupt existing techno-power advantages of the West. As an added benefit, the new AI would also bring commercial as well as military advancements. There was a massive national program to try to dominate AI, and this led directly to Xi Jinping's *China 2025* program and its national AI initiative.

Where We Are: Branch Point and Backlash

A branch point is a point at which a problem or trend changes fundamentally. Before this point, the problem develops in a particular way. After this point, it develops altogether differently. For China, 2016 marked a branch point. The Chinese had many successes in global business, including in automobiles and 5G, going into 2016, and the strategic concept underlying China's modernization of the PLA began to look like it could work.

Then came the backlash. Before 2016, it was reasonable to draw a straight-line projection of China's growing economic and military power. There were expert debates over the growth rate, access to China's markets, financial liberalization, and how close Beijing was getting to Moscow. But these things could be covered by reasonable high-medium-low estimates of different variables.

As in every social system, if developments go too far in one direction, opposing forces build up to pull it in another direction. In the 2010s, many voices warned of China's unfair business practices, espionage, and rising military capacity. In governments and boardrooms across the world, it became clear where this process would go if it continued unchecked.

Something had to give. Either China was going to change voluntarily—and this seemed unlikely—or other countries and companies were going to have to do something to stop the military and technology buildup.

The peculiar fact of Donald Trump's election in 2016 smashed the widely accepted story line of American progress since the end of the Cold War. The Trump administration was more amenable to a big policy shift against China than previous administrations had been. Regardless of the distinctive features of the Trump White House, any administration coming into office in 2016 or afterwards would have had to switch gears away from business as usual in dealing with Beijing. There were just too many examples of China's espionage, intellectual property theft, spying, unfair business practices, military buildup, and recalcitrance in dealing with big problems like North Korea's nuclear weapons.

So US policies fundamentally shifted. China's military buildup was called out and made a centerpiece of a US strategy of long-term competition against authoritarian regimes. There was a crackdown on China's technology transfer of intellectual property and on its cyber espionage. Key business takeovers by China's companies or those thought to be aligned with them were blocked in the areas of semiconductors, financial services, and technology.[15]

A straight-line projection of China's advances in business and technology in the 2000s suggested an unstoppable global dynamo, one that would dominate global automobiles, communications, and manufacturing. This view, however, exaggerated China's strengths, and surely overlooked China's weaknesses. China's centralized, top-down direction of industry and technology had succeeded. But inside China, this created a crisis of success. This is the argument made by China scholar and business expert William Overholt.[16] He argues that the strategy that brought China up in the world economy cannot deliver comparable growth in the future. Nor will the successful Chinese strategies of the 1990s and 2000s effectively deal with China's huge internal problems of environmental degradation, infrastructure, or of a growing middle class demanding more rights. Pressure is growing in China for solutions to all of these problems.

On the business side, China's central control had worked well for quickly entering new industries. But it worked less well as economies matured and grew more complex. The need to meet market needs required a freer market, and this clashed with the political structures of the Communist Party, overcentralized government agencies, and bankrupt but politically powerful state-owned enterprises. A corrupt crony capitalism was the inevitable result.

Overholt's argument that China faces a "crisis of success" at home— that a straight-line projection of China's 1995–2016 growth into the indefinite future wasn't accurate—is important. It suggests inevitable self-correcting changes regardless of any outside resistance by the US and others to derail China's growth. It may even suggest that a significant decline in performance would result, as measured by GDP growth and employment.

But on top of China's own contradictions, there *was* a backlash from abroad, and it greatly compounded China's internal difficulties, which were peaking independently of this in 2016. The backlash put major obstacles in China's plans, and brought attention to its dangerous behavior. It also stripped away the veil that surrounded Beijing's high-tech military strategy for turning the western Pacific into a Chinese lake.

The New Sources of Complexity in National Security

China faces a national security situation that is highly dynamic and quite different from what it has faced for the past twenty years. It is unfamiliar in that the country has little experience to draw on for dealing with it, and since the issues themselves are so new, their policy implications are not yet clear. The key issue here is complexity, and how China will deal with it across many sectors. It is important to detail what these complexities are. They can be analyzed in five clusters.

- Advanced technology
- Nuclear forces and advanced technology
- Extended conventional operations
- US counter-strategies and arms races
- Arms control

Advanced Technology

China is building an enormously complex network whose purpose is to track mobile targets. The purpose is to locate and respond to US ships, submarines, aircraft, drones, and satellites. This network monitors fixed US bases in Japan, South Korea, Guam, and elsewhere. But the distinctive new emphasis is on reconnaissance of mobile targets.

In order to track moving assets, a reconnaissance system is needed that collects multiple sensor data types and fuses the information into an operational military picture. This collection system, in turn, is linked to a strike force of Chinese missiles (conventional, hypersonic, and nuclear), aircraft, submarines, and drones that receive the target locations and adapt to it. That is, they update target location and select the best warhead or cyber weapon for the task given their orders.

Here, by the way, is the significance of hypersonic weapons that China is investing in. These weapons travel at five times the speed of sound. They get to the target very quickly, and that is the point. For warfare against a target set in motion, the "seeker"—here China—requires very low-latency weapons. Otherwise the target in question will have moved. Low latency is also a consideration in 5G technologies. They offer faster communications within networks in which to coordinate strikes.

Many different kinds of sensors are used to "feed" this system. Radar, satellites (infrared, ocean surveillance, electronic, photographic), and also drones and electronic intercepts and cyber penetrations of enemy computers and electronics. A staggering amount of data must be processed in real time if the system is to track moving targets.

The reconnaissance challenge is especially complicated because, at the same time, US forces are moving and actively trying to hide. They can interfere with China's tracking system through deception, stealth, and cyber attacks of their own against Chinese collection systems.

This collection requires super-large databases, cloud computing, and data analytics to store and process the massive amounts of data involved. And the data sets are common to the military side of the network. That is, they are used to assign weapons to targets, inform China's ships when a US satellite is passing overhead, and advise information warfare teams in China of the need to disrupt particular information flows.

By themselves, these reconnaissance technologies are not enough to do the job of tracking moving targets. The truly difficult challenge is the fusion of information streams that can automatically direct certain actions to take place. The only way to tackle this is to use AI to direct and coordinate the various elements of the collection and strike systems, that is, to link the reaction forces of the PLA to potential targets.

This is the reason for China's extraordinary interest in AI.[17] Only AI can handle the complexity of these tasks. A simplified example may give a sense of the intricacy of the problem. China has to coordinate drone-based sensors with its own submarines trailing US ships, and employ land-based radar to locate a US aircraft carrier. It may need to degrade the communication links aboard the carrier, or introduce false targets into its defense systems. At the same time, anti-satellite attacks may be necessary to cut US communications back to headquarters. Ground-based lasers or anti-satellite weapons in space need to be readied and fed the proper information about their target's trajectory. Finally, land-based mobile missiles need to be prepped in case they need to be fired at targeted ships.

No general staff organization can plan such an attack in the face of such a dynamic—moving—set of targets. Against fixed targets, it could. This is what happened in the Cold War, as each superpower was heavily reliant on fixed-site ICBMs. Then, the SSBNs of each side were much harder to track, as were the airborne bombers. In these conditions, where many of the targets were in fixed locations, a staff could come up with a complicated war plan (e.g., the Single Integrated Operational Plan), essentially assigning missiles and bombers against targets that didn't move (e.g., radars) or against slow-moving armies. The same was also true in conventional warfare. It was limited by the range of a radar on an aircraft or by the very limited scan of a passing satellite.

The shift from fixed to mobile targeting is the key characteristic of the technological changes in major power rivalry now underway. And only

AI can have any chance of tackling this complex problem. The human mind simply cannot handle the number of elements and the rapidity of changes. There are just too many "subsystems"—drones, satellites, submarines, hypersonic missiles, China's own mobile missiles, radar, cyber war and espionage—that have to synchronize together for it to work. The *amounts* of data are staggering, and even more important, the *diversity* of data is overwhelming without automated systems like AI to process it.

It's no wonder that AlphaGo captured the imagination of China's technologists. The game of Go comes as close as any to a metaphor for the continuous shifting of power positions of strength and weakness that modern conflict with advanced technology involves. So far, only China and the US have enough technical potential to handle it. But other countries are likely to develop some of these capabilities. And they are also likely to buy it from the US, China, or others.

Nuclear Forces and Advanced Technology

Nuclear modernization adds another layer of complexity.[18] China is not just building a larger nuclear force, but a full triad of bombers, ICBMs, and submarine-launched ballistic missiles for its submarines. They are also developing multiple independently targeted re-entry vehicles and hypersonic nuclear missiles.

China's "triad" is a remarkable historical development, one whose significance few people have understood. Now, *four* countries either have nuclear triads or are developing them. The US, Russia, China, and India are all going down this road. This is quite astounding because it is a reproduction of superpower nuclear force structures circa 1975—but for a world with four big powers.[19] More countries will probably join this club in the future. To say the very least, it complicates world order.

Another very important issue needs to be brought up. Most analysts look at nuclear weapons as a separate category of war that has little to do with conventional war. It is, so to speak, a world of its own, with stability measures and targeting strategies like counterforce and countervalue. Together, these define a separate type of conflict.

But this view is a constructed academic framing of the role of nuclear weapons, ignoring how the revolution in advanced technology discussed earlier upsets Cold War notions of nuclear stability. It is short sighted in the extreme. This is because the extraordinary changes in advanced technology impact nuclear operations.

The hunt for mobile targets driving China's modernization is part of a general technological shift toward a world of hunting fleeting targets that is driving US and Russian modernization as well. Since most nuclear weapons around the world are in fact mobile missiles of various kinds, advanced technology threatens the nuclear forces of many countries, including those of China, North Korea, Pakistan, India, and others.

Another way of saying this is that advanced technologies are making the hunt for mobile missiles faster, cheaper, and better. Mobile *nuclear* weapons are therefore becoming open to attack with conventional, cyber, and nuclear weapons in a way never previously imagined. This engenders new uncertainties having to do with escalation control that almost no one has analyzed. I cannot imagine that China has developed some new framework for it.

But even this technological development doesn't address the complexity that a nuclear context for advanced technology warfare introduces. For one thing, the behavior of highly automated AI systems is especially complex, with many unintended consequences. Recent experience offers multiple examples. Automated systems were at least partly responsible in the Boeing 737 MAX airliner crashes.[20] The US Navy ship collisions in the western Pacific in 2017 arose at least in part from the use of sophisticated automated navigation systems.

AI systems offer many ways to fail. A bad sensor could give a faulty reading—of an attack, for example, when in fact there was no attack. Or a sensor could be taken over and programmed to incorrectly give a reading that everything is working properly, when it isn't. This was what happened when the Stuxnet virus was revealed in 2010 to have infected Iran's uranium centrifuges. This cyberattack was purposefully designed to lull Iran's engineers into not intervening because their meters and control systems indicated that everything was normal, when in fact the rotation of the centrifuges sped up, disintegrating them. Many other failure paths exist that we are only beginning to understand.

In addition, conventional forces now use the same command and control networks used in nuclear operations. This is very different than the Cold War, when a considerable effort was made to keep the two systems separate and distinct. Now, the satellite communication and tracking systems, ocean surveillance sensors, and other networks used to locate enemy ships, planes, drones, and underwater and space targets are also used for nuclear operations. In in China, Russia, and the US, conventional and nuclear command and control systems are merging. Yet most strategic thinking about nuclear strategy dates back to a technological world of 1975 that no longer exists.

Dangerous uncertainties are developing from the increasing use of advanced technology like AI, cyber war, and computer disruptions. What must be understood is that these same systems are connected to nuclear forces.

Extended Conventional Operations

China's strategic push into Southeast Asia and the expanding PLA Navy are another source of complexity. China has ostensible allies in North Korea, Cambodia, and Pakistan. These "allies" could create serious problems for China. By no means can they be considered to be any kind of mutual defense system. Now that China has aircraft carriers that can reach these areas, the whole gamut of conventional war issues emerges.[21] Two of these countries have nuclear weapons. The nightmare possibilities here are not the topic of this chapter. Suffice it to say that China has to consider itself as a target of these countries. It is useful to note that Chinese companies like Huawei and ZTE are building these countries' telecommunications systems, as well as India's. These systems would be critical in a crisis or war.

US Counterstrategies and Arms Races

Another new source of uncertainty facing China comes in the form of—at a minimum—a technology arms race with the US. This is something that could intensify and go off in a number of different, dangerous directions—for China and for the world. Relations with the US have always been complicated, but they are on a path to an entirely new level of complexity. They could spill over into more intense trade wars, business restrictions on Chinese companies, and boycotts of various kinds.

At the same time, US nuclear modernization clearly affects China. For example, the US wants to deploy an X-band radar in South Korea to defend against North Korea. These radars could serve to defend against Chinese missiles, as well, both nuclear and conventional. Another issue for China is how to offset American cyberwar efforts that have recently been invigorated with enormous budget increases and the removal of restrictions on certain operations.[22]

Long-term competition also brings in new and unfamiliar problems. This isn't like the Cold War, when amassing warheads, tanks, and aircraft gave one an advantage. Today, the advanced technologies have to work in a much more integrated fashion. This tight integration can be a hindrance to performance as software, rather than hardware, takes on a more central role. The large number of software stumbles in the corporate world in this regard—at GE, IBM, and Boeing—shows just how complex these challenges are. In short, the new systems might not work. They are subject to catastrophic rather than gradual failure. Moreover, such failures can be produced by enemy cyberattacks. In extremis, attacks could strip away most defenses, making one vulnerable to conventional attack or nuclear blackmail.

Arms Control

Arms control is very much out of fashion these days. For decades, China has refused to be drawn into arms control talks or treaties with the US and Russia.[23] Nor did either Washington or Moscow want to bring China in. Doing so would have detracted from their unique "superpower" status as the largest nuclear-weapon states.

But we are seeing changes in this position, and it seems likely that China itself will have to embrace a more active arms control stance, if for no other reason than to try to restrain US nuclear modernization. In 2019, the US justified its exit from the Intermediate Nuclear Forces Agreement in part by declaring that the treaty didn't restrain China from building more than 2,000 missiles on its coast.

It seems clear that we are moving into a multipolar nuclear world, whether or not anyone wants to admit it. In this world, major powers have an interest in restraining further nuclear buildups by their rivals. Related to this is the desire of the major powers to restrain the arsenals of smaller states like North Korea, Pakistan, Israel, and others. It cannot be in China's interest for North Korea to field 200 nuclear weapons, something that is possible in the next decade. And while at the moment there is little action by Washington, Moscow, or Beijing to stop North Korea, this is something that could easily change. If the first "big" crisis of this second nuclear age occurs, in Pakistan or North Korea, conditions will look very different than they do at the moment. It's worth recalling that the way the Cold War superpowers changed their attitudes to arms control came after crises in Berlin, Taiwan, Cuba, and elsewhere. It was *crises*, not *doctrine* or *theory* that drove changed attitudes to arms control.

Conclusion

This chapter offers two conclusions about China's national security policy and how it will change. First, Beijing cannot stay on the same pathway of the past twenty years because it faces an altogether greater level of complexity in its security environment. The security environment is changing rapidly for Beijing. It faces a long-term competition with the US and others. The dynamics are changing quickly, because of political changes in Washington. And they are changing because so much of China's defense uses a far greater technology input than ever before. I would argue that China's national security policy is now greatly shaped by the technology innovation cycles in AI, big data, and cloud computing. Many uncertainties and complexities accompany this.

It should be emphasized here that such uncertainties are not necessarily negative. There is the chance that China will "solve a problem." By this I mean that they will get cyberwar, AI, machine learning, and other areas right, or right enough to sharply alter the military balance against the US in the western Pacific. This kind of surprise, disruptive upset has shown up repeatedly in business rivalry where technology is a key element.

The second conclusion of this chapter is that a key question—and a very interesting one—is how China will deal with the increased complexity it faces. I would argue that China will deal with it through what

I would call an organizational transformation of its military apparatus. In simple terms, the argument is this: China's strategic environment is changing. Its military and intelligence organizations will have to change, too, if they are to avoid a decline in performance.

We already see this organizational change in several areas. In late 2015, China launched the most sweeping reorganization of the PLA since its founding. The thrust of the reorganization was to emphasis "jointness," that is, greater coordination across the various services, to better compete in an "informatized environment."[24] The reorganization called for changing the legacy bureaucracies of the PLA to better match the conditions of modern war and technology.

Another example of organizational transformation is the restructuring of China's nuclear forces that was included in this reorganization.[25] This move should have been anticipated. The addition of SSBNs and nuclear bombers, along with the overall expansion of its missile force of intercontinental and intermediate-range ballistic missiles, creates institutional issues of launch authority, communications, and deterrence. With a small force, China had a handful of missiles with the warheads separated from them. It was not a survivable force, and for this reason did not constitute the minimum deterrent most Western analysts imputed as China's doctrine. Regardless, putting nuclear weapons to sea aboard submarines, and on coastal runways of airfields. raises altogether new complexities. The coordination of alerts, assurance of communications, and the physical protection of the weapons against rogue and insider threats are some of the issues that come with a nuclear triad.

So too do the complex nuclear head games that national leaders play with their nuclear forces. China may, for example, fly a nuclear bomber over the Sea of Japan or over North Korea, land a bomber on an offshore island, closely hug and trail enemy submarines. China is entering this world of nuclear head games. The reality that China is now surrounded by five nuclear-weapon states is part of this. I would bet that every one of these five countries have targets in China. And all of them have missiles with the range to get there.

I would further argue that China cannot handle this greater complexity in its security policy simply by updating its doctrine. The complexities, internal linkages, and interactions of the moving parts, and of the enemy, are so great, with so many conceivable variants, that it is impossible to formalize this in written doctrine.

As a result, China's military is entering an era in which doctrine lags behind technology. This point has some very important implications for all competitors. Technology is racing ahead of doctrine in advanced technology warfare. The chance of a mistake, an accident, a big escalation that no one saw coming—is growing.

So too is the possibility that China will actually find a breakthrough that provides it with a decisive military advantage. The Chinese may, so to speak, get a lucky technological break that "solves a problem." There are many examples of this in history. Britain's Enigma breakthrough in code breaking and the US employment of chaff against German air defense radars in the Second World War are examples. Many technical breakthroughs have this character, resulting from stumbling into some major advance. I think Beijing understands this, and it's one more reason to pour resources into military AI, machine learning, and quantum computing.

Finally, a nuclear context must be layered on top of this advanced technology competition. No one can know what happens when a communications system for nuclear command and control is blacked out in a limited conventional war. It depends on the interconnected actions of at least two nuclear powers—and maybe more, since North Korea is also a nuclear-weapon state, and its action could cause a "standard" US-China crisis to explode in violence.

China's high-tech military modernization has radical potential. It can lead to complicated entanglements and crisis management interactions with the US. And it can give China a decisive military advantage, one China could exploit for a number of political reasons. All of this may work out on its own. But there is enough reason to think that it won't. The dynamism of technology is one of these. So is the reality that a much more complicated nuclear environment is developing, one that isn't separated off from other military systems. For these and other reasons, my final thought is that the system cannot be trusted to get us out of the competitive dangers that are building up without a comprehensive look at the interaction of moves by the major powers. More professional, systematic work on China, advanced technology, and other areas is badly needed.

NOTES

1 See Bracken, *Fire in the East*; Bracken, *The Second Nuclear Age*.

2 Remarks of Lt. Gen. Robert P. Ashley, Jr., Director Defense Intelligence Agency. See Ashley, "Russian and Chinese Nuclear Modernization Trends."

3 For a history of China's military strategy, see Fravel, *Active Defense*.

4 Halperin, *The 1958 Taiwan Straits Crisis* is a formerly top-secret, now declassified, RAND study of decision making on the US side.

5 Ellsberg, *The Doomsday Machine*, chaps. 2 and 5.

6 I use "MAD" here in two senses of the word: as in mutual assured destruction and as in the transcendental madness of fielding tens of thousands of nuclear weapons by the superpowers.

7 The first two Taiwan crises were in 1953 and 1958. The 1996 crisis involved Beijing's opposition to political developments in Taiwan.

8 The author was a member of a Department of Defense advisory body at the time and reviewed these studies.

9 See Chase et al., *China's Incomplete Military Transformation*.

10 White House Office of Trade and Manufacturing Policy, *How China's Economic Aggression Threatens the Technologies and Intellectual Property of the United States and the World*.

11 Sciutto, *The Shadow War*, 41–60.

12 An insightful description of China's entry into the flow of US venture capital deals is Brown and Singh, "China's Technology Transfer Strategy."

13 "China's Car Revolution Is Going Global."

14 The significance of the win is described in Lee, *AI Superpowers*, 1–10.

15 Specifically, in semiconductors, the Singapore-based company Broadcom tried to buy US owned Qualcomm; Alibaba's Ant Financial Services tried to acquire US-based MoneyGram; and Huawei was blocked from selling hardware to the Department of Defense and many local governments in the US. All three of these deals involved major AI, software, and technology elements.

16 Overholt, *China's Crisis of Success*.

17 I am not considering here the uses of databases, cloud computing, and AI for internal security and control.

18 On China's nuclear strategy and modernization, see Cunningham and Fravel, "Assuring Assured Retaliation."

19 See Bracken, "Nuclear Command, Control, and Communications in a Multipolar Nuclear World."

20 Pasztor and Tangel, "MAX Crashes Strengthen the Resolve of Boeing to Automate Flight."

21 For an overview of China's naval expansion, see Tobin, "Beijing's Strategy to Build China into a Maritime Great Power."

22 Volz, "White House Expands Use of Cyber Weapons but Stays Secretive on Policies."

23 See Cimbala, *United States, Russia, and Nuclear Peace.*
24 See Mulvenon, "China's 'Goldwater-Nichols'?"
25 See Chase, "PLA Rocket Force Modernization and China's Military Reforms."

BIBLIOGRAPHY

Ashley, Robert P., Jr. "Russian and Chinese Nuclear Modernization Trends: Remarks at the Hudson Institute." US Defense Intelligence Agency. Updated May 29, 2019. www.dia.mil.

Bracken, Paul. "Nuclear Command, Control, and Communications in a Multipolar Nuclear World: Big Structures and Large Processes." Nautilus Institute for Security and Sustainability, May 14, 2019. https://nautilus.org.

Bracken, Paul. *Fire in the East: The Rise of Asian Military Power and the Second Nuclear Age.* New York: HarperCollins, 1999.

Bracken, Paul. *The Second Nuclear Age: Strategy, Danger, and the New Power Politics.* New York: Times Books, 2012.

Brown, Michael, and Pavneet Singh. *China's Technology Transfer Strategy: How Chinese Investments in Emerging Technology Enable a Strategic Competitor to Access the Crown Jewels of US Innovation.* US Department of Defense, Defense Innovation Unit Experimental (DIUx), January 2018. https://admin.govexec.com.

Chase, Michael S. "PLA Rocket Force Modernization and China's Military Reforms" (testimony presented before the US-China Economic and Security Review Commission). Santa Monica, CA: RAND Corporation, 2018. www.rand.org.

Chase, Michael S., Jeffrey Engstrom, Tai Ming Cheung, Kristen A. Gunness, Scott Warren Harold, Susan Puska, and Samuel K. Berkowitz. "China's Incomplete Military Transformation: Assessing the Weakness of the People's Liberation Army (PLA)." Santa Monica, CA: RAND Corporation, 2015. www.rand.org.

"China's Car Revolution Is Going Global." *Bloomberg Businessweek*, April 23, 2018. www.bloomberg.com.

Cimbala, Stephen J. *The United States, Russia, and Nuclear Peace.* New York: Palgrave Macmillan, 2020.

Cunningham, Fiona S., and M. Taylor Fravel. "Assuring Assured Retaliation: China's Nuclear Posture and US-China Strategic Stability." *International Security* 40, no. 2 (2015): 7–50.

Fravel, M. Taylor. *Active Defense: China's Military Strategy since 1949.* Princeton, NJ: Princeton University Press, 2019.

Halperin, M. H. *The 1958 Taiwan Straits Crisis: A Documented History.* Santa Monica, CA: RAND Corporation, 1966. www.rand.org.

Lee, Kai-Fu. *AI Superpowers: China, Silicon Valley, and the New World Order.* New York: Houghton Mifflin Harcourt, 2018.

Mulvenon, James. "China's 'Goldwater-Nichols'? The Long-Awaited PLA Organization Has Finally Arrived." *China Leadership Monitor*, no. 49 (Winter 2016): 1–6.

Overholt, William H. *China's Crisis of Success.* Cambridge: Cambridge University Press, 2018.

Pasztor, Andy and Andrew Tangel. "MAX Crashes Strengthen Resolve of Boeing to Automate Flight." *Wall Street Journal*, December 31, 2019. www.wsj.com.

Sciutto, Jim. *The Shadow War: Inside Russia's and China's Operations to Defeat America.* New York: HarperCollins, 2019.

Tobin, Liza. "Beijing's Strategy to Build China into a Maritime Great Power." *Naval War College Review* 71, no. 2 (Spring 2018): 16–48.

Volz, Dustin. "White House Expands Use of Cyber Weapons but Stays Secretive on Policies." *Wall Street Journal*, December 30, 2019. www.wsj.com.

White House Office of Trade and Manufacturing Policy. *How China's Economic Aggression Threatens the Technologies and Intellectual Property of the United States and the World.* June 2018. www.whitehouse.gov.

2

China's Economic and Technological Strategy in the Age of Xi Jinping

HE LI

Economic performance has been the deciding factor of maintaining the legitimacy of the regime in China since the reform and open-door policy began in 1978.[1] The Nineteenth Party Congress Report states firmly that "development is the Party's primary task," which echoes Deng Xiaoping's saying that "only development is the indisputable truth [*fazhan cai shi ying daoli*]." The Chinese Communist Party (CCP) sets the purpose for the whole nation, providing the coordination and integration that are critically important for such a vast and diverse country, and effectively mobilizes resources to achieve developmental goals.[2] Sulmaan Khan suggests that while economic policy has shifted over time, and even though personalities at the helm have varied, the CCP's "overarching goal" has "remained the same."[3] China's current grand strategy reveals that economic development is the top priority and a crucial component of the government's core interests.

Meanwhile, technology is a vital part of China's efforts to build global political and economic influence. In 1988, Deng Xiaoping pointed out that science and technology are primary productive forces [*kexue jishu shi diyi shengchanli*]. In a similar vein, Xi Jinping insists that innovation is central to the country's standing on the world stage. Given the many inherent obstacles, Chinese policy makers naturally see economics as a potentially more effective instrument to advance its overall foreign policy interests.[4]

According to the joint China/World Bank report *China 2030*, China should complete its transition to a market economy through enterprise, land, labor, and financial sector reforms, strengthen its private sector, open its markets to greater competition and innovation, and ensure equality of opportunity to help achieve its goal of a new structure for economic growth.[5] But the party-state under Xi quickly abandoned this design in favor of a state-led growth model. At the 2017's Nineteenth Party Congress, Xi set out a two-stage development plan for the nation. In the first stage, from 2020 to 2035, the primary goal is to build on the foundations of China's modern economy. In the second stage, from 2035 to 2050, China will seek to become a state with substantial global influence.[6] The goal is to complete the process by 2049, the year marking the centennial anniversary of the founding of the People's Republic of China (PRC). To this end, Beijing has intertwined its economic, technological, and strategic initiatives. This chapter explores the key components and prospects of China's economic and technological strategy in the era of Xi Jinping.

National economic strategy, as defined by Bruce R. Scott of the Harvard Business School, comprises a vision of a desired future state of the economy, a time frame within which that state is to be achieved, and a set of policies and institutions for influencing the mobilization and allocation of resources and for promoting their efficient utilization.[7] This chapter is divided into three parts. The first section presents the major elements of China's economic and technological strategy under Xi. The second part explores the readjustment of China's strategy in recent years. The final section discusses the major challenges the country is facing.

Key Elements of China's Economic and Technological Strategy

China's economic and technological strategy in the age of Xi contains four pillars: state-led development, core technologies self-sufficiency, moving up the value-added ladder, sustainable development, and poverty eradication.

Maintaining the State-Led Economic Model

The first defining feature of economic strategy under Xi is the promotion of a statist orientation toward the economy. The Beijing leadership under Xi favors a state-led economic model, assuming that the role of the government needs to be brought into play in order to create steadier economic growth.[8] A number of experts and policy makers reckon that the secret of the East Asian economic miracle is the state-led market economy. The fifth generation of the Chinese leadership also wants to give the state a more important role in guiding the post-socialist economy.

China's extraordinary economic development is often said to be a product of neoliberal market reforms. The private sector has contributed nearly two thirds of the country's growth and nine tenths of the new jobs created in the early 2010s.[9] Under the Xi government, China is stepping back from the free-market, pro-business policies that the country had pursued since Deng Xiaoping. Liberal scholars call it *guo jin min tui* [advance of the state sector and retreat of the private sector]. Contrary to key elements of the decision of the Third Plenum of the Central Committee of the Eighteenth Party Congress held in 2013, in which the Chinese leadership called for the market to play a decisive role in the allocation of resources across the economy, "Made in China 2025" instead appears to reaffirm the government's central role in economic planning.[10]

The Chinese leadership regards one of the greatest strengths of the PRC's political system as the opportunity to set long-term development priorities and concentrate powers to accomplish major undertakings [*jizhong liliang ban dashi*]. Medium and long-term development planning plays a key role in coordinating and directing state activities across various policy areas in the PRC. Development planning represents the political leadership's aspirations to perpetuate macro-management [*hongguan tiaokong*] through the CCP and the government.[11]

The Beijing leadership has convinced itself that to stay ahead of the technology curve, a national team [*guojia dui*] is needed.[12] The central government further deems that to catch up with the West, certain industries such as the high-technology sector require government support through subsidies and trade protection. Policy makers in Beijing regard the ongoing trade tussle with the United States as further evidence that the government should take a leading role to defend national economic security.

Engaging in industrial policy and fusing public and private entities and interests is nothing new in China. Nevertheless, it has important consequences for security as well as the economy. For instance, at the Eighteenth National Congress in 2012, Xi set forward the importance of *junmin ronghe* [military-civilian fusion]. Its objective is to accelerate the transfer of people and technologies between the military and civilian sectors.[13] China's state-led economic strategy not only fuses economic and security interests, but also relies on coordination between state and market actors across multiple areas. Qiao Liang and Wang Xiangsui, two Chinese military officers, contend that no country could challenge the military supremacy of the US through conventional means, or so-called kinetic warfare. The only hope, they claim, is to wear the US down gradually with what term economic and information warfare.[14]

The Chinese decision-making body also includes a contingent of reformers who favor liberalizing the Chinese economy. They argue that market reforms will make the economy more vibrant. Many reform-minded bureaucrats and scholars hold that China should complete its transition to a market economy through enterprise, land, labor, and financial sector reforms, and that it should strengthen its private sector, open its markets to greater competition and innovation, and ensure equality of opportunity to help achieve its goal of a new structure for economic growth. They insist that such reforms will benefit the country in the long run.[15] The reformers provide two prescriptions for dealing with the clash with the US: deepen the opening and accelerate market-oriented reform. At present, however, the reformers within the party-state do not have sufficient clout to induce such reform.

Achieving Self-Sufficiency in Core Technologies

Technological innovation plays an increasingly important role in China's rise on the global stage. China has set a long-term goal to become a nation of innovation and creativity. Beginning in the 2000s, the Chinese state emphasized the technological competitiveness of domestic firms (this was known as *zizhu chuangxin* [independent innovation]). However, China's state-led innovation has been focusing more on practical technologies, and not so much on basic science. For this reason, this section concentrates on China's technological strategy.

With the rapid change of technology, profits in the global economy are shifting to those who own knowledge and control the distribution of knowledge-intensive goods and services. To the surprise of many, China is fast becoming a world leader in areas of technology including 5G and artificial intelligence. A recent report by the US China Economic and

Security Review Commission finds that Chinese companies utilize a variety of methods—many of them covert or coercive—to acquire valuable technology, intellectual property, and know-how from US firms. These efforts are often made at the direction of and with assistance from the central government, part of Beijing's larger effort to develop its domestic market and become a global leader in a wide range of technologies.[16]

Despite signs of slowing economic growth, China's innovation continues to blossom. China has climbed from the seventeenth to the fourteenth position in the *Global Innovation Index*, which ranks nearly 130 nations.[17] We have seen an increase in state efforts to nurture core technologies, by whatever means, so that China can move up the production value chain and try to escape the middle-income trap, which has been a top priority for the Chinese state.

After years of rapid growth, China's research and development spending reached some $410 billion in 2016—more than that of Japan, Germany, and South Korea combined. Such state investment has helped Chinese firms to take the lead in many tech-focused fields.[18] Over the past decade, Chinese companies have achieved a tenfold increase in their share of US patents. China became one of the top five US patent recipients for the first time in 2017, behind the US, Japan, South Korea, and Germany.[19]

China can be described as a "learning state" that has adapted to changing conditions and has frequently turned outward to learn its lessons. The past four decades have seen the Chinese central government investing heavily in education. According to *The Diplomat*, China opened more than 1,800 new universities between 2001 and 2014, and produces nearly five million science, technology, engineering and mathematics (STEM) graduates a year—nearly ten times the equivalent American figure.[20] In the meantime, China has benefited from having a large diaspora of scientists living in the West. With lucrative funding, salary, and benefits, a growing number of Chinese scholars have returned home with their American or European degrees, taking up important positions in the government, science, and business community. It goes without saying that the Trump administration's crackdown on university scholars with ties to China has triggered a reverse brain drain. According to government data, about one million Chinese people were studying at higher-education institutions outside of China in 2015.

According to SupChina, "In 2012 alone, 159,600 overseas students re-turned, and four years later, this number grew to 432,500."[21]

The Innovation and National Security Task Force of the Council on Foreign Relations finds that China is likely to spend more than any coun-try on research and development by 2030. China is expected to invest over $200 billion in the upcoming decade in industrial policies focused on strategic technology industries. It is, or will soon become, one of the leaders in artificial intelligence, robotics, energy storage, 5G, quantum information systems and, potentially, biotechnology.[22] According to the *Global Innovation Index*, even though China is now churning out a great many patents, it is still way behind the US and other rich countries when it comes to innovation quality. Several studies conclude that although the US continues to lead the world in innovation, China is closing the gap.[23] With significant backing from the Chinese government and the anticipated involvement of the world's largest public sector, China will likely catch up with the existing intellectual-property powers more quickly than many have anticipated.[24]

ZTE, one of China's leading telecom equipment manufacturers, was briefly banned from doing business with US partners but settled with a hefty fine in 2018. The "ZTE incident," as it is known in China, may be the country's Sputnik moment. The country is determined to become a technological powerhouse in order to reduce reliance on the West in general and on the US in particular. In May 2019, due to national se-curity concerns, the Commerce Department placed Huawei, another Chinese tech giant that is also a symbol of the US-China tech rivalry, on its "Entity List," which is basically a trade blacklist that bars anyone on it from buying parts and components from US companies without the government's approval. In the aftermath of the Huawei debacle, the country is trying its best not to rely on the US in the field of core technologies.

As the trade war with the US continues in 2020, there is a growing consensus in China's policy world that the country must make break-throughs and maintain self-reliance in core technologies at any cost. It is expected that China will double down on its efforts to upgrade to higher value-added industries and technologies, and invest more aggressively in science and education. China missed the Industrial Revolution but is determined not to miss the current high-tech revolution.

There is little likelihood that China will abandon its "Made in China 2025" plan. The country will avoid talking about it but do more to achieve that goal. The ZTE incident exposed China's weakness in high tech, and the subsequent conflict over Huawei made China uneasy about its technical security. Under such circumstance, industrial plans like "Made in China 2025" have accelerated.

While the research environment in China has improved substantially in the past two decades, it is not yet on par with its American counterpart. Xi has acknowledged that a lack of innovation is China's "Achilles heel." He has also bemoaned the economy for being big yet not yet strong. China's technological prowess is still at the low end of the global value chain, and the "reserves" the country has set aside for science and technology are far from enough.[25] To stay ahead of the technology curve, more investment in science and technology is needed. Yet, so far, most Chinese firms lag considerably behind in this area and neglect it. Huawei is one of the few exceptions. Much state funding goes to applied science rather than to basic science projects. According to *The Economist*, despite the name of its plan to develop advanced industries—"Made in China 2025"—which has caused so much concern in the US, the bureaucrats who drew up the plan did not think that China could rival foreign prowess until 2049.[26]

Miao Wei, Minister of Industry and Information Technology, has made it clear that China still lags behind the US by about thirty years in technology, manufacturing development and other areas, and it will take around three decades for China to catch up with the US, let alone beat it.[27] Without any doubt, this will be difficult, as China struggles to master real innovation and research. Only so much can be gained by *wan dao chao che* [reverse engineering].

Climbing the Value-Added Ladder

Another element of China's strategy is to move up to products with higher value added. This industrial upgrading strategy is called *teng long huan niao* [vacating cage to change bird]. This policy was initiated in 2008 by Wang Yang, then the party secretary of Guangdong Province, and endorsed by the CCP leadership under Xi. Since then, the old "Made in China" model—with its reliance on cheap labor and thin profits—has begun to wane.

For years, China's economy was widely known for low-cost, labor-intensive manufacturing and imitation of foreign goods. With the rise of the cost of production at home, China could no longer depend on labor-intensive industry. The nation is thus now endeavoring to move up the value-added chain by focusing on high-tech and high-end industry sectors.

Apparently, middle-income nations can easily lose their cheap labor advantage as they grow but can hardly gain a technological advantage fast enough to compensate for the loss of manufacturing industries. To prevent this from happening, industrial upgrading is imperative. The country aims to transform its brand from "Assembled in China" to "Created in China." Through determined efforts in industrial upgrading, the country has slowly but gradually abandoned "high production" in the sense of cheap, low tech, and labor-intensive goods. "Made in China 2025" is the strategic plan through which Xi Jinping hopes to turn China into a high-tech superpower in the twenty-first century.

For the past ten years, China has sought to move up the technological ladder by attracting foreign direct investment (FDI) in technology sectors and encouraging private firms in research and development spending. To accomplish this goal of becoming a high-tech power, it is essential for China to vastly increase its spending on higher education and research and development, set up high-tech zones, recruit high-tech scientists and researchers from all over the world, and develop cutting-edge industries in artificial intelligence, robotics, telecommunications, and the like. The focus on tech has worked. In 2018, China was home to nine of the world's twenty most valuable tech companies—a big leap over the two it had claimed five years earlier, according to a report by venture capital firm Kleiner Perkins.[28]

China has become the world's largest electric-vehicle market and the dominant player in drones. Skylogic Research reports that "one Shenzhen-based company alone has a 74 percent share of the worldwide drone market"; moreover, "Huawei and ZTE's advances in 5G network technology are also the result of massive government support."[29] High tech is seen as crucial to industrial upgrading. According to Qin Hailin, a senior industrial economics researcher at the China Center for Information Industry Development, China's rapid advancements in digital economy and local companies' readiness to embrace cutting-edge internet, artificial intelligence, big data, and cloud technologies will help expedite industrial upgrades.[30]

It is worth noting that as the Carnegie Mellon University Professor Vivek Wadhwa and others have demonstrated, the quality of engineering education in China, especially before 2010, was well below international standards. Many engineering degrees would barely qualify as technical certificates in the US.[31] The country will remain weak when it comes to the production of core technologies. It is, however, becoming a major global producer of intellectual property. The American pressures on China on intellectual property should, in the long run, propel China's ascent in this area. In fact, some Chinese firms are transforming themselves from "copycats" to "fast followers." China's telecom sector, for instance, has evolved from a follower in 2G into a pioneer in the era of 5G.

Promoting Sustainable Development and Poverty Alleviation

Last but not least, China's economic strategy includes a commitment to sustainable development and poverty reduction. China lacks natural resources and lags far behind the industrialized countries when it comes to energy efficiency. Beijing has realized that the country's development cannot follow the traditional path of industrialization, which comes with high energy consumption and heavy pollution. With increasing concerns over economic inequality and environmental degradation, the CCP has gradually shifted its economic strategy from a growth orientation to sustainable development. Beijing has moved to put more emphasis on the "quality and efficiency" of future economic development. Other than economic growth, the Party has devoted more attention to environmental protection and improving people's quality of life.[32]

The CCP also sees eliminating poverty as a source of its legitimacy. In 2013, Xi coined the term "precise poverty alleviation" [jingzhun fupin] to suggest that he would take a more strident approach to eliminating the impoverished conditions that have persisted for forty million Chinese citizens under his leadership.[33] Since 2012, Beijing has addressed the negative consequences of rapid growth by launching an ambitious program of poverty alleviation on the one hand and promoting sustainable development on the other. Since Xi came to power, Beijing has spent generously on poverty reduction. Poverty alleviation funds allocated under the central government budget amounted to 282.2 billion yuan ($41.7 billion) during Xi's first term (2012–17), more than double the level of the previous five years under the Hu Jintao–Wen Jiabao administration.[34] Xi's pledge to eliminate poverty by 2020 is in line with the larger CCP goal of developing China into a "moderately prosperous society" at the party's centennial in 2021. According to the World Bank, China experienced "the fastest sustained expansion by a major economy in history—and more than 850 million people have lifted themselves out of poverty."[35]

Meanwhile, the central government's approach has moved from relying solely on growth to sustainable development. In 2013, Beijing declared a "war on pollution." Although China has long confronted serious environmental degradation, the recent efforts of the Chinese authorities to shut down a large number of heavily polluted factories and promote clean-energy cars seem to have yielded positive results. In December 2018, the State Council released an ambitious "zero-waste city" pilot plan in eleven cities, aiming to minimize solid-waste generation and maximize recycling in urban areas. China, one of the world's biggest users of plastic, announced that single-use plastic bags will be banned in major cities by the end of 2020 and in all cities and towns by 2022.

Xi's appeal for green development is a nod to the widespread middle-class discontent over air, water, and soil pollution, and the environmental degradation that has resulted from China's rapid economic growth. The new vision of building a "beautiful China" or "ecological civilization" has broad popular appeal. The catchphrase "ecological civilization" was enshrined in the CCP Constitution in 2012. Under its framework, Xi claims to lead climate change cooperation, push for energy transformation, and cultivate China's renewable energy sector.[36]

Readjustment of Economic Strategy

China is well-known for its long-term planning. Yet its strategic plans have been constantly revised, updated, and adjusted. With the slowdown of the Chinese economy, the term "new normal" was adopted by policy makers in Beijing in 2014; it refers to a transition from high-speed growth to mid-to-high-speed growth.[37] Beijing has acknowledged the need for China to embrace a new growth model that relies less on fixed investment and exporting and more on private consumption, services, and innovation to drive economic growth.

Since the founding of the PRC, the Party's strategy has changed from "politics in command" to "economics in command" to "governance in command." The effectiveness of governance has emerged as a critical element for strengthening the legitimacy of the regime.[38] Facing the sternest test of its economic development model, the Xi administration has apparently readjusted China's economic strategy. The following readjustments have been put into practice.

Boosting Domestic Demand and Stabilizing Supply Chain

About four decades ago, Chinese economic strategy shifted from a closed-door policy to one of export-led growth. China's subsequent remarkable economic growth has hinged on investment-driven, export-led industrialization that capitalized on labor-intensive manufacturing industries and efficient infrastructure. Infrastructure spending has been crucial in shoring up the economy. But this model reached its developmental limit by the early 2010s, when Xi came to power. China has since faced a mounting industrial overcapacity. China has benefitted significantly from the liberal international economic order. Yet its export-led industrialization is now facing the severe headwinds of de-globalization and protectionism. Donald Trump's policies have exposed a vulnerability in this export-dependent economic model. On top of the US-China trade war, the pandemic has wreaked further havoc. Under such circumstances, China is making another transition in its economic strategy from export-led growth toward more balanced development that relies on both international and domestic markets.

In the new McKinsey Global Institute China-World Exposure Index, China's exposure to the world in trade, technology, and capital has fallen in relative terms. Conversely, the world's exposure to China has increased. This reflects the rebalancing of the Chinese economy toward domestic consumption. In eleven of the sixteen quarters since 2015, consumption contributed more than 60 percent of total GDP growth.[39] In spite of these efforts, exports continue to play a major role in economic growth. An endogenous dynamic for sustained and steady economic development has been lacking. In the wake of the corona crisis, Beijing has intensified its efforts to boost domestic demand and has taken steps to stabilize foreign trade. Obviously, it takes a long time for any country to shift its growth model from an export and investment–driven orientation to a consumption and innovation–led model.

FDI has played a very important role in China's economic development. China's participation in the globalization is not a short-term tactic but a long-term strategy. The rapid growth of China's economy, export boom, and job creation vindicated this strategic choice. *Yinjinlai*, literally meaning "inviting in" (inflow FDI), has been integral part of China's reform and opening up policies since 1978. So far, China remains the second largest recipient of FDI globally. Beijing is expected to carry on this type of policy.

Diversifying Trading Partners

China was a closed economy for much of the twentieth century but aggressively opened up to the world since the late 1970s, joining the World Trade Organization and forging free trade agreements (FTAs) with a growing number of countries. Since opening its door to the world, the country has become one of the largest beneficiaries of globalization. FDI and cross-national trade are major drivers of the country's economic miracle. From the Chinese perspective, the "New Cold War" between the US and China does not benefit anyone, but rather drains funds from the education and healthcare systems of both countries, diverting resources that would be put toward infrastructure projects, alleviating poverty, and more. Yet there is little Beijing could do to stop or reverse it. China has a lot more stake outside its border today than it did in the past.[40]

Disruption caused by the trade war and global pandemic has prompted many businesses and governments to think again about relying too much on a single country in a global supply chain. A growing number of countries are trying to reduce their dependence on China and are rerouting supply chains. Some call it the ABC supply chain, as in "anywhere but China." Take Japan, for example. In April 2020, the Japanese government announced that it would provide $2.2 billion in direct loans to help its manufacturers shift production out of China as the coronavirus disrupted supply chains between the major trading partners. Last year saw companies actively rethinking their supply chains, either convincing their Chinese partners to relocate to Southeast Asia to avoid tariffs, or by opting out of sourcing from China altogether.[41] Many in China worry that it might be the beginning of the end of globalization.

A "divorce" between the US and China will have some consequences for the US, but it will be devastating for China. As Xi stressed at the extraordinary G20 Leaders' Summit in March 2020, "We need to jointly keep the global industrial and supply chains stable." With supply chains disrupted and demand falling, the global economic outlook has shifted to "more dire scenarios" as the International Monetary Fund recently warned. To reverse that trend, Beijing is attempting to form alliances, both with neighboring nations like Russia, Japan, South Korea, and Southeast Asia, as well as the rest of the world. Over the last few years, China has rallied countries around its ambitious Belt and Road Initiative as a global vision to shift the economic center of gravity away from traditional powers like the US. Developing this initiative may also help compensate for the loss of supply chain. China is taking proactive steps to help adjacent countries and EU member states to contain the pandemic. In October 2017, the Belt and Road Initiative was added into the Party's Constitution, signaling an all-out effort to realize the vision.

Re-emphasizing Market-Oriented Reform

The outbreak of the coronavirus and the trade conflict with the US have driven the government to reinvigorate the reform and opening process. On March 30, 2020, the CCP and the State Council issued a guideline on improving the market-based allocation mechanism of production factors in a bid to further facilitate the free and orderly flow of factors and stimulate market vitality. China will promote a market-based allocation of factors of production including land, labor, and capital, while accelerating the development of the market for technology and data factors. The country will push forward the reform of the rural land expropriation system, adjust policies on industrial land use, and optimize its land management mechanism. To further promote labor mobility, it will take more steps to advance household registration system reforms. China will improve the basic mechanisms of the stock market, accelerate the development of the bond market, increase the supply of effective financial services and expand the opening of financial markets. Access requirements for foreign-funded financial institutions will be gradually relaxed.[42]

Implementing supply-side structural reform is another strategic adjustment devised by the party-state. Such reform is a major component of new strategy. Xi has noted that although China's developing economy faces cyclical and aggregate issues, the most prominent hindrances are of a structural nature. To deal with these obstacles, the government has announced a series of economic stimulus measures, including tax cuts, targeted bank reserve-ratio and lending-rate cuts, and intensive investment projects. The pension contribution rate of employers in China will be reduced from a ceiling of 20 percent to 16 percent of the overall wage bill, as part of a wide-ranging package of new measures designed to ease the burdens on small and medium-sized enterprises.

Despite the popularity of the notion of "Beijing Consensus" or "China Model," which emphasizes the strong role of the state and strengthening of the state sector, liberal reformers believe that this approach is not the right prescription for China since it can only lead to state capitalism or so-called "crony capitalism."[43] Huang Qifan, former mayor of the megacity of Chongqing, has spoken at various public forums, expounding the need for Beijing to embrace the "zero for zero" solution, also known as the "three zeros" [san ling]: zero tariffs, zero subsidies, and zero non-tariff barriers. He believes that by embracing the three zeros, the Chinese economy will have a breakthrough similar to the one it experienced after the country's accession to the World Trade Organization in 2001, which helped pave the way for its economic lift-off. It should be noted that Huang has been able to repeat his comments at various forums, a fact that indicates that he has supporters within the central government.[44]

In the minds of the reformers, monetary stimulus packages are the most direct way to promote economic growth, but they only work in the short term and are unable to alter the long-term economic trajectory. A decade of easy money after the global financial crisis has only compounded the difficulties. Many of China's problems, such as massive debt and excess industrial capacity were caused by China's past stimulus packages. Reformers argue that China needs to restart its structural reforms and transform its semi-command and semi-market economy into a full-fledged market economy based on the rule of law.[45]

The danger of returning to a nationalist-populist path is of great concern. Liberal thinkers contend that China must give greater sway to market forces and rein in its bloated state sector, warning that not doing so will lead to economic stagnation and stoke continuing tensions with the West. In the eyes of the reformers, competition, not state protectionism, is the answer to China's economic problems. If the government continues to dominate the process of resource allocation, it will distort the market and stifle incentives for innovation. Pragmatic leaders such as Vice Premier Liu He, Politburo Standing Committee Member Wang Yang, and Vice President Wang Qishan understand that China is still weak and cannot easily win the trade war with the US. But the conservative camp advocates nationalism and wants to continue the fight.

In the words of Elizabeth Economy, "with the exception of anticorruption, no issue is as central to China's leadership's legitimacy as ensuring rising income levels. Yet the country's economic model has also reached an inflection point."[46] Sorted by per capita income, China is now in the "middle-income range" or the "middle-income trap" where emerging market economies are likely to get stuck. The economists who originally came up with this term explained the phenomenon as a loss of comparative advantage. To be sure, it is in the long-term interests of the party-state to speed up economic reform, and China's pursuit of state-led growth is inconsistent with the repeated pledges of President Xi to further open China's economy and promote globalization.[47]

Cheng Li, director of the John L. Thornton China Center at Brookings, pointed out recently that China is promoting market reform in some ways (such as pushing for private-sector development) and foreign investment in some ways, while asserting greater state control in others.[48] China made a series of commitments to reform when it joined the World Trade Organization in 2001, yet the country still falls far short of a free-market economy.

Challenges ahead

Along with a deft combination of economic liberalism and neo-mercantilist policies, China's economically oriented strategy has been an astonishing success. In just a few decades, China has moved from the periphery to the semi-periphery of the world system. Only a handful of low and middle–income nations have managed to power into the high-income ranks since 1960—just twenty-five out of 156 as of 2016, according to *Capital Economics*.[49] The country has now reached a critical juncture in its economic development. Whether it can escape the middle-income trap is probably one of the most important questions of our time. Liberal reformers posit that unless China is able to implement further structural reforms, the country will be caught in the middle-income trap and be unable to join the ranks of the developed countries. China's grand economic strategy under Xi have been largely successful. But the country faces serious headwinds, including the impacts of the trade war, the coronavirus crisis, mass protest in Hong Kong, an aging population, state inefficiency, and looming debt, among others. I now examine each of these challenges in turn.

The Impacts of the Trade War

President Trump's tariffs and other sanctions are hitting China at a vulnerable moment. Data from the China State Statistics Bureau shows that the country's economy is now experiencing its longest deceleration of the post-Mao era.[50] As this book goes to press, Phase I of the new trade agreement with the US, the most difficult bilateral economic negotiation in recent decades, has concluded. In exchange for some tariff relief, China promised to buy an additional US$200 billion in American goods and services over the next two years and make structural reforms that would provide more protection for US intellectual property. As part of the trade agreement, China allows full foreign ownership of life insurers and futures and mutual fund companies starting April 1, 2020. Chinese leaders have described the moves as a useful way to improve the competitiveness of the domestic industry—without challenging its dominance—as well as to allocate capital more efficiently and attract foreign investment. Yi Gang, central bank governor, described the moves as "prudent, cautious, gradualist."[51] In fact, the trade war forced China to accelerate market reform.

Phase II will be much more difficult. A common view in China is that signing the Plaza Accord led to Japan's "two lost decades," and that the country should not compromise with the US on the key issues relating to economic security. Under rising nationalism, any major compromises with the US may be politically unacceptable. The leadership in Beijing can't be seen by the Chinese people as kowtowing to American demands to alter its development model in exchange for removing tariffs. Given that competition over technology between the US and China is intensifying alongside the trade war, China is unlikely to abandon its industrial policy. The negotiation process could last a long time, as Beijing and Washington face such additional uncertainties as the American election, a global economic slowdown, and the deadly coronavirus. Trump and Xi might resolve the trade dispute, but state capitalism is likely to continue. In the long run, even if the trade war comes to an end through negotiations, the competition between China and the US in the high-tech sector can only become fiercer. The trade and technology conflict between the US and China shows no signs of thawing at present.

Challenges of the COVID-19 Pandemic

Already reeling under the trade tensions, the coronavirus chaos has dealt another, more dramatic blow to the Chinese economy. The survival of the one-party state depends on performance legitimacy. Beijing has made clear that fighting the virus is a national priority. As this book goes to press, the country appears to have had a drastic reduction in cases and deaths but is still struggling to get back on its feet. There are signs that Chinese economy is sputtering back to life, supported by a growing number of government measures to reduce the impact of the lockdowns. Likewise, the government has announced a temporary reduction in social security contributions and valued-added taxes for businesses in affected regions. Although activity has restarted, it is still not back to normal levels, with many service businesses struggling and the outlook for exporters grim as the outbreak covers the rest of the world.

To offset the economic impact of the COVID-19, China is looking at investing in "new infrastructure" projects, which are different from the "old infrastructure," like railways, airports, and power plants. These new infrastructure projects typically include 5G, extra-high-voltage power transmission, inter-city rail transit, vehicle charging facilities, big data centers, artificial intelligence, industrial internet, and the internet of things—areas where China sees ample space for development and a new growth point for China's future economy.

The COVID-19 crisis has apparently tipped the world into recession. China's economy is likely to show a record contraction in the first quarter. Actual economic recovery remains a distant prospect. The greatest cost will come to China's reputation as a reliable trade partner. The most important longer-term outcome would appear to be a strengthening of a trend for global companies to "de-Sinicize" their supply chains.[52] China is moving into uncharted territory, and risks instability if the economic slowdown continues.

China's economy will continue to suffer from falling global demand as it spreads throughout Europe and the US. The highly contagious COVID-19 is circulating widely, portending a profound global impact on public health, consumer spending, logistics supply chains, and capital investments. Even if factories open back up, they will have far fewer customers to buy their goods. China's economy can only recover fully when the world economy gets back on track.

A growing number of countries are seeking to become self-sufficient in the production of "strategic" commodities, contributing to a further rollback of globalization. The World Trade Organization expects that world trade will fall by between 13 percent and 32 percent in 2020. Estimates of the expected recovery in 2021 are equally uncertain.[53] If the global slowdown lasts a long period of time, it might take long time for the world's second-largest economy to bounce back.

Mass Protest in Hong Kong

In 2020, widespread protests, along with the uncertainties of the US-China trade war and COVID-19, sent the Hong Kong economy into a recession for the first time in a decade. And many agree that Hong Kong's tide of economic woes may have only just begun.

Hong Kong remains very important for China. Thanks to its sound legal and financial systems, the city serves as the mainland's gateway to the outside world and has long played a functional go-between role, benefiting both the city itself and many foreign businesses, including American interests. Meanwhile, the city acts as the main offshore renminbi clearing center and the main channel of FDI. Beijing has taken measures that will help mitigate the effects of the mass protests. For instance, Beijing plans to let the Guangdong-Hong Kong-Macau Greater Bay Area, a megalopolis also known as the Pearl River Delta, play "a key role" in science and technology.

In the past few decades, most Hong Kong factories relocated to the Pearl River Delta in the mainland. Manufacturing industry has largely been replaced by service industries, particularly in finance and real estate. The Yangtze River Delta and Guangdong Province used to produce garments and shoes, and assemble electronics. Nowadays, they have become hubs for high-tech innovation. Beijing believes that vast economic inequality, among other factors, underpins Hong Kong's great political divide and hopes that robust economic growth and fairer income distribution could enhance political stability in the city. The central government is determined to integrate the Guangdong-Hong Kong-Macau Greater Bay Area into an economic and business hub, as well as a center for commerce and trade that can facilitate relations between China and the rest of the world.

An Aging Population

The aging of the Chinese population is an additional obstacle for Beijing. For many years, China benefitted from a growing workforce, which boosted GDP both by adding workers and because younger workers tend to be more productive than older ones. But around 2012, the working-age population began to shrink, an inevitable result of the one-child policy enacted in 1979.[54] In the new century, China is an aging society with the unique characteristic of growing old before getting rich. China already has 180 million people over the age of sixty, and this could reach 240 million by 2020 and 360 million by 2030. The share of the population that is over the age of sixty could reach 20 percent by 2020 and 27 percent by 2030.[55]

Some observers have pointed to China's aging population as evidence that the momentum of consumption growth may weaken.[56] Too few young workers will be forced to support too many dependent elderly family members. The wellsprings of creativity, innovation, and risk-taking—long associated with youth—will inevitably decline. China is losing manufacturing production shares to other low-cost producing countries, and is still not able to take more technological production shares from the rich nations. It could therefore be stuck in a middle-income trap for decades. These unfavorable demographic trends are creating heavy headwinds for the Chinese economy.[57]

The Inefficiency of the State Sector

It is increasingly clear that inefficiency of the state sector impedes economic growth. China's state-owned enterprises have used too much capital inefficiently and have generated poor returns at the expense of China's private sector. So far China's government is still omnipotent. State-owned enterprises and governments at various administrative levels control too many economic resources, especially land and capital. Economically, Xi has strengthened the state sector and imposed more constraints on the private sector. A fierce anti-corruption campaign has led to the dismissal of a large number of powerful figures and has brought more power under Xi's control. Xi's consolidation of power, however, has led a large number of Chinese bureaucrats to become less creative, less likely to take responsibility, which indirectly slows the economy. China's top leadership appears to be willing to pay the price of slower economic growth in order to enhance political control.[58]

Looming Debt and the Housing Bubble

China's growth is also undermined by rising debt and the housing bubble. Government policies have created tremendous economic imbalances and have saddled China with debt. China's total debt—corporate, household and government—rose to over 300 percent of its GDP in the first quarter of 2019, according to a report by the Institute of International Finance.[59] Comprehensive structural reform is unlikely in the near term. There is little indication that Beijing will, in the foreseeable future, privatize the huge state-owned enterprises that account for about 30 percent of China's economy, serve the regime's goals and enrich political elites. As then-Premier Wen Jiabao recognized in March 2007, "There are structural problems in China's economy which cause unsteady, unbalanced, uncoordinated, and unsustainable development."[60] Whether

China will be able to marshal its economic, intellectual, and political resources to overcome these obstacles remains to be seen.

Conclusion

Beijing is keenly aware that reform is now in "deep water."[61] The country can no longer afford to "cross the river by feeling the stones." The easier reform tasks are mostly complete, but tough impediments are growing quickly. Some observers think that China is approaching collapse.[62] But alarmist forecasts have been proven wrong repeatedly in the past three decades. Others forecast that China will become a leading economic power by 2030.[63] Given potential black swans—sudden, unexpected events that can harm the economy—Beijing will continue to adjust its national economic strategy.

China's economic success builds on a mixture of state-led and market-led approaches, its will to catch up with the West, and a solid plan. Rapid industrialization and economic development of the PRC has been achieved through pragmatic policies that combine flexible market reforms with strong state control over the pace and scope of economic opening. In 2017, the Nineteenth Party Congress laid out a roadmap for China's development in the coming thirty years. Beijing leadership has demonstrated ambition and determination in pursuing a new path for economic growth. In spite of the strengthening of state control under Xi Jinping, it is unlikely that China will go back to autarky and a planned economy.

China remains a fragile power. For years to come, it will continue to depend on the West for technology and export markets. Furthermore, the Chinese economy still trails behind the US in GDP and the gap is even more extreme in GDP per capita. China's per capita GDP in 2019 was just above $10,000, well below the world average of $18,000. And its economic growth might continue to slow down. In sum, without further, meaningful reform, it will be difficult to transform China into a developed country with sustainable development.

NOTES

1 An earlier version of this chapter was presented at a private conference hosted by Professor David Denoon at New York University on June 10, 2019. I would like to thank Professor Denoon, Nele Noesselt, Guoli Liu, Fujia Lu, and other conference participants for their thoughtful feedback.

2 Gore, "China's Party-Dominated Governance System."

3 Khan, *Haunted by Chaos*, 3.

4 Wong and Lim, "The Economic Card in China's Pro-active Diplomacy."

5 World Bank and the Development Research Center of the State Council, *China 2030*.

6 "China Focus: Xi Unveils Plan to Make China 'Great Modern Socialist Country' by Mid-21st Century."

7 Scott, "The Concept of National Economic Strategy."

8 For an excellent study on the model of developmental state, see Wade, "The Developmental State: Dead or Alive?"

9 Yuan, "Private Businesses Build Modern China."

10 US Chamber of Commerce, "Made in China 2025," 9.

11 For detail, see Heilmann, *Red Swan*, 7–9.

12 The "national team" [*guojia dui*] refers to key domestic companies that the government nurtures to promote long-term economic development.

13 Roberts, Moraes, and Ferguson, "Geoeconomics."

14 Qiao and Xiangsui, *Unrestricted Warfare*.

15 World Bank and the Development Research Center of the State Council, *China 2030*.

16 Sean O'Connor, "How Chinese Companies Facilitate Tech Transfer from the US."

17 World Intellectual Property Organization, "Global Innovation Index 2019."

18 Emanuel, Gadsden, and Moore, "How the US Surrendered to China on Scientific Research."

19 China Power Project, "Are Patents Indicative of Chinese Innovation?"

20 Frolovskiy "China's Education Boom."

21 McCarthy, "Why Are Growing Numbers of Overseas Chinese Students Returning Home?"

22 Manyika, McRaven, and Segal, "Innovation and National Security."

23 Manyika, McRaven, and Segal, "Innovation and National Security."

24 Yu, "Building the Ladder."

25 "President Xi Stresses Innovation to Bolster Economy."

26 "The Story of China's Economy as Told through the World's Biggest Building."

27 Si, "Nation Can Withstand Manufacturing Risks."

28 Meeker, "Internet Trends 2018."

29 Emanuel, Gadsden, and Moore, "How the US Surrendered to China on Scientific Research."

30 Si, "Industrial Upgrading Will Continue."

31 Palmer, "China's Overrated Technocrats."

32 PricewaterhouseCoopers China, "China's New Leadership Rolls Out New Blueprint for Future Development: Business Review of China's 19th Party Congress." .

33 Jinping, "*Tan jingzhun fupin: Kai duile 'yaofang zi', caineng ba diao 'qiong genzi.*'"

34 Cheng Li, "Xi Jinping's 'Proregress.'"

35 World Bank and the Development Research Center of the State Council, *China 2030.*

36 For detail, see Wang-Kaeding, "What Does Xi Jinping's New Phrase 'Ecological Civilization' Mean?"

37 Noesselt, "Introduction: 'New Normal' under Xi Jinping."

38 Li, "The Chinese Discourse on Good Governance."

39 McKinsey Global Institute, "China and the World."

40 For a detailed analysis of the topic, see Cordesman, "China and the US."

41 Rapoza, "New Data Shows US Companies Are Definitely Leaving China."

42 "China Unveils Guideline on Improving Market-based Allocation of Production Factors."

43 Wu and Ma, *Whither China?*, iii.

44 Xiangwei, "The Bold Zero-tariff Plan That Could Settle the US-China Trade War in Beijing's Favour."

45 Wu and Ma, *Whither China?*, iii.

46 Economy, *Third Revolution*, 95.

47 Lardy, *The State Strikes Back*, 128.

48 Li, "Xi Jinping's 'Proregress.'"

49 Taplin, "China Could Lose Face, Get Rich from a Trade Deal."

50 National Bureau of Statistics of China, *China Statistical Year Book 2018.*

51 "China's Finance World Opens Up to Foreigners, Sort of."

52 Urcosta, "The Geopolitical Consequences of the Coronavirus Outbreak."

53 "Trade Set to Plunge as COVID-19 Pandemic Upends Global Economy."

54 Balding, "What's Causing China's Economic Slowdown and How Beijing Will Respond."

55 Balding, "What's Causing China's Economic Slowdown and How Beijing Will Respond."

56 Roberts and Mehlman, "What Does Population Aging Mean for Growth and Investments?"

57 Eberstadt, "With Great Demographics Comes Great Power."

58 Lardy, *The State Strikes Back*, 122.

59 "China's Debt Tops 300% of GDP, Now 15% of Global Total."

60 Quoted in Pettis, "China's Troubled Transition to a More Balanced Growth Model."

61 "Xi Says China's Reform Enters Deep-Water Zone."

62 Chang, *The Coming Collapse of China.*

63 For detailed analysis on the topic, see Cordesman, "China and the US."

BIBLIOGRAPHY

Atkinson, Robert D. and Caleb Foote. "Is China Catching Up to the United States in Innovation?" Information Technology and Innovation Foundation, April 8, 2019. https://itif.org.

Blackwill, Robert and Jennifer Harris. *War by Other Means: Geoeconomics and State-craft*. Cambridge, MA: Harvard University Press, 2016.

Boutin, Kenneth. *Economic Security and Sino-American Relations: Progress under Pressure* Northampton, MA: Edward Elgar Publication, 2019.

Carfagno, Bart and Michelle Ker. "Policy Analyst, Economics and Trade," U.S.-China Economic and Security Review Commission Staff Research Report, July 19, 2018. www.uscc.gov.

Cheng, Siwei. *Financial Reforms and Developments in China*. Singapore: World Scientific, 2013.

"China Power Project. "Are Patents Indicative of Chinese Innovation?" ChinaPower. February 15, 2016. https://chinapower.csis.org.

"China Unveils Guideline on Improving Market-based Allocation of Production Factors." *China Daily*, April 10, 2020. www.china.org.cn.

"China's Debt Tops 300% of GDP, Now 15% of Global Total: IIF." Reuters. July 18, 2019. www.reuters.com.

"China's Finance World Opens Up to Foreigners, Sort of." Bloomberg Quint. Updated May 18, 2020. www.bloombergquint.com.

Cordesman, Anthony H. "China and the US: Cooperation, Competition and/or Conflict: An Experimental Assessment." Center for Strategic and International Studies. October 1, 2019. www.csis.org.

DeLisle, Jacques and Avery Goldstein eds. *China's Challenges*. Philadelphia, PA: University of Pennsylvania Press, 2016.

Eberstadt, Nicholas. "With Great Demographics Comes Great Power: Why Population Will Drive Geopolitics," *Foreign Affairs* 98, no. 44 (July 2019): 146.

Economy, Elizabeth. *The Third Revolution: Xi Jinping and the New Chinese State*. New York: Oxford University Press, 2018.

Emanuel, Ezekiel, Amy Gadsden, and Scott Moore. "How the US Surrendered to China on Scientific Research." *Wall Street Journal*, April 20, 2019. www.wsj.com.

Frolovskiy, Dmitriy. "China's Education Boom." *Diplomat*, December 29, 2017. https://thediplomat.com.

Gore, Lance L. P. "China's Party-Dominated Governance System: How Does It Achieve Efficiency, Legitimacy and Accountability?" *EAI Background Brief*, no. 1444, April 2019.

Heilmann, Sebastian. *Red Swan: How Unorthodox Policy Making Facilitated China's Rise*. Hong Kong: Chinese University Press, 2018.

Jinping, Xi. "*Tan jingzhun fupin: Kai duile 'yaofang zi', caineng ba diao 'qiong genzi.'*" ["On Precision Poverty Alleviation: When You Have Found the Right 'Medical Formula,' You Can Unplug the 'Poor Roots.'"] *Renmin wang* [People's Daily website], February 18, 2019, http://cpc.people.com.cn.

Kenneth Rapoza, "New Data Shows US Companies Are Definitely Leaving China." *Forbes*, April 7, 2020. www.forbes.com.

Khan, Sulmaan Wasif. *Haunted by Chaos: China's Grand Strategy from Mao Zedong to Xi Jinping*. Cambridge, MA: Harvard University Press, 2018.

Lardy, Nicholas R. *The State Strikes Back: The End of Economic Reform in China?* Washington, DC: Peterson Institute for International Economics, 2019.

Lau, Lawrence Juen-yee. *Is the Chinese Economy a Miracle or a Bubble?* Hong Kong: Chinese University Press, 2019.

Li, Cheng. "Xi Jinping's 'Proregress': Domestic Moves toward a Global China." Brookings. September 2019. www.brookings.edu.

Li, He. "The Chinese Discourse on Good Governance: Content and Implications." *Journal of Contemporary China* (2020): 1–14.

Manyika, James, William McRaven, and Adam Segal. "Innovation and National Security: Keeping Our Edge." Council on Foreign Relations. Updated September 2019. www.cfr.org.

McCarthy, Simone. "Why Are Growing Numbers of Overseas Chinese Students Returning Home?" *SupChina*. https://supchina.com.

McKinsey Global Institute. "China and the World: Inside the Dynamics of a Changing Relationship." McKinsey. July 1, 2019. www.mckinsey.com.

Meeker, Mary. "Internet Trends 2018." Kleiner Perkins. May 30, 2018. www.kleinerperkins.com.

Morrison, Wayne M. "China's Economic Rise: History, Trends, Challenges, and Implications for the United States," *Congressional Research Service Report*, updated June 25, 2019. https://crsreports.congress.gov.

National Bureau of Statistics of China. *China Statistical Year Book 2018.* China Statistics Press, 2018. www.stats.gov.cn.

Naughton, Barry J. *The Chinese Economy: Adaptation and Growth*, 2nd ed. Cambridge, MA: MIT Press, 2018.

Noesselt, Nele. "Introduction: 'New Normal' under Xi Jinping." *Journal of Chinese Political Science*, 22, no. 3 (2017): 321–25.

O'Connor, Sean (2019). "How Chinese Companies Facilitate Tech Transfer from the US." US-China Economic and Security Review Commission. May 6, 2019. www.uscc.gov.

Palmer, James. "China's Overrated Technocrats." *Foreign Policy*, no. 233 (Summer 2019): 9.

Pettis, Michael. "China's Troubled Transition to a More Balanced Growth Model." New America. March 1, 2011. www.newamerica.org.

"President Xi Stresses Innovation to Bolster Economy." *China Daily*, May 11, 2016. www.chinadaily.com.cn.

PricewaterhouseCoopers China. "China's New Leadership Rolls Out New Blueprint for Future Development: Business Review of China's 19th Party Congress." 2017. www.pwccn.com.

Qiao, Liang and Wang Xiangsui. *Unrestricted Warfare: China's Master Plan to Destroy America.* Panama City, Panama: Pan American, 2002.

Roberts, Anthea, Henrique Choer Moraes, and Victor Ferguson, "Geoeconomics: The Chinese Strategy of Technological Advancement and Cybersecurity." Lawfare. December 3, 2018. www.lawfareblog.com.

Roberts, Paula Campbell and Ken Mehlman. "What Does Population Aging Mean for Growth and Investments?" KKR, February 13, 2018. www.kkr.com.

Scott, Bruce R. "The Concept of National Economic Strategy." In *International Friction and Cooperation in High-Technology Development and Trade: Papers and*

Proceedings, ed. National Research Council, 239–66. Washington, DC: The National Academies Press, 1997.

Si, Ma. "Industrial Upgrading Will Continue." *China Daily*, September 21, 2019. www .chinadaily.com.cn.

Si, Ma. "Nation Can Withstand Manufacturing Risks." *China Daily*, September 28, 2018. www.chinadailyhk.com.

Taplin, Nathaniel. "China Could Lose Face, Get Rich from a Trade Deal." *Wall Street Journal*, May 14, 2019. www.wsj.com.

"The Story of China's Economy as Told through the World's Biggest Building." *Economist*, February 23, 2019. www.economist.com.

"Trade Set to Plunge as COVID-19 Pandemic Upends Global Economy." World Trade Organization. April 8, 2020. www.wto.org.

Urcosta, Ridvan Bari. "The Geopolitical Consequences of the Coronavirus Outbreak." *Diplomat*, January 31, 2020. https://thediplomat.com.

US Chamber of Commerce. "Made in China 2025: Global Ambitions: Built on Local Protections." March 16, 2017. www.uschamber.com.

Wade, Robert H. "The Developmental State: Dead or Alive?" *Development and Change*, 49, no. 2 (2019): 518–46.

Wang-Kaeding, Heidi. "What Does Xi Jinping's New Phrase 'Ecological Civilization' Mean? An Investigation of the Phrase is Pressing." *Diplomat*. March 6, 2018. https://thediplomat.com.

Wong, John and Tai Wei Lim. "The Economic Card in China's Pro-Active Diplomacy." *East Asian Policy* 7, no. 3 (2015): 99–101.

World Bank and the Development Research Center of the State Council. *China 2030: Building a Modern, Harmonious, and Creative High-Income Society.* Washington DC: World Bank, 2013.

World Bank. "World Bank in China," accessed November 21, 2020. www.worldbank.org/.

World Intellectual Property Organization. "Global Innovation Index 2019." Accessed September 1, 2020. www.wipo.int.

Wu, Jinglian and Ma Guochuan. *Whither China? Restarting the Reform Agenda.* New York: Oxford University Press, 2016.

"Xi Says China's Reform Enters Deep-Water Zone." *Global Times*, April 1, 2014. www.globaltimes.cn.

Xiangwei, Wang. "The Bold Zero-Tariff Plan That Could Settle the US-China Trade War in Beijing's Favour." *South China Morning Post*, June 1, 2019. www.scmp.com.

Xin Li, Bo Meng, and Zhi Wang. "Recent Patterns of Global Production and GVC Participation." In *Technological Innovation, Supply Chain Trade, and Workers in a Globalized World: Global Value Chain Development Report 2019*, 9–43. Washington, DC: World Bank Group, 2019. http://documents.worldbank.org.

Yu, Peter K. "Building the Ladder: Three Decades of Development of the Chinese Patent System." *WIPO Journal*, 4, no. 1 (2013): 1–16.

Yuan, Li. "Private Businesses Build Modern China. Now the Government Is Pushing Back." *New York Times*. October 3, 2018. www.nytimes.com.

3

Xi Jinping's Vision of Chinese Foreign Policy

A Coherent Chinese Diplomatic Strategy?

ROBERT SUTTER

Since taking top governing positions in late 2012 and early 2013, strongman leader Xi Jinping has directly controlled China's policy making, including over foreign affairs. Expanding Chinese economic and military power accompanies a rise in China's international influence and activism. Against that background, Xi has put aside the low profile in world affairs recommended by China's last dominant leader, Deng Xiaoping (d. 1997), declaring a "new era" in which China leads in nearby Asian countries and throughout the world.

The vision Xi proposes for China's diplomatic strategy is ambitious, clear, and coherent. It centers on his grand "China Dream" of a rejuvenated Middle Kingdom with primacy in Asia and wide influence on world affairs, in which a strong and confident China gains ever more economic, military, and political power and influence and uses it to foster peace and development in ways that benefit friendly countries and global governance.

Many abroad echo the hagiographic accolades for Xi's foreign approach that emanate from China's powerful party and government publicity mechanisms. The US and other governments and specialists disagree. For them, China is rising at the expense of others; it is changing the international order in ways that disadvantage them. Some critics discern a long-term Chinese strategy of seeking ever-broader dominance, targeting the United States. For others, China's behavior belies a coherent diplomatic strategy.[1]

This chapter's assessment of the vision and realities of contemporary Chinese foreign policy and practice demonstrates that strong and changing circumstances, often outside the control of Chinese leaders, are making it difficult for the Chinese government to chart a coherent diplomatic strategy. Such circumstances have been evident throughout the history of the People's Republic of China (PRC). Dealing with them has caused Chinese leaders to shift diplomatic strategy on various occasions. This chapter illustrates the circumstances that are prominent today—notably, the deepening strategic US-China divide reinforced most recently by the COVID-19 pandemic. I find that Xi's vision will continue to encounter major obstacles in the days ahead. Readers are advised to watch for shifts in the Chinese diplomatic strategy going forward.

Does China Have a Consistent and Coherent Diplomatic Strategy?

The literature arguing that China follows a consistent and coherent diplomatic strategy cites variables influencing a nation's grand strategy: (1) the country's strategic environment; (2) national resources—tangible and intangible; (3) the ambitions and effectiveness of leaders; (4) the country's strategic culture.[2] Mao Zedong directed Chinese foreign policy until his death in 1976. Consistency was not seen in that period, which saw Mao shift dramatically in his dealings with the Soviet Union and the US. In the post-Mao period, specialists in China and abroad often judged that Deng Xiaoping and later leaders were following a coherent strategy focused on peace and development; they assumed this would last well into the twenty-first century.[3] In contrast, American and other foreign specialists critical of China's rise argued that China's strategy was hidden—it notably sought regional and in some cases global dominance—goals explicitly denied by Beijing.[4] Other specialists argued that, as in the Maoist period, China's approach was subject to change, particularly as major uncertainties and variables pushed its foreign policy in directions different from the avowed strategy of the time. As shown below, this writer judges that the record of past and recent Chinese foreign behavior supports the latter view. What seems constant in China's diplomatic strategy is that it continues to change over time.[5]

Important enduring aspects of Chinese foreign policy making that support the image (if not the reality) of a consistent strategy in Chinese foreign policy are the beliefs of Chinese leaders and the Chinese people, heavily influenced by conditioning controlled by Chinese leaders: (1) China's foreign policy is consistent; (2) China follows morally righteous principles in dealing with foreign affairs; (3) abiding by principles and seeking moral positions provide the basis for effective Chinese strategy and approaches in world affairs; (4) such strategy and approaches ensure that China does not make mistakes in foreign affairs, an exceptional position reinforced by the fact that the PRC is seen to have avoided publicly acknowledging foreign policy mistakes or apologizing its actions in world affairs.[6] In reality, however, this self-righteous attitude hinders effective management of disputes and adds to circumstances that impede pursuit of Chinese ambitions.

Xi Jinping's Foreign Policy Vision

Xi Jinping and supporting publicists craft a vision called the China Dream that builds on gains in China's rising influence in Asian and world affairs. The vision also seeks the approval of Chinese elite and popular opinion and support for Xi's rule. However, the image of a powerful and benign China moving smoothly to international leadership proves weak in the face of realities constraining China.[7]

The China Dream: The Central Mission

Xi Jinping's China dream of "national rejuvenation" comes after two centuries of struggle against national weakness and foreign exploitation. It seeks a unified and powerful China as Asia's leader and a great power. As noted, Xi broke with the more restrained policies of previous leaders who followed Deng Xiaoping's instructions in foreign affairs. Unlike his predecessor, Hu Jintao (2002–12), Xi is bolder and no longer emphasizes reassurance of the US, Asian neighbors, and others that China's rise will be peaceful; those gestures are now seen as signs of weakness.

Salient manifestations of Xi's new foreign policy approach include:

- Using growing military, paramilitary, economic, and other state power coercively, though generally short of military attack, to advance China's broad territorial claims and other interests at the expense of neighbors and the US. Concurrent and often hidden efforts by Chinese spies and other government, party, and military agents foster influence and favorable elite and public opinion in a wide range of developed and developing countries.

- Using large foreign exchange reserves and massive excess industrial capacity to launch various self-serving international economic development programs (e.g., the Belt and Road Initiative) and institutions that undermine US leadership and/or exclude the US.
- Advancing China's military buildup, targeted mainly at the US in the Asia-Pacific region, and building capacity for far-reaching military deployments, including the nurturing of states beholden to China to host Chinese military forces overseas.
- Cooperating ever more closely with Russia as both powers increasingly support one another to pursue, through coercive and other means, revisionist ambitions in their respective spheres of influence, taking advantage of weaknesses in the US, Europe, the Middle East, and Asia.
- Continuing cyber theft of economic assets; widespread violations of intellectual property rights; grossly unfair market access restrictions on US and other developed countries' companies; state-directed industrial policies leading to targeted acquisition of US and other high-technology; large-scale overcapacity disadvantaging US and other foreign producers; and currency practices disadvantaging US and other foreign traders. "Made in China 2025," a massive effort benefiting from these economic practices, seeks dominance in high technology industries to protect China from feared US technological leadership.
- Intensified internal repression and tightened political control—all with serious adverse consequences for US interests and those of other developed countries.

The US was slow in responding effectively to Xi Jinping's advances. President Barack Obama began to complain publicly about Chinese practices that came at US expense, but President Xi publicly ignored the complaints. The Obama government believed US interests were best served by managing growing differences in order to preserve positive US engagement with China. American critics, who rose in influence after President Obama left office, believed that Xi Jinping was duplicitously playing a double game, pretending to seek cooperation while relentlessly undermining the US.[8] At this time, US opinion was negative toward the Chinese government but sought to avoid confrontation. The media and elites in both political parties increasingly shifted against Xi and his practices; calls for a tougher US approach toward China came from both leading candidates and most others in the 2016 US presidential election campaign, though most candidates did not deem China a high priority.[9]

Internationally, key factors facilitating Xi's foreign advances were an irresolute American government; a decline in the ability and willingness of US allies and partners to counter China's affronts; weaknesses in Asia, notably Southeast Asia, allowing Chinese to expand into the disputed South China Sea. Meanwhile, Russia, facing strong sanctions in the West, became more dependent on China.[10]

Newly Prominent Elements in Xi's Foreign Policy Vision

Supporting the foreign policy implications of Xi Jinping's China Dream are three other elements in China's foreign policy that have featured prominently in official Chinese discourse since the start of Xi's second five-year term at the Chinese party and government congresses of 2017–18. The first is the idea that China is building "A Community with a Shared Future." Commentary on this aspect of current Chinese foreign policy argues that China recognizes its rising global status and seeks to do more to protect world peace, advance development, and promote international cooperation. Xi Jinping's speech at the international economic meeting in Davos, Switzerland, in January 2017, and an article by leading foreign policy spokesperson Ambassador Fu Ying in June 2017 both underlined the concept of a community of a shared future.[11] The concept prioritizes an United Nations-based international order and includes support for the World Trade Organization and the World Bank; it opposes a US-led world order based on alliances and US-backed interventions beyond UN norms. China's officials continue at times to call for a new world order, but the more recent emphasis on a community of a shared future implies preserving much of the existing US-led world order and changing it along lines favored by China.

In this regard, on security disputes, China depicts itself as favoring consultations and as very reluctant to resort to force; it opposes US alliances and international interventions. On economics, China sees its so-called Silk Road or One Belt, One Road plans, now known as the Belt and Road Initiative (BRI), as an exemplary way to promote mutually beneficial (or what China calls "win-win") economic development. On diplomacy, China argues for inclusiveness, allowing different government systems to develop without prejudice or interference. In this context, it opposes Western promotion of human rights, democracy, and good governance.

The second newly publicized element in the Xi Jinping government's foreign policy plans is an emphasis on the idea that China undertakes more international costs and leadership risks, contrary to its past reputation as a "free rider," leaving such costs and risks to the US and other developed countries. Highlighted here are reports that China's UN dues and payments for UN peacekeeping now are in line with its economic advances, unlike in past decades when China worked hard to portray itself as a developing country warranting very small UN dues and payment responsibilities. Also, China has put aside its past status as a net recipient of foreign assistance, even though it still annually receives several billion dollars of international assistance. In particular, Chinese loans supporting foreign infrastructure projects and other ventures are deemed very important for promoting development among BRI participants and elsewhere in the developing world. Also, China's commitment to the Paris Agreement on climate change is portrayed as crucial to world support for the agreement. And China's support for economic globalization is welcomed amid signs of populist resistance in the US and the West.

The third newly emphasized feature of the Xi Jinping government's foreign policy approach has to do with the Chinese government's long-standing practice of manipulating Chinese historical interpretation to serve the needs of the ruling authorities. In the current period, the interpretation being stressed is one that supports China's identity as historically peaceful—a benign leader of *Tianxia*—translated as "all under heaven" and historically referring to China and all of the surrounding territories that fell within the scope of the civilization of Chinese imperial dynasties in the previous two millennia.[12]

This emphasis is designed to influence the idea, in China and abroad, that Chinese governments and people have always been peace-loving. Xi Jinping is among the leading Chinese officials who use such a depiction of history to underline the assertion that peace and harmony are integral in the spirit and blood of Chinese people.[13] Responding to

Xi's leadership, Chinese scholars reconstruct Chinese history to show a benevolent Chinese empire (*Tianxia*) based on royal ethics or the so-called *Wangdao* (translated as "righteous rule") shown by the Chinese leader.

The governance model seen here is one of subjects and neighboring states being subservient to the Chinese ruler, whose governance secures lasting peace and order for the benefit of all. This image of past Chinese rule is contrasted favorably against Western practices of using coercive power to advance narrow state interests. This Chinese identity of benevolence and righteousness fits well with the aforementioned government conditioning of opinion in China to view Chinese foreign policy as uniformly moral and correct. Thus, Chinese opinion is inclined to support the Chinese government's positions in disputes with other countries. Many abroad also echo Chinese claims of benevolence and righteousness. In contrast, foreign historians often find the interpretations historically wrong and professionally offensive. The many foreigners subjected to past and recent Chinese expansion and intimidation often see them as propaganda and self-serving lies.

Image Meets Realities: Constraints on China's Rise

Circumstances impacting China's diplomatic strategy of power and influence abroad seriously limit China's rise.[14] They include China's domestic preoccupations, the strong interdependence of the US and China, China's insecure position in Asia, gaps and shortcomings in China's international economic policies, the US position in Asia and the world, enduring US strengths in the Asia-Pacific region, and the current American hardening against China.

Domestic Preoccupations

Chinese leaders face a major challenge in trying to maintain one-party rule in the world's largest country, a very dynamic and economically vibrant society. To sustain one-party rule requires massive expenditures and widespread leadership attention regarding internal security and control and strong continued economic growth that advances the material benefits of Chinese people and ensures general public support and legitimacy for the Communist government. These domestic concerns are multifaceted, expensive to deal with, and very hard to resolve.[15] They involve:

- weak leadership legitimacy that is highly dependent on how the leaders' performance is seen at any given time;
- pervasive corruption that saps public support and undermines government efficiency;
- widening income gaps that are contrary to Communist ideals and are sources of social division;
- widespread social turmoil (reportedly involving 100,000–200,000 mass incidents annually) that require domestic security budgets bigger than China's large national defense budget;[16]
- a highly resource-intensive economy and enormous related environmental damage; and
- over sixty major reforms proposed in 2013 for an economic model at the point of diminishing returns with no clear plan of how they can be implemented.

Domestic preoccupations, reinforced by extraordinary measures to deal with the COVID-19 pandemic, make China reluctant to undertake the costs and risks of international leadership because it has so many important requirements at home. One result is that China continues to rely on the US-led world order where it benefits China, moving only incrementally to displace US leadership.

Strong Interdependence with the United States

The so-called trade war with the US has brought home to Chinese leaders how strongly China depends on the US economically. The US has much greater influence than China on the international flows of technology, finance, and trade that China depends on. The economic face-off with the US causes major harm to Chinese economic development—the linchpin of regime legitimacy in China.[17] China also depends on the US for secure passage of its growing imports of oil and gas from the Persian Gulf. Moreover, neither side can deal effectively with North Korea without the other. Additional areas of interdependence involve climate change, antiterrorism, nuclear nonproliferation, and cyber security.

The respite in the trade war provided by the so-called Phase I trade agreement was quickly overshadowed by strident acrimony and acute rivalry prompted by the COVID-19 pandemic. Notably, China launched a world propaganda campaign that covered up responsibility for initially mishandling the virus and causing global plague. China portrayed itself as effectively curbing the virus at home and generously offering medical supplies abroad. Some prominent Americans argued for closer US government cooperation with China to deal with the crisis, but President Trump, Democratic presidential candidates, bipartisan congressional majorities, mainstream media, and public opinion all viewed China more negatively. US hardening deepened as it became clear that in the initial stages of the outbreak, China cornered the world market in medical equipment and supplies needed to fight the virus. The result was that the many states that were ill-prepared to deal with the outbreak, including the US, found no available supplies because of Chinese hoarding, profiteering and using targeted international donations to burnish China's world image. The broadly negative US view of China also prompted forecasts that Republican political strategists would continue through the election year to blame China in order to distract attention from the Trump administration's initial handling of the crisis.[18]

China's Insecure Position in Asia

The areas of Asia adjacent to China is where it devotes the lion's share of its foreign policy attention. Nearby Asian countries have security and sovereignty issues (e.g., Taiwan) of top importance. This is also the main arena of interaction with the US. The region's economic importance for China far surpasses the rest of world. Without a secure foundation among its Asian neighbors, China will have difficulty undertaking major leadership roles in other world areas.

An inventory of China's relationships with other leading regional powers, notably Japan and India, and with important mid-level powers like South Korea and Australia, shows serious reversals over the past two decades. Similarly serious downturns have occurred in areas keenly sensitive to Chinese interests, notably Taiwan, Hong Kong, and North Korea. In particular, Beijing's passivity in the face of protracted anti-China mass demonstrations in Hong Kong in 2019 and its failure to influence Taiwan's elections in 2020 project a constrained rather than decisive Chinese leadership. These setbacks offset the widely touted gains China has made in the South China Sea and among some Southeast Asian and other neighboring countries.

This mixed record has persisted for thirty years as China has tried, with mediocre results, to expand its influence in nearby Asian countries after the Cold War. But negative legacies of past violent and coercive policies and practices prompt regional wariness of contemporary Chinese intentions. Chinese foreign policy in post–Cold War Asia also shows conflicting objectives involving peaceful development of mutual interests, on the one hand, and steely determination to gain control of disputed territories and resources at neighbors' expense, on the other. China has repeatedly switched postures, at times stressing reassurance and peaceful development and at other times stressing determination and intimidation in pursuing sensitive issues of sovereignty and security.

Looking to the future, it is hard to predict whether or not China's importance as a powerful military force and prime trader and investor with nearby Asian countries will override security, sovereignty, and other differences, and these issues are unlikely to be resolved anytime soon. Uncertainty over US resolve to sustain regional leadership remains an important determinant in China's quest for Asian primacy, though, as shown below, recent US government hardening toward China clearly complicates and constrains China's rise going forward.

Gaps and Shortcomings in China's International Economic Policies

Xi Jinping's BRI, begun in 2013, advances and modifies the strong "going out" policies of Chinese investment and financing abroad seen in the previous decade[19] That past effort focused on attaining access to the oil and other raw materials needed for China's resource-hungry economy. Recent Chinese economic reforms seek to reduce such intense resource use. The new push for Chinese foreign investment and financing is meant to enable construction abroad of Chinese-supplied infrastructure provided by the enormous excess capacity of Chinese companies for such construction and supply now that major infrastructure development inside China is curtailed under recent economic reforms. Locating some of China's heavily resource-intensive and polluting industries abroad eases China's serious pollution problems and enhances its ability to meet commitments to international climate-change agreements. Economically, the new push also helps to connect the poorer regions of central and western China to international markets and thereby advance their development; to provide investment opportunities promising better returns for China's $3 trillion foreign exchange reserves invested in low-yield foreign securities; and to broaden the international use of China's currency. Strategically, it improves Chinese access to key international land and sea corridors, reduces China's vulnerability to actual or possible US military control of transit choke points for Chinese shipping, and advances overall Chinese relations with important countries.

The BRI also is the centerpiece of China's push to build an exaggerated image of itself as a confident and generous global economic leader. The realities seen in summing up the results of China's decades-long "going out" strategy and the trends in recent Chinese economic behavior show substantial growth in Chinese economic activism, influence, and power, but also pervasive constraints and strong negative international reactions.

Since China joined the World Trade Organization in 2001, Beijing has relied on its burgeoning trade with Asian and international markets as the primary source of its international economic influence. For several years, China's volume of trade grew at double the rate of its economic growth of around 10 percent. In contrast, while the Chinese economy continued to grow by around 7 percent in 2015 and 2016, the growth of Chinese trade collapsed—its rate was zero in those two years. The value of trade began to rise again in 2017, but a return to the days of high annual growth seemed unlikely even before the major negative impacts of the US-China trade war and the COVID-19 pandemic.[20]

The "going out" policies begun twenty years ago were accompanied by massive publicity for Chinese multi-billion-dollar agreements to invest in various developing countries and to promote infrastructure constructed by Chinese companies with loans from Chinese banks. The recent BRI and related initiatives are accompanied by the same kind of positive publicity. Foreign experts' assessments, in contrast, are more sober. China's actual investment in developing countries remains limited. Its more important position as the leading world provider of financing for infrastructure has resulted in only a few, often very controversial, countries taking on China as the dominant international economic power. More commonly, Beijing is seen as a growing source of influence, but still only "one among several" foreign sources of economic influence and support.[21]

As a provider of infrastructure financing to developing countries, serious shortcomings emerge. China's past record of announcing massive deals and delivering much less continues. The reasons focus on the difficulty of carrying out large projects in poorly governed countries that are bad credit risks. Other factors include changes in governments and much greater opposition to Chinese practices by the US and some other developed countries. The American government, think tanks, and the media in the US and other developed countries have been in the lead recently in exposing how the Chinese government uses loans and economic dependency to infiltrate and influence decision making in vulnerable developing countries to benefit Chinese expansion abroad. Special attention has been devoted to China's pursuit of ports in the Indo-Pacific region for its forces, the expansion of Chinese telecommunications to dominant positions in these countries, backing for Chinese expansion in the South China Sea, and its egregious crackdown on dissent in the Xinjiang region.[22]

The US Position in Asia and the World

Until the past decade, a comparison of Chinese policies and practices with those of the US in the Asia-Pacific region (of top importance to China) and the rest of the world underlined how far China had to go to supersede American leadership.[23] However, after the US for many years accommodated China's rise through constructive engagement and the downplaying of differences, the erratic behavior of the current, unpredictable US president has added to regional and international uncertainty about American leadership. Extraordinary domestic distractions—notably the congressional impeachment of the president in 2019 and the pandemic of 2020—have compounded the difficulties leaders throughout the world have faced in attempting to weigh American resolve to stay the course in Asian and world affairs. Going forward, will the US persist in its past leadership role in competition with China in the Asia-Pacific region? Other possibilities range from retrenchment to conflict. In particular, retrenchment means that existing constraints on China in Asia will weaken substantially and China will have a freer hand in advancing toward regional dominance.

Nevertheless, the realities of US power and practice demonstrate enduring strengths. And the past three years have seen a sharp US policy shift away from its previous drift toward a new confrontation the China, now widely viewed as America's number-one opponent. The new American toughness is led by the administration and bipartisan congressional leaders. It is reinforced by an ever-growing outpouring of government and nongovernmental assessments disclosing in detail China's heretofore often hidden measures to expand at American expense while publicly avowing cooperation. Beijing is now widely viewed as duplicitous, which makes meaningful agreements and accommodation more difficult in the foreseeable future. Media and public opinion have become significantly more negative and sharp criticism of China comes from leading Democratic presidential candidates, as well.[24]

China's leaders did not anticipate the recent American shift and the array of troubles it poses for China's economy, international influence, security, and sovereignty. Facing an aroused US, Xi Jinping's strategy in pursuit of the China Dream is now under revision, the latest episode of China being compelled by circumstances to shift its strategy in order to accommodate a changing situation and rising constraints.

Enduring US Strengths in the Asia-Pacific Region

The deeply rooted US military and intelligence relationship with almost all Asia-Pacific governments has made the head of the US Indo-Pacific Command an active senior US government representative in the region; these relationships remain of mutual benefit and do not depend on sentiment. And despite withdrawing from the Trans Pacific Partnership (TPP), the US market still absorbs a massive amount of manufactured goods from regional exporters and their component suppliers in the regional production chains. The US has a unique and remarkably strong foundation of nongovernment connections with Asian countries, topped off by the influence of the many millions of Asians who are now settled there and participating constructively in interchanges connecting the US and Asia.

The basic determinants of US strength and influence in the Asia-Pacific region involve five factors. The first is security. In most of Asia, governments are viable and make the decisions that determine their direction in foreign affairs. Popular and elite opinion, the media, and other spheres may influence government officials in policy toward the US and other countries, but in the end the officials make decisions on the basis of their own calculus. In general, such officials see their governments' legitimacy and success resting on nation building and economic development, which require a stable and secure international environment. Asia is not particularly stable, however, and most regional governments are privately wary of each other. As a result, they look to the US to provide the security that they need to pursue goals of development and nation building in an appropriate environment. They recognize that the US security role is very expensive and involves great risk, including large-scale casualties if necessary, for the sake of preserving Asian security. They also recognize that neither China nor any other Asian power or coalition of powers is able or willing to undertake even a small part of these risks, costs, and responsibilities.

Second, the nation-building priority of most Asian governments depends greatly on export-oriented growth. Much of Chinese and Asian trade depends heavily on exports to developed countries, notably the US. The US has run a massive trade deficit with China, and a total annual trade deficit with Asia valued at more than US $500 billion. Asian government officials recognize that China, which consistently runs an overall trade surplus, and other trading partners in Asia, are unwilling and unable to bear even a fraction of the cost of such large trade deficits, which are nonetheless very important for Asian governments. The recent US-China trade war seriously disrupts existing production chains valued by Asian governments, forcing expensive adjustments in their export-oriented economies that nonetheless still depend substantially on exports to the US.

Third, despite the negative popular view in Asia of the George W. Bush administration's policies in Iraq and the broader war on terror, it was generally effective in its interactions with Asia's powers—notably China, Japan, and India. The Obama administration built on these strengths. The Obama government's broad rebalancing with regional governments and multilateral organizations had a scope ranging from India to the Pacific island states to Korea and Japan. Its emphasis on consultation with and inclusion of international stakeholders before coming to policy decisions on issues of importance to Asia and the Pacific was also broadly welcomed and stood in contrast with the previously perceived unilateralism of the Bush administration. Meanwhile, the US Indo-Pacific Command and other US military commands and security and intelligence organizations have been at the edge of wide-ranging and growing US efforts to build and strengthen webs of military and related intelligence and security relationships throughout the region. Such cooperation has advanced in recent years. The Trump government's tougher policies toward China are a disruptive surprise to regional governments that nonetheless generally see their interests best served by dealing constructively with the US president.

Fourth, the US has long engaged the Asia-Pacific region through business, religious, educational, media, and other interchanges. Such active nongovernmental interaction puts the US in a unique position and reinforces overall American influence. Meanwhile, more than fifty years of generally color-blind US immigration policy, since the ending of discriminatory American restrictions on Asian immigration in 1965, has resulted in the influx of millions of Asia-Pacific migrants who call the US home and who interact with their countries of origin in ways that underpin and reflect well on the US position in the region. The Trump government's stricter immigration policies reduce this dimension of US soft power, but the flow of migrants remains substantial.

Fifth, part of the reason for the success of US efforts to build webs of security-related and other relationships with Asia-Pacific countries has to do with active contingency planning by many Asia-Pacific governments. As power relations change in the region, notably on account of China's rise, regional governments, on the one hand, generally seek to work positively and pragmatically with China, but, on the other hand, they also seek the reassurance of close security, intelligence, and other ties with the US, in case China shifts from its avowed benign approach to one of greater assertiveness or dominance. Xi Jinping's pursuit of the China Dream has notably precipitated ever-greater security contingency planning by the US and its allies and partners in Asia. The US, Japan, Australia, and India, sometimes under the rubric of the so-called Quad, engage in an ongoing exchange of views regarding how to deal with the adverse consequences of China's rise.

American Hardening against China

The breadth and depth of hardening American attitudes toward China continues to grow, even with debate over the Trump administration's tariffs and trade policy.[25] The hardening is reinforced by criticism across the political spectrum in US government of a wide range of Chinese state policies and practices. Think tank and academic specialists have revealed a long list of often hidden or disguised actions by the Chinese government as it seeks greater advantage and influence at American expense while professing positive intentions toward the US, its allies, and partners.

Well-documented reports criticizing Chinese trade, investment, and other economic practices produced by the US Trade Representative get much greater media and specialist attention in the Trump administration, supporting tariffs and other measures targeting a wide range of Chinese practices that US Trade Representative Robert Lighthizer views as an existential threat to the American economy. China's intention to use "Made in China 2025" to advance the country to a controlling position in the high-tech manufacturing of the future features prominently; a prevailing judgment is that Beijing is at a stage of economic development where it represents a peer of the US, and it could surpass it in the years ahead in global economic and security leadership.

The Departments of Justice and Homeland Security and the FBI publicize Chinese economic and military espionage intended to strengthen China and weaken the US. They disclose overt and covert influence operations, propaganda, and penetration of key sectors of American society for the purpose of distracting and limiting American opposition to Chinese policies and practices adverse to US interests. China's use of such influence operations abroad also receives official attention from the Department of Defense. The Chinese state uses so-called hybrid warfare tactics including economic and political intimidation and coercion as well as enticement and corruption in seeking to advance China's control abroad. Recent nongovernmental studies showed fifteen categories and nine instances of Chinese practices that have negative implications for US interests.

The Department of Defense and nongovernmental think tanks have disclosed the networks of the Chinese Communist Party, media, high technology communications, economic influence, espionage, special payments and other means that have accompanied Chinese infrastructure projects abroad under the rubric of the BRI. While Beijing's reported use of indebtedness to gain greater control of developing countries is a common refrain in US government and other criticism of China's BRI, the evidence in these studies shows a range of tools Beijing uses covertly as well as overtly to support its foreign ambitions. The Defense Department gives special attention to Beijing seeking military bases abroad in countries heavily indebted to Chinese lenders.

Think tank studies have documented Beijing's Janus-faced approach to the South China Sea, pledging peace and development on the one hand while secretly confronting small Asian neighbors and disputing China's egregious (and illegal) claims in the South China Sea with the type of crude bullying seen in gangster movies. These revelations show that although the extensive and growing cooperation between China and Russia has multiple objectives, it has a single common target—to diminish the international influence of the US. Although China differs from Russia in wanting to preserve and exploit aspects of the existing US-led international order, Beijing is actively seeking to undermine the US-led order and replace it with elements supportive of authoritarian regimes like their own.

Outlook

Xi Jinping's China is unlikely to back away publicly from its ambitious diplomatic strategy focused on the China Dream, if only to sustain China's image as following a consistent, morally correct and effective foreign policy. But Chinese leaders have clearly underestimated the American resolve shown in the past three years. The US under President Trump was commonly seen by Chinese officials as pragmatic; Trump was viewed as a business dealer with whom China could advance its agenda smoothly. Beijing was among the last in the world to acknowledge the seriousness of American challenges to China's ambitions.[26]

Today, the economic, security, and diplomatic challenges facing Chinese ambitions are enormous and growing. COVID-19 has caused massive unexpected domestic expenditures amid widespread questioning of the competence of the regime, and it has deepened the strategic divide with the US. The setbacks and failures of Chinese policy in dealing with the US come in tandem with stronger pushback in Europe and elsewhere against China's mercantilist economic policies, influence operations, and the egregious violations of human rights seen most glaringly today in its incarceration of over a million Muslims in the Xinjiang region for purposes of thought reform. While Xi Jinping remains dominant at home, Chinese officials are publicly calling for a new foreign policy strategy to deal with the adverse situation. Thinly disguised grumbling is even being aired over the hubris of Chinese leadership in throwing off Deng's cautious approach in favor of unrealistic ambitions.[27]

On important foreign policy issues close to home, Beijing is maneuvering to ease longstanding tensions with Japan and India in order to focus on the US. It has failed to still the remarkable protests in Hong Kong that rebuked China's direction as the PRC ceremoniously marked its seventieth anniversary in October 2019. Pressure on Taiwan to elect a pro-China president in January 2020 met with a backlash on the island and was offset by unprecedented US support for the Taiwanese government. Relations with both North and South Korea remain uncertain, recovering from major Chinese pressures on both in recent years. The economic losses China faces (from the trade war and from the overall decline of its growth rate and that of the world economy in the wake of the ongoing pandemic) forecast a retrenchment of Chinese outlays to poor credit risks in the BRI. China is improving relations with Russia and Central Asian countries and Beijing's double game of economic enticement and coercion regarding South China Sea and other disputes advances its influence in Southeast Asia. But regional leaders also cling to US ties as a hedge against feared Chinese ascendency. In sum, readers are advised to watch for more adjustments and shifts as Chinese leaders respond to obstacles and constraints, many outside their control, in their avowed but flawed efforts to devise a consistent and coherent diplomatic strategy.

NOTES

1 On debates over China's diplomatic strategy, see my review of the works of Thomas Christensen, Dai Bingguo, Aaron Friedberg, Bates Gill, Avery Goldstein, David Michael Lampton, Evan Medeiros, Michael Pillsbury, Denny Roy, Phillip Saunders, David Shambaugh, Susan Shirk, Tang Shiping, Ashley Tellis, Wang Jisi, Zhang Yunling, and Zheng Bijian in Sutter, *Chinese Foreign Relations*, 3–16.

2　Tellis, "Pursuing Global Reach."

3　Goldstein, *Rising to the Challenge*; Bates Gill, *Rising Star*.

4　Friedberg, *The Contest for Supremacy*; Roy, *Return of the Dragon*; Tellis, *Balancing without Containment*; Pillsbury, *Hundred Year Marathon*.

5　Shirk, *China*; Sutter, *Foreign Relations of the PRC*. On the PRC's often changing military doctrine in response to other countries' capacities and other circumstances, see Fravel, *Active Defense*.

6　Roy, *China's Foreign Relations*, 36–39; Kim, "China's International Organizational Behavior," 401–5; Harding, "China's Changing Role in the Contemporary World," 177–79; Ford, "Realpolitik with Chinese Characteristics," 31–37; Sutter, *Foreign Relations of the PRC*, 10. Contributors to this volume discuss whether or not Xi Jinping's adjustments regarding problems in the Belt and Road Initiative (BRI), made at the 2019 BRI summit, represented public acknowledgement of China's mistakes. This writer's review of the record sees a variety of reasons offered for the adjustments involving foreign countries as well as China, but no direct acknowledgement that China made mistakes.

7　For background and sources regarding this section, see Sutter, *Foreign Relations of the PRC*, 297–301.

8　Sutter, "Obama's Cautious and Calibrated Approach to an Assertive China."

9　Sutter and Limaye, *America's 2016 Election Debate on Asia Policy and Asian Reactions*.

10　Weitz et al., *Russia-China Relations*.

11　"Full text of Xi Jinping Keynote at World Economic Forum"; Ying, "China's Vision for the World."

12　Zhao, "Reconstruction of Chinese History for a Peaceful Rise."

13　Ching, "Does Chinese Blood Really Lack DNA for Aggression?"

14　For background and sources for this section, see Sutter, *Foreign Relations of the PRC*, 301–313 and Sutter, *United States and Asia*, chap. 11.

15　See Shambaugh, *China's Future*.

16　Blanchard and Ruwitch, "China Hikes Defense Budget, to Spend More in Internal Security."

17　Shih, "US-China Relations in 2019."

18　Rogin, "The Coronavirus is Turning Americans in Both Parties against China"; Heer, "Why the Coronavirus is a Hinge for the Future of US-China Relations"; Sutter, Schwarzenberg and Sutherland, *COVID-19*.

19　For background and sources for this section, see Sutter, *Foreign Relations of the PRC*, 305–310, and Sutter, *United States and Asia*, chap. 11. See also Shinn, "China's Just Another Great Power in Africa"; Myers, "The Reasons for China's Cooling Interest in Latin America."

20　Shih, "US-China Relations."

21　Shinn, "China's Just Another Great Power in Africa"; Myers, "The Reasons for China's Cooling Interest in Latin America."

22　Tellis, Szalwinski, and Wills, eds., *Strategic Asia 2020*.

23 Sutter, *United States and Asia*, chaps. 1, 5, and 11; "Special Report"; Schell and Shirk, *Course Correction*; Paal, "America's Future in a Dynamic Asia."
24 Sutter, "Has US Government Angst over the China Danger Diminished?"
25 Sutter, "Strong Evidence Targeting China."
26 Sutter, "Trump, America and the World."
27 Shih, "US-China Relations"; Gang, "Time for China to Forge a New Strategy toward the US"; Yinhong, "Nostalgic Past, Stark Present, and Hopeful Future for Sino-US Ties."

BIBLIOGRAPHY

An, Gang. "Time for China to Forge a New Strategy towards the US." *China-US Focus Newsletter*, June 4, 2019. www.chinausfocus.com.

Barshevsky, et al. "US Policy toward China: Recommendations for a New Administration." New York: Asia Society, 2017.

Blackwill, Robert and Ashley Tellis. *Council Special Report: Revising US Grand Strategy toward China*. Washington, DC: Council on Foreign Relations, April 2015.

Blanchard, Ben, and John Ruwitch. "China Hikes Defense Budget, to Spend More in Internal Security." Reuters. March 5, 2013. www.reuters.com.

Ching, Frank. "Does Chinese Blood Really Lack DNA for Aggression?" *South China Morning Post*, July 1, 2014. www.scmp.com.

Christensen, Thomas. *The China Challenge*. New York: Norton, 2015.

Dai Bingguo. "Stick to the Path of Peaceful Development." *Beijing Review* 51 (December 23, 2010). www.bjreview.com.

Deng, Yong. "China: The Post-Responsible Power." *Washington Quarterly* 37, no. 4 (Winter 2015): 117–32.

Diamond, Larry, and Orville Schell. *Chinese Influence and American Interests*. Stanford, CA: Hoover Institution, 2018.

Dittmer, Lowell. *China's Asia: Triangular Dynamics since the Cold War*. Lanham MD: Rowman & Littlefield, 2018.

Economist. "Special Report: China and America," May 18, 2019, 3–16.

Economy, Elizabeth. *The Third Revolution: Xi Jinping and the New Chinese State*. New York: Oxford University Press, 2018.

Ellings, Richard, and Robert Sutter, eds. *Axis of Authoritarians: Implications of China-Russia Cooperation*. Seattle, WA: National Bureau of Asian Research, 2018.

Ford, Christopher. "Realpolitik with Chinese Characteristics: Chinese Strategic Culture and the Modern Communist Party-State." In *Strategic Asia 2016–17: Understanding Strategic Cultures*, edited by Ashley Tellis, Alison Szalwinski, and Michael Wills, 29–60. Seattle, WA: National Bureau of Asian Research, 2016.

Fravel, M. Taylor. *Active Defense: China's Military Strategy Since 1949*. Princeton, NJ: Princeton University Press, 2019.

Friedberg, Aaron. "Competing with China," *Survival* 60, no. 3 (June 2018): 7–64.

Friedberg, Aaron. *A Contest for Supremacy: China, America, and the Struggle for Mastery in Asia*. New York: W. W. Norton, 2011.

"Full Text of Xi Jinping Keynote at World Economic Forum." *China Global Television Network*, January 17, 2017. https://america.cgtn.com.

Garver, John. *China's Quest*. New York: Oxford University Press, 2016.

Gill, Bates. *Rising Star: China's New Security Diplomacy*. Washington, DC: Brookings Institution Press, 2007.

Goh, Evelyn, ed. *Rising China's Influence in Developing Asia*. New York: Oxford University Press, 2016.

Goldstein, Avery. *Rising to the Challenge: China's Grand Strategy and International Security*. Stanford, CA: Stanford University Press, 2005.

Harding, Harry. "China's Changing Role in the Contemporary World." In *China's Foreign Relations in the 1980s*, edited by Harry Harding, 177–224. New Haven, CT: Yale University Press, 1985.

Heer, Paul. "Why the Coronavirus is a Hinge for the Future of US-China Relations." *National Interest*, April 7, 2020. https://nationalinterest.org.

Johnson, Christopher. *Decoding China's Emerging "Great Power" Strategy in Asia*. Washington, DC: Center for Strategic and International Studies, June 2014.

Kang, David. "Getting Asia Wrong: The Need for New Analytical Frameworks." *International Security* 27, no. 4 (Spring 2003): 57–85.

Kim, Samuel Kim. "China's International Organizational Behavior." In *Chinese Foreign Policy: Theory and Practice*, edited by Thomas Robinson and David Shambaugh, 401–34. New York: Oxford University Press, 1994.

Lampton, David M. *The Three Faces of Chinese Power: Might, Money, and Minds*. Berkeley, CA: University of California Press, 2008.

Medeiros, Evan. "China Reacts: Assessing Beijing's Response to Trump's New China Strategy." *China Leadership Monitor*, March 1, 2019.

Medeiros, Evan. "The Changing Fundamentals of US-China Relations," *Washington Quarterly* 42, no. 3 (Fall 2019): 93–119.

Myers, Margaret. "The Reasons for China's Cooling Interest in Latin America." *Americas Quarterly*, April 23, 2019. www.americasquarterly.org.

Paal, Douglas. *America's Future in a Dynamic Asia*. Working paper. Washington, DC: Carnegie Endowment for International Peace, January 2019.

Pillsbury, Michael. *The Hundred Year Marathon*. New York: Holt, 2015.

Rogin, Josh. "The Coronavirus is Turning Americans in Both Parties against China." *Washington Post*, April 8, 2020. www.washingtonpost.com.

Rolland, Nadege. *China's Eurasian Century? Political and Strategic Implications of the Belt and Road Initiative*. Seattle, WA: National Bureau of Asian Research, 2017.

Roy, Denny. *China's Foreign Relations*. Lanham, MD: Rowman & Littlefield, 1998.

Roy, Denny. *Return of the Dragon: Rising China and Regional Security*. New York: Columbia University Press, 2012.

Schell, Orville, and Susan Shirk. "Course Correction: Toward an Effective and Sustainable China Policy. Task Force Report." New York: Asia Society and University of California San Diego, February 2019.

Shambaugh, David, ed. *China and the World*. New York: Oxford University Press, 2020.

Shambaugh, David. "US-China Rivalry in Southeast Asia: Power Shift or Competitive Coexistence." *International Security* 42, no. 4 (Spring 2018): 85–127.

Shambaugh, David. *China's Future*. Cambridge, UK: Polity Press, 2016.

Shi, Yinhong. "Nostalgic Past, Stark Present, and Hopeful Future for Sino-US Ties." *China-US Focus*, July 3, 2019. www.chinausfocus.com.

Shih, Victor. "US-China Relations in 2019: A Year in Review." Testimony before the US-China Economic and Security Review Commission, September 4, 2019. www.uscc.gov.

Shinn, David. "China's Just Another Great Power in Africa." *East Asia Forum*, May 17, 2018. www.eastasiaforum.org.

Shirk, Susan. *China: Fragile Superpower*. New York: Oxford University Press, 2007.

Smith, Sheila. *Intimate Rivals*. New York: Columbia University Press, 2015.

Snyder, Scott. *South Korea at the Crossroads: Autonomy and Alliance in an Era of Rival Powers*. New York: Columbia University Press, 2018.

Strategic Asia 2020: US-China Competition for Global Influence. Seattle WA: National Bureau of Asian Research 2020.

Sun, Yun. *Chinese National Security Decision-making: Process and Challenges*. Washington, DC: Brookings Institution, May 2013.

Sutter, Karen M., Andres B. Schwarzenberg, and Michael D. Sutherland. *COVID-19: China Medical Supply Chains and Broader Trade Issues*. Congressional Research Service Report R46304, Congressional Research Service, Library of Congress, Washington DC, April 6, 2020. https://crsreports.congress.gov.

Sutter, Robert, and Satu Limaye. *America's 2016 Election Debate on Asia Policy and Asian Reactions*. Honolulu, HI: East-West Center, 2016.

Sutter, Robert. "Has US Government Angst over the China Danger Diminished?" *Asia-Pacific Bulletin*, January 22, 2020. www.eastwestcenter.org.

Sutter, Robert. "Obama's Cautious and Calibrated Approach to an Assertive China." *Yale Global*, April 19, 2016, http://yaleglobal.yale.edu.

Sutter, Robert. "Strong Evidence Targeting China—Lasting Constraints on US Engagement." *PACNET Newsletter* #50, September 10, 2019. www.pacforum.org.

Sutter, Robert. "Trump, America and the World—2017 and Beyond." *H-Diplo/ISSF POLICY Series*, January 19, 2019. https://networks.h-net.org.

Sutter, Robert. *Chinese Foreign Relations*. 4th ed. Lanham, MD: Rowman & Littlefield, 2016.

Sutter, Robert. *Foreign Relations of the PRC*. Lanham, MD: Rowman & Littlefield, 2013.

Sutter, Robert. *The United States and Asia*. 2nd ed. Lanham, MD: Rowman & Littlefield, 2020.

Swaine, Michael, and Ashley Tellis. *Interpreting China's Grand Strategy, Past, Present and Future*. Santa Monica, CA: RAND Corporation, September 2001.

Swaine, Michael, with Wenyan Deng and Aube Rey Lescure. *Creating a Stable Asia*. Washington, DC: Carnegie Endowment for International Peace, 2016.

Swaine, Michael. *America's Challenge: Engaging a Rising China in the Twenty-First Century*. Washington, DC: Carnegie Endowment for International Peace, 2011.

Tellis, Ashley. "Pursuing Global Reach: China's Not So Long March toward Preeminence." In *Strategic Asia 2019: China's Expanding Strategic Ambitions*, edited by Ashley Tellis, Alison Szalwinski, and Michael Wills, 3–48. Seattle, WA: National Bureau of Asian Research 2019.

Tellis, Ashley. *Balancing without Containment*. Washington, DC: Carnegie Endowment for International Peace Report, January 22, 2014.

Wang, Jisi. "China's Search for a Grand Strategy." *Foreign Affairs* 90, no. 2 (March/April 2011): 68–79.

Weitz, Richard, Robert Sutter, J. Stapleton Roy, Eugene Rumer, Michael S. Chase, and Evan S. Medeiros. *Russia-China Relations: Assessing Common Ground and Strategic Fault Lines*. Seattle, WA: National Bureau of Asian Research, July 2017. http://nbr.org.

White, Hugh. *The China Choice*. Collingwood, Australia: Black Inc., 2012.

Yahuda, Michael. *The International Politics of the Asia-Pacific*. 4th ed. London: Routledge, 2019.

Yan, Xuetong et al. *Ancient Chinese Thought, Modern Chinese Power*. Princeton, NJ: Princeton University Press, 2011.

Ye, Zicheng, *Inside China's Grand Strategy: The Perspective from the People's Republic*. Lanham, MD: Lexington Press, 2011.

Ying, Fu. "China's Vision for the World: A Community of Shared Future." *Diplomat*, June 22, 2017. https://thediplomat.com.

Zhao, Suisheng. "Reconstruction of Chinese History for a Peaceful Rise." *Yale Global*. June 13, 2017. https://yaleglobal.yale.edu.

Zhu, Liqun, *China's Foreign Policy Debates*. Brussels: Chaillot Papers, September 2010.

4

China's Grand Strategy toward Northeast Asia

RALPH A. COSSA

Describing China's "grand strategy" toward Northeast Asia requires as much analysis—some would say speculation—as it does research, since China does not produce a public strategy document like the American *National Security Strategy Report* and much of the Chinese government's pronouncements about strategy, like those about principles, must be considered suspect when matched against its actions and policies. The 2017 State Council white paper "China's Policies on Asia-Pacific Security Cooperation," for example, asserts that Beijing's overall strategy and its Asia-Pacific policy are founded on the five principles of peaceful coexistence; foremost among these principles is "noninterference in others' internal affairs."[1] Yet few nations (Russia being a notable exception) interfere in the internal affairs of its neighbors on a scale matched by China. One only needs to watch Beijing control tourism levels in advance of Taiwan's January 2020 presidential elections, comment repeatedly on the content of Japanese textbooks, or punish Korean firms after Seoul allowed Washington to install a missile defense system aimed at North Korea on its soil, or coach—if not control—Chinese student organizations in Australia or elsewhere in Asia (and beyond) to understand Beijing seldom practices what it preaches when it comes to noninterference.

As a result, while this chapter looks at Chinese pronouncements regarding relations and intentions vis-à-vis its Northeast Asian neighbors, it also includes the author's own analysis regarding China's "true" long-term intentions and grand strategy. This analysis is based on two basic premises. The first is that Chinese President Xi Jinping appears set on moving beyond "Deng Xiaoping thought," which instructed China's leaders to "hide your strength and bide your time,"[2] in order to pursue his own vision of the "China Dream."[3] The decision by the rubber-stamp

National Peoples' Congress in March 2018 to remove the two-term limit on the presidency that Deng had installed—essentially permitting Xi to become president for life—put the final nail in Deng's coffin.[4] It is Xi Jinping thought that now prevails.

Xi's dream is to restore China to its "rightful place" in Asia and the world. This leads to a second premise: when Xi Jinping looks to China's Northeast Asia neighbors, he longs for a return to what many Chinese would believe to be the natural order of things. During the second half of the twentieth century, when the leaders of Japan, North and South Korea, Taiwan, and, indeed, even China itself woke up each morning, the first thing they wondered about, foreign policy-wise, was "what is Washington thinking about today?" When making foreign policy decisions, a primary (if not determinative) factor was, "how will this play in Washington?"

Since Xi Jinping came to power, this phenomenon has been changing. Most Northeast Asian leaders still wonder first about what Washington is thinking, especially given President Trump's generally nontraditional (dare we say erratic) approach to foreign policy—but their next thought is about how Beijing will respond. Xi would like to accelerate and institutionalize this change in priority, as the Middle Kingdom takes up what is to him its proper role as the regional (if not one day global) hegemon, replacing the United States. While each of his neighbors will be handled in different ways, the overall objective is to put China's priorities and concerns, rather than Washington's, first in their minds, just like in the good old days before the "century of humiliation."[5]

Xi first laid out his China Dream shortly after assuming the role of Party General Secretary in November 2012: "In my view, to realize the great renewal of the Chinese nation is the greatest dream for the Chinese nation in modern history."[6] He went on to set a timeline:

> I believe that by the time when the Communist Party of China marks its one-hundredth founding anniversary [July 23, 2021], the goal to complete the building of a moderately prosperous society in all respects will be inevitably achieved. When it comes to the one-hundredth founding anniversary of new China [October 1, 2049], the goal of building an affluent, strong, civilized and harmonious socialist modern country will certainly be fulfilled, and the dream of great renewal of the Chinese nation will inevitably be accomplished.[7]

Xi is believed to have taken inspiration for the "China Dream" from a book by the same title written in 2010 by Colonel Liu Mingfu of China's National Defense University in 2010.[8] While Xi did not talk about grand strategy or Northeast Asia in rolling out his "grand renewal" concept, there is an entire chapter on strategy in Liu's book.[9] Liu notes that "The Communist Party of China's grand strategy to save and revive the nation features two distinctive breakthroughs: first is the strategy's global reach—it is intimately linked with the world beyond China; second is its phased implementation."[10] He describes the phases as follows: "China's strategy is to deal with itself first, then Asia, then the world. The grand strategy of twenty-first-century China has to answer three questions: what kind of a China should we build, what kind of Asia should we build, and what kind of a world should we build?"[11]

In answering the first question, Liu stresses that economic development is key to China's future success, even though "China's rise and revival cannot be limited to a strictly economic rise"—China also needs a powerful military and a compelling ideology.[12] While internally focused, this first stage, which coincides with Xi's first one-hundredth anniversary milestone, has foreign policy implications. As Xi himself noted as early as October 2013, the period leading up to 2021 is "a period of strategic opportunity" for China, during which it must "consolidate its friendly relations with neighboring countries and make the best use of the strategic opportunities [that] China now has. . . . We must strive to make our neighbors more friendly in politics, economically more closely tied to us, and we must have deeper security cooperation and closer people-to-people ties."[13]

Laying out the strategy that has largely been followed to date, Xi noted that great efforts must be made toward "accurately identifying convergence points for cooperation; making use of China's advantages in economy, trade, technology, and finance; and actively taking part in regional economic cooperation." He also said China should work with its neighbors "to hasten inter-connectivity and establish a Silk Road Economic Belt and a Maritime Silk Road for the twenty-first century . . . ; accelerate establishment of free trade zones, with neighbors as the foundation stone; expand trade and investment; and create a new pattern of regional economic integration."[14]

In pursuit of this strategy, China has, in fact, become the largest trading partner of all of its Northeast Asian neighbors, with regional trade accounting for nearly a quarter of China's overall trade.[15] As Chi Fulin, president of the China Institute for Reform and Development, explained, China "highly values comprehensive planning of integrated development with its neighbors, and prioritizes economic and trade ties with neighboring countries in its efforts to build a new type of economic partnership, most importantly with Northeast Asia." Xi has also been pursuing a trilateral trade agreement with Japan and Korea for several years, although the lingering tensions between these two US allies (which suits Beijing's larger purpose) have been a restraining factor.[16]

Writing in the National Bureau of Asian Research's annual *Strategic Asia* report, Patricia Kim argues that:

> China seeks to build a Northeast Asian regional order centered on economic development in which it enjoys superiority across all dimensions and can freely protect its interests while retaining the respect and support of its neighbors. It is working to achieve these objectives through: (1) a public diplomacy strategy that aims to win support for its great-power ambitions, (2) an economic strategy that draws regional states into Chinese-led initiatives, and (3) a security strategy based on expanding military capabilities, strengthening territorial claims in the East China Sea, and weakening the US-led alliance system.[17]

All of this is consistent with Liu's and Xi's China dreams. Ironically, in laying out his dream in 2013, Xi also noted that "the basic tenet of diplomacy with neighbors is to treat them as friends and partners, to make them feel safe and to help them develop."[18] This, however, is one area where Xi has not fully practiced what he preached; "hide your strength" has not been one of his defining characteristics. As noted China expert Bonnie Glaser observed in testimony before the US-China Economic and Security Review Commission in early 2014, "since coming to power, Xi Jinping has repeatedly emphasized that China's good-neighborly policy does not mean compromising on disputes over sovereignty, territory, and jurisdiction."[19] According to Glaser, Xi "appears to believe that growing Chinese economic and military clout will over time persuade its neighbors that there is more to gain from accommodating Chinese interests than from challenging them."[20] This logic is prevalent in Colonel Liu's analysis as well.

In Liu's section on "What Kind of Asia Should Be Built?" he asserts: "To lead the world China first needs to lead Asia."[21] He further notes that "if China wants to manage the world, it first needs to manage Asia. . . . Most of the world's key nations are in Asia, or will be in the future. We must manage their rise, *and they will resist our management* [emphasis added]."[22] He identifies Japan and India as the primary challengers to China's leadership—"Today China, Japan, and India are acting out the Wars of the Three Kingdoms over the entire continent"[23]—but is confident that China will prevail, both in Asia and globally.

Xi set out early to manage his neighbors. Again, according to Glaser, "In handling relations with its neighbors, China is employing both carrots and sticks to deter countries from pursuing policies that inflict damage on Chinese interests. Beijing's periphery policy is also aimed at countering the US rebalance to Asia [the Obama administration's Asia policy at the time], preventing the formation of anti-China coalitions on its periphery, and weakening US alliances."[24]

Criticism of the US alliance network in Asia has been a constant feature of China's Northeast Asia policy since long before Xi came to power. Concern about US alliances is a central theme in Liu's China Dream book. When arguing that "A Peaceful Rise is Contingent on a Strong Military" to counter the threat posed by the US, Liu talks about the US "strategic encirclement of China," specifically noting that "in the East, it established a military alliance with Japan and South Korea, and used Taiwan to pin down China," and that it "acted aggressively to promote the formation of an alliance of states to deal with China."[25] The US, he warns, "creates anti-enemy alliances and creates a unified front in the world, controlling Western countries and containing rising countries to guarantee its status and interests as a hegemonic power."[26]

This rhetoric of opposition to the US alliance can be found in almost every Chinese presentation on US-Asia strategy today, where it is decried as an example of a "Cold War mentality." In fact, accusing the US of a "Cold War mentality" or "Cold War mindset" has become a favorite theme of Cui Tiankai, current Chinese Ambassador to Washington.[27] Central Party School scholar Chen Jimin has also argued that "a renewed Cold War mentality has entangled the US,"[28] even as China's senior-most defense official, State Councilor and Minister of Defense General Wei Fenghe warned at the 2019 Shangri-La Dialogue in Singapore that "no approaches to regional issues should resort to military blocs."[29] China's 2019 "Defense White Paper" also complains that "the US is strengthening its Asia-Pacific military alliances and reinforcing military deployment and intervention, adding complexity to regional security."[30] The foreign ministry's Asia-Pacific policy paper was even more explicit: "Major countries should treat the strategic intentions of others in an objective and rational manner, reject the Cold War mentality, . . . and pursue partnerships rather than alliances."[31]

One can safely surmise from all this that one of Xi's strategic priorities in Northeast Asia continues to be the weakening, if not the breaking, of the US alliance network, including Washington's *de facto* alliance with Taipei. The US-China Economic and Security Review Commission's *2018 Annual Report to Congress* reached a similar conclusion: "Beijing seeks to undermine US alliances and partnerships in the Indo-Pacific to reorder the region to its advantage. China seeks a dominant role in Asia and views US military alliances and influence as the primary obstacle to achieving this objective."[32]

As Xi continues his "building of a moderately prosperous society in all respects," it raises the question as to what China's grand strategy toward its neighbors is or will become once China reaches its 2021 centennial goal and he focuses more intently on Liu's second phase; namely, "managing Asia."

While crafting their strategy, neither Xi nor Liu could foresee the impact that a China-originated global pandemic could have on the achievement of their dream. While the long-term impact is yet to be determined, the initial cover-up and mishandling of the coronavirus outbreak in Wuhan has demonstrated the weaknesses inherent in Xi's authoritarian regime.[33] Once the government acknowledged the problem and responded, it was praised. But the praise was short-lived once Beijing launched a massive (and hugely disingenuous) campaign to shift the blame for the virus' origins to the West, with the US and Italy being the most frequent victims of this "fake news" campaign.[34] China's handling of the pandemic and its aftermath impacted its relations with all of its neighbors, but none as much as with its brothers and sisters on Taiwan.

Grand Strategy toward Taiwan

China's stated long-term objective regarding Taiwan remains clear and consistent: reunification, preferably peaceful. The good news about Xi laying the groundwork to become president for life (or at least beyond his current second term) is that, to the extent he sees resolving the Taiwan problem as part of his desired legacy,[35] at least the clock is not ticking down dangerously.[36]

Xi's January 2, 2019 remarks commemorating the fortieth anniversary of Deng Xiaoping's "Message to Compatriots in Taiwan" clearly articulated his thinking regarding Taiwan: "China's complete reunification as a historic task" following "the basic principles of 'peaceful reunification' and 'one country, two systems.'"[37] While the Western press focused on Xi's refusal to rule out the use of force,[38] "peaceful reunification" or "peaceful development" were used more than a dozen times in the China Daily's summation of Xi's remarks[39] and the overall tone was nonthreatening, especially since Xi did not set a timeline for reunification. His comments on the use of force were pretty standard: "We make no promise to renounce the use of force and reserve the option of taking all necessary means."[40] He further noted that China "will leave no room for any form of separatist activities" but prefaced this by stating that "we are willing to create broad space for peaceful reunification."[41]

Nonetheless, long-time Taiwan-watcher David G. Brown observed that Xi's "reformulations took a decidedly tougher tone," as Xi asserted that the 1992 Consensus—the basis of cooperation between Beijing and the former Kuomintang (KMT) administration in Taipei—meant not only that both sides "belong to one China" but also that they "will work together toward national reunification," and that China's "One China principle" and not the 1992 consensus was "the political basis for cross-Strait relations."[42]

Most notable about Xi's January 2 remarks was his repeated reference to the "one country, two system" formula (originally formulated to facilitate Hong Kong's reversion to the mainland's control) as "the best approach to realizing national reunification," which was further defined by Xi as follows: "On the basis of ensuring China's sovereignty, security, and interests of development, the social system and way of life in Taiwan will be fully respected, and the private property, religious beliefs and legitimate rights and interests of Taiwan compatriots will be fully protected after peaceful reunification is realized."[43]

China's white paper on the practice of the "one country, two systems" policy in Hong Kong states that the Hong Kong Special Administrative Region "exercises a high degree of autonomy in accordance with the law, and is vested with executive, legislative and independent judicial power, including that of final adjudication." It further states that the policy "enjoys growing popularity in Hong Kong, winning the whole-hearted support from Hong Kong compatriots as well as people in all other parts of China," which presumably includes Taiwan, since it is seen as a "part of China" by Beijing.[44]

All of this was patently and demonstrably false, even before the 2019 pro-democracy protests in Hong Kong, but these have clearly put the final nail in the "one country, two systems" formula, at least as far as Taiwan is concerned. Taiwan President Tsai Ing-wen, after noting that Hong Kong was "on the verge of chaos due to the failure of 'one country, two systems,'" declared (correctly) during her 2019 National Day address that "the overwhelming consensus among Taiwan's twenty-three million people is our rejection of 'one country, two systems,' regardless of party affiliation or political position."[45] The continuing, broadly supported demonstrations in Hong Kong show that the people there share Tsai's assessment.[46]

The main lesson to be drawn from Hong Kong is not whether "one country, two systems" can work for Taiwan—it can't—but whether a re-surgent China will live up to its past obligations. As US Assistant Secretary of State David Stillwell testified before the US Congress:

> The world fully expects that the Chinese government will honor its bind-ing treaty, made with the British and registered with the United Nations, in which China commits to protect Hong Kong's freedom, legal system, and democratic ways of life. How China chooses to handle the situation will say a great deal about its role in the world in the future.[47]

There is little cause to be optimistic about China living up to its promises if its adherence to the Basic Agreement with the UK is the new norm. Xi's direct promise to then-President Obama not to militarize what have now become heavily fortified islands in the South China Sea is yet another example, as is Beijing's refusal to honor its promises made upon entry into the World Trade Organization.

In my many years of discussions with officials from the Taiwan Affairs Office in Beijing, I have never met a Chinese official or scholar who truly believed that any Taiwanese administration would ever accept the "one country, two systems" formula or that President Tsai would be politically capable of accepting the rival KMT's "1992 consensus" formulation as a basis for cross-Strait discussion.[48] Yet, under Xi, Beijing has insisted on this approach, indicating that there really is no sense of urgency behind a resumption of cross-Strait dialogue, at least as long as Tsai's Democratic Progressive Party (DPP) remains in power. Even under the more acceptable (or at least less confrontational) KMT, the prospects of Taiwan willingly becoming a province of the People's Republic of China (PRC) under any type of formula is considered extremely remote, and again, I have met few Chinese who believe this is likely, even as all must continue to religiously support peaceful reunification as the ultimate goal.

Public opinion polls in Taiwan provide justification for Chinese pessimism, with support for reunification with the PRC consistently falling under 3 percent of the population. Instead, most prefer the status quo (*de facto* independence), even while arguing that there is no need for a formal declaration of independence "since the Republic of China is already independent."[49] Both KMT and DPP leaders have traditionally made the "already independent" argument, understanding that a formal declaration of independence—declaring a *Republic of Taiwan* instead of the *Republic of China*, for example—would likely generate a military response from the mainland.[50] The best Beijing can hope for under the current DPP leadership is to prevent a further move toward independence.

Meanwhile, Beijing continues to take steps to "punish" the Tsai government for its "splittist" tendencies, while attempting to further isolate it internationally.[51] These activities were also clearly aimed at persuading "Taiwan compatriots" to support the KMT candidate in the 2020 presidential elections.[52] It is equally clear that this effort failed. As with any election, numerous factors no doubt contributed to Tsai's overwhelming victory—57 percent of the vote in a three-person race—but most analysts saw the "Hong Kong factor" as a major contributor.[53]

It should have become clear under the past KMT leadership, however, that no Taiwan leader will willingly work toward true reunification. While no Chinese leader or official (or even most scholars) would say so publicly, peaceful reunification remains a pipe dream, especially if the country continues to be ruled by the Chinese Communist Party.

While the threatened use of military force may be sufficient to prevent an independence declaration, its actual use would have staggering economic and political costs for the mainland. Chinese military capabilities, while considerably enhanced over the past decade or so, remain insufficient to militarily conquer, much less pacify the island, especially if the US remains poised and ready on its unsinkable Japanese aircraft carrier to prevent such an outcome. Even if it were not to fire a shot, the US could take economic measures that would cripple China's economy (albeit, of course, at great cost to its own) in response to Chinese-instigated cross-Strait hostilities.[54]

It would seem Chinese grand strategy toward Taiwan today is merely to prevent independence, not achieve true unification. This is why Beijing's former "hearts and minds" strategy seems to have been replaced by a "soft hand, hard hand" strategy that is aimed, less ambitiously, at preventing independence.[55] This was the primary intent of the Anti-Secession Law, which remains the essential piece of PRC legislation regarding Taiwan. It stresses that reunification "through peaceful means best serves the fundamental interests of the compatriots on both sides of the Taiwan Straits" and that the state "shall do its utmost with maximum sincerity to achieve a peaceful reunification." Should secessionist activities occur, however, "the state shall employ non-peaceful means and other necessary measures to protect China's sovereignty and territorial integrity."[56]

Beijing's handling of the coronavirus pandemic has put yet another (and likely final) nail in the peaceful reunification coffin. For starters, Beijing has continued its diplomatic isolation tactics, keeping Taipei from direct participation in the World Health Organization (WHO) pandemic prevention and response efforts, as it did during the SARS epidemic in 2003.[57] Chinese netizens, posing as Taiwan citizens, also fueled the flames of discontent and disinformation in hopes of driving a deeper wedge between Taiwan officials and WHO Director-General Tedros Adhanom Ghebreyesus, who demonstrated an unusual (dare we say unhealthy) deference to Beijing during the pandemic.[58] Meanwhile, those who might claim that Beijing's authoritarian system was best suited for managing such a crisis need only look across the Strait to see how a democratic society was even more effective in dealing with the challenge.[59]

The greatest hope for Xi to achieve his and his nation's One China dream is to redefine the term. Today the Chinese mantra is "there is only one China and Taiwan and the mainland are both part of that China." Changing one word could make this a more acceptable slogan to Taiwan: "there is only one China and Taiwan and the PRC are both part of that China." If Xi were strong and secure enough to seek such a win-win solution, he could accept the idea of "shared sovereignty" that I have previously described as "one nation, two states; one country, two governments." Otherwise, continuing to prevent *de jure* Taiwan independence may be the best Xi or any future Chinese leader can hope for, at least as long as the CCP prevails in Beijing.

Grand Strategy toward Japan

China's overall grand strategy toward its Northeast Asian neighbors has already been discussed in some detail above. It boils down to speaking loudly and waving a big (economic and military) stick to "persuade its neighbors that there is more to gain from accommodating Chinese interests than from challenging them."[60] For Japan, this includes cautious saber-rattling toward the Senkaku/Diaoyu Islands as part of its security strategy "based on expanding military capabilities, strengthening territorial claims in the East China Sea, and weakening the US-led alliance system."[61] As Patricia Kim further notes (and Colonel Liu would agree), "China desires stable economic relations with Japan but also views Tokyo as its primary regional competitor that must be prevented from assuming a greater security role in the region."[62]

Xi's predecessors probably saw some value in the US-Japan alliance during a period when Japan was strong and China was weak. The alliance helped prevent Japan's remilitarization; it helped keep Japan in a box in which Tokyo was quite content to remain. But this has changed.[63] As China becomes stronger, it becomes less and less concerned about a remilitarized Japan. It is Japan's role as an "unsinkable aircraft carrier" facilitating a forward US military presence that presents the greatest challenge to China's regional hegemony and reunification with Taiwan.

As a result, Chinese statements against the US-Japan alliance as part of both sides' "Cold War mentality" are frequent and readily available, as are admonitions to Japan that, given the new realities (including "an unpredictable US"), it should stop "playing second fiddle" to Washington: "Japan has recognized the historical trend of China's further development. China remains a future world power and Japan's neighbor, thus developing strategic relations with Beijing has become inevitable for Tokyo."[64]

In a May 2019 interview with the *Asahi Shimbun* in Beijing, Colonel Liu Mingfu amplified this point:

> I believe Japan now faces a third turning point. Now is the perfect opportunity for Japan to utilize the emergence of China and Asia, which is geographically close to it. Now is the time for Japan to escape from an excessive dependence on the United States and "return to Asia." With China breaking through the efforts by the United States to contain it, Japan should move away from being controlled by the United States and cooperate with China to create a new order in East Asia.[65]

If the handling of the COVID-19 pandemic is any example, there is little fear that Tokyo will take Liu's advice. Although the aftershocks of Beijing's mismanagement of the crisis affected Taipei and Seoul to a much greater degree, they also served to further deepen inbred Japanese suspicions and hostilities toward China. Even those who have argued that cooperation on dealing with the crisis could positively impact relations in the near term have been more pessimistic regarding any positive long-term impact from Sino-Japan pandemic cooperation.[66]

As a result, while some Chinese may dream of a Japan firmly in the Chinese camp, the most they can realistically hope for is a neutral and neutralized Japan. There is a catch-22 in all this, however. Most serious analysts agree that, were the US-Japan alliance to disintegrate or were Japan to lose faith in the US extended deterrent, Tokyo's most likely alternative would not be an alliance with Beijing but the development of an independent nuclear capability.[67] Given these two alternatives, I would argue that even a nuclear weapons-equipped, non-aligned Japan would seem less of a challenge to Beijing that a non-nuclear Japan closely aligned with the US, but others would no doubt debate this point.

Meanwhile, Tokyo's greatest leverage vis-à-vis Beijing is China's continued reliance on Japanese foreign direct investment and the Japanese factories in China that employ millions of Chinese workers.[68] This limits the degree to which Beijing can try to demonize and neutralize Japan, but as Japanese foreign direct investment shrinks and Chinese state-owned enterprises replace Japanese factories (after stealing their intellectual property), the nature of the relationship is likely to become more antagonistic.[69]

The success of China's grand strategy toward Japan depends in large part on how successfully Japan, in concert with the US, counters China's economic and political actions. It also depends, at the end of the day, on the strength of the US-Japan alliance. The current Trump administration's strategy toward Japan began with the rejection of the Obama-negotiated Trans-Pacific Partnership multinational trade agreement. It now includes economic pressure and tariffs along with a demand, at this writing, for a five-fold increase in the already sizable Japanese contribution toward the mutually beneficial basing of US forces in Japan. If not managed correctly, such demands may serve Beijing's strategic interests much more than either Washington's or Tokyo's. As Patricia Kim has summarized the situation, "To compete with China and signal commitment to the region, the US must demonstrate both military and economic engagement, and continue to reaffirm the values of democratic governance, political freedom, and rule of law that have long underpinned US soft power." Foremost among these efforts must be a reaffirmation and then strengthening of the Japan-US alliance.

Finally, Washington needs to be especially attuned to Japanese (and South Korean) concerns about the credibility of its extended deterrence. Any agreement with Pyongyang regarding the denuclearization (or not) of the Korean Peninsula must keep the credibility of US security assurances to Tokyo and Seoul in mind.[70]

Grand Strategy toward the Korean Peninsula
Republic of Korea (ROK or South Korea)

Even more than in the case of Japan, Beijing would love to see an end to the US-ROK alliance relationship (and is likely encouraged by the transactional approach to the alliance currently being taken by Washington).

As a general rule, Beijing prefers progressive rather than conservative leadership in Seoul since the former is less committed to sustaining the alliance and includes some downright anti-US elements (even though the current progressive Moon administration at a minimum continues to pay lip service to the alliance, provided it does not undermine North-South rapprochement).[71] Regardless of the party in power, however, Beijing's aim remains the same: the weakening, if not the abolition, of the ROK-US Alliance.

In the early days of China's re-emergence under Deng Xiaoping, Beijing placed a high priority on South Korean investment and economic/technical assistance. The Chaebol model was at one time seen as a useful model for Beijing to emulate (or exploit).[72] Under Xi, China has outgrown the ROK and no longer sees the need to handle Seoul with kid gloves. If anything, the reverse is now true. Xi's heavy-handed response to the ROK's decision to allow Washington to deploy its Terminal High Altitude Area Defense (THAAD) missile system to the Peninsula to protect against the growing North Korean missile threat certainly revealed China's more arrogant approach to Seoul when it dares to takes steps contrary to Beijing's clearly expressed desires (read: demands).[73]

While the missile system is purely defensive in nature, Beijing has alleged that its deployment "has severely undermined the regional strategic balance and the strategic security interests of regional countries."[74] China's political and economic reaction was harsh and largely continues to this day, even though Seoul has backed down on additional future THAAD deployments.[75] While Xi Jinping has been to Pyongyang (more on this below), his meetings with ROK President Moon have been limited to international gatherings. Meanwhile, Beijing's heavy-handed approach continues in ways that stretch the credibility of the US-ROK alliance and remind Seoul of Beijing's ever-present and increasing military capabilities. As Scott Snyder and See-Won Byun have summarized the issue,

> the China-South Korea relationship has also been hobbled by more aggressive Chinese intrusions into South Korean-claimed air and naval jurisdictions. Chinese vessels have reportedly attempted to normalize their presence on the South Korean side of the equidistant line between China and South Korea in the Yellow Sea. In addition, Chinese air patrols have

more actively entered portions of the Korean Air Defense Identification Zones (KADIZ) adjacent to Chinese-controlled zones and in the East Sea/Sea of Japan between Japan and South Korea.[76]

The handling of the coronavirus pandemic by both the Xi and Moon administrations has also increased hostile feelings toward China within the ROK. Unlike President Trump and other world leaders, President Moon gave in to Chinese pressure and refused to block travel from China, a step that no doubt contributed to South Korea becoming the Asian country (other than China) most affected by the virus.[77] Moon's decision to send medical supplies to China just prior to his own nation subsequently suffering a shortage of such equipment when the pandemic struck home resulted in calls for Moon's impeachment.[78] Adding insult to injury, once the situation appeared under control (or at least manageable) in China, many Chinese provinces banned travel from Korea.[79] It's no wonder that Korean attitudes toward China, already low, have plummeted.[80]

When it comes to the subject of the reunification of the Korean Peninsula, most Chinese would privately agree that if and when it occurs, is likely to take place under the political, economic, and social system prevalent in Seoul today. They would also agree that a reunified Korea, especially if denuclearized, would potentially be more stabilizing than a divided peninsula led by the Kim family in the Democratic People's Republic of Korea (DPRK). This latter outcome would first require an end to the US-ROK security relationship that could otherwise potentially place US military forces along the Yalu River on China's doorstep.[81]

China professes to support the on-again, off-again direct US-DPRK dialogue and North-South rapprochement, and this is likely true, with one important caveat, as noted in the *USCC 2018 Annual Report*: "China supports US and South Korean diplomatic engagement with North Korea, although Beijing is wary of being isolated in the process or losing out if North Korea commits to a full-scale strategic realignment with the United States and South Korea."[82] As a Chinese colleague once confided to me, "China adopts a 'Goldilocks approach' toward US-DPRK and North-South talks: they are OK as long as they are not too cold [resulting in conflict] or too warm [resulting in true rapprochement at China's expense]."

The *USCC 2018 Annual Report* sees China's immediate geopolitical goals as "avoiding war or instability in North Korea and, eventually, rolling back the US-South Korea alliance"; ending the North's nuclear and long-range missile programs is seen (by Beijing) as "a worthwhile but secondary goal."[83] The means of achieving its primary goals are "by advocating for a peace treaty to formally end the Korean War, seeking the suspension of joint US-South Korean military exercises, and pushing for a reduction of US forces in South Korea."[84] Not coincidentally, these mirror Pyongyang's demands to Washington in return for denuclearization discussions. The current government in South Korea also supports the first means and has voiced no strong objective to the second and third, raising questions about its long-term commitment to the alliance.

Meanwhile, Beijing has clearly tilted toward Pyongyang in recent years, since Xi's series of summits with Kim Jong Un began. Compare, for instance, Xi's visit to Pyongyang to commemorate the "new chapter" in China-DPRK relations after seventy years of diplomatic ties with his brief meeting along the sidelines of the Osaka G-20 with ROK President Moon. As Snyder and Byun noted, the Kim-Xi summit "aimed to advance the bilateral friendship to a new phase of comprehensive development and drive regional coordination on the Korean Peninsula," while the brief Xi-Moon meeting in Osaka "seemed to marginalize Moon, subordinate the relationship with South Korea, and place Xi as an intermediary between North Korea and the rest of world."[85]

Democratic People's Republic of Korea (DPRK or North Korea)

The one country where China's strategy of creating a situation of economic dependence has been at once the most successful and the least successful has been with the DPRK. Most successful, since over 90 percent of North Korea's official or legal trade is with China, and one suspects a similar amount of its illegal or clandestine commerce is with the PRC as well.[86] But also least successful, since the North Koreans seem unfazed by this dependency, acting like China needs them more than they need China. All too often, Chinese behavior reinforces this impression.

Pyongyang's handling of the coronavirus underscores both its dependency and its disdain. Nine days before the WHO declared a global health emergency and ten days before the US and a number of other countries declared limited China travel restrictions, North Korea closed its borders to outside tourism (with almost all of it coming from China) and implemented a quarantine on incoming cargo.[87] This has had a severe impact on the North's already failed economy, although some experts, including the Korean Economic Institute's Troy Stangarone, suspect that illegal smuggling will help keep the North afloat.[88]

North Korean disdain for China long predates the coronavirus, however. I have been meeting with North Korean officials and government-sponsored think tank scholars two or three times annually for over two decades and have never heard a kind word uttered about China or any expression of gratitude for China's role, neither for preserving their survival during the Korean War nor for keeping them on life support economically ever since.[89] Even in the face of Pyongyang's most egregious behavior (nuclear tests, missile tests, and acts of terrorism) it has been Beijing that has either blocked or watered down UN Security Council Resolutions aimed at changing (and punishing) the North's behavior and inhibiting future banned activities.

There was one period, after Pyongyang's sixth nuclear test in 2017, in which China, apparently angered by Pyongyang's dismissal of Xi's admonitions not to conduct the test, decided to tighten the screws, not to bring about the North's collapse but merely to cause enough pain to compel Pyongyang to resume nuclear talks. Beijing's actions were apparently also prompted by promises, since broken, that the US would not pursue economic penalties against China for its unfair trade practices as long as it was cooperating with the Trump administration's "maximum pressure" campaign. This all ended with the announcement of the first Trump-Kim Summit, as Xi was presumably worried about being left out of the Peninsula peace process and opened the door for his own series of summits with Kim Jong Un, along with an apparent relaxation of sanctions enforcement measures (or more accurately, turning a blind eye to out-and-out sanctions violations by China).[90] One can only guess at what was requested and/or promised when the two leaders met, but the White House has accused Xi of complicating, if not undermining the US-DPRK negotiating process, which is likely not too far from the truth.[91] At any rate, Pyongyang's demands to the US in its negotiations with Washington, as previously noted, closely mirror China's long-standing objectives.

It would appear that the one thing that has not (yet) changed under Xi Jinping is the longstanding Chinese belief regarding the importance of maintaining North Korea as a buffer state. Beijing would prefer that Pyongyang give up its nuclear weapons but is not prepared to push it to (much less beyond) the brink of collapse to make this happen. To the degree the North's belligerent behavior provides Washington with the rationale to keep forces deployed in Northeast Asia, this is a bad thing in Beijing's eyes. To the degree that Washington is preoccupied with the North Korean threat, though, this is a good thing, especially in the (currently unlikely but not impossible) event that Chinese military action is needed to prevent or respond to Taiwan independence.

At any rate, China clearly places a higher priority today on regional stability and the preservation of its buffer zone than it does on North Korean denuclearization. This has allowed the DPRK leadership to be somewhat dismissive of Chinese preferences and concerns in the apparent belief that the North is too important to China for Beijing to allow it to fail. This may be true now, but one can speculate that the day Beijing feels confident that a reunified Peninsula will look to China rather than the US for its security, its calculus could change.

Unified Korea

Most Chinese Korea specialists acknowledge that the North is living on borrowed time and that reunification, under the South's political and economic system, is the most likely, if not inevitable, long-term outcome.[92] China would prefer that a reunified Korea look to Beijing as its primary benefactor, however, and not to the US. Beijing is prepared to take whatever steps are necessary, including continuing to prop up an otherwise failed North Korean state, to prevent a unified Korea that remains a close alliance partner with the US.[93]

It is this disconnect in one another's long-term objectives that has limited the prospects of Sino-US cooperation vis-à-vis North Korea, even though our short-term objectives—regional stability, no war, and eventual complete denuclearization—continue to overlap. It is not the fear of North Korea's collapse *per se* that worries Beijing, but a unification that would place a US military ally on its border, presumably with American military bases now clearly directed at countering Chinese primacy in the region. This is not to downplay Chinese concerns about regional instability or managing refugee flows in the event the DPRK were to collapse, but Chinese interlocutors acknowledge that such concerns are temporary and manageable. What China desires, at a minimum, is a neutral and neutralized unified Korea that no longer serves as a forward base for US military forces that even today, in Chinese eyes, are aimed as much against China as they are against North Korea.

Were Seoul prepared to end its alliance with Washington and turn to Beijing as its security guarantor, it is my assessment that Beijing would quickly and readily abandon Pyongyang in favor of the more prosperous and stable South. Standing in the way of this Chinese dream is the South's strong reluctance—based on an awareness of its own history and reinforced by China's current heavy-handed behavior—to become a Chinese client state. And it is the firm US commitment to the alliance that makes the South's resistance possible and credible.

Conclusion

China, under Xi Jinping, has already been successful in putting China foremost (even if not always first) in the minds of its neighbors' leaders. As Beijing's economic, military, and political clout continues to grow, it will attempt to accelerate this trend toward Chinese centrality. The extent to which China's Northeast Asian neighbors will respond by hedging *with* rather than hedging *against* China will depend in large part on how reliably they continue to see Washington as their best and only alternative.

NOTES

1 "China's Policies on Asia-Pacific Security Cooperation." See also "The Five Principles of Peaceful Coexistence."

2 See Xiaoping, "Revitalizing the Chinese People."

3 For an assessment of Xi's rejection of Deng's approach, see, for example, Clover, "Xi Jinping Signals Departure from Low-Profile Policy."

4 For an assessment, see "China's Xi Allowed to Remain 'President for Life' as Term Limits Removed."

5 I hasten to add that there is nothing sinister *per se* in this approach. To the Chinese (and to many others) it merely reflects the emerging "new reality" as China's global strength—economic, military, political, and some would argue ideological—continues to grow.

6 Gang and Shuang, "Xi Jinping Pledges 'Great Renewal of Chinese Nation.'"

7 Gang and Shuang, "Xi Jinping Pledges 'Great Renewal of Chinese Nation.'"

8 Liu, *China Dream*. This was written in 2010 and first published in Chinese by the PLA National Defense University. According to Jeremy Page in "For Xi, a 'China Dream' of Military Power," the book flew off the shelves but was pulled over concerns it could damage relations with the US. The day after Xi's first "China Dream" speech, however, Colonel Liu received approval to launch a new edition (Liu, *China Dream*). One can find a number of direct quotes from Liu's book in Xi's China Dream speeches.

9 Liu, *China Dream*, chap. 5.

10 Liu, *China Dream*, loc. 2588. In stressing China's strategic reach, Lui had earlier noted [loc. 2569] that "China's development goal isn't just to be king of Asia, China wants to become king of the world."

11 Liu, *China Dream*, loc. 2624.

12 Liu, *China Dream*, loc. 2633. He further notes, "A China that rises and develops without an ideology is a China without a soul, a brawny China without the IQ to match" (loc. 2636).

13 "Xi Jinping: China to Further Friendly Relations with Neighboring Countries."

14 "Xi Jinping: China to Further Friendly Relations with Neighboring Countries." The Belt and Road Initiative (BRI, also called "One Belt, One Road") is a key part of China's global strategy but, beyond inroads into North Korea (which were happening regardless), it is not that significant a factor in Northeast Asia and thus I do not dwell on it in this chapter. China's overall economic strategy is covered elsewhere in this volume.

15 Fulin, "Northeast Asia Gateway for Growth."

16 For details, see, for example, "China, ROK, Japan Vow to Further Enhance Mutual Trust." "China's Policies on Asia-Pacific Security Cooperation" also lays out China's hopes for greater trilateral economic cooperation with the ROK and Japan.

17 Kim, "China's Quest for Influence in Northeast Asia."

18 Kim, "China's Quest for Influence in Northeast Asia."

19 Glaser, "Statement before the US-China Economic and Security Review Commission.'"

20 Glaser, "Statement before the US-China Economic and Security Review Commission.'"

21 Liu, *China Dream*, see loc. 2642.

22 Liu, *China Dream*, loc. 2645.

23 Liu, *China Dream*, loc. 2652.

24 Glaser, "Statement before the US-China Economic and Security Review Commission.'"

25 Liu, *China Dream*, loc. 4710.

26 Liu, *China Dream*, loc. 4177.

27 See, for example, "Chinese Ambassador Urges US to Abandon Cold War, Zero-Sum Mentality"; "Transcript of Ambassador Cui Tiankai's Interview with China-US Focus."

28 Jimin, "Back to Cold-War Mentality?"

29 Fenghe, "Speech at the 18th Shangri-La Dialogue."

30 State Council Information Office of the People's Republic of China, *China's National Defense in the New Era*. Andrew Erickson's website is particularly useful since it contains all back issues of China's Defense White Papers along with assessments of each (Erickson, "Full Text of 2019 Defense White Paper").

There are few if any great insights into China's grand strategy to be gained from reading this "Defense White Paper." China's military strategy (examined elsewhere in this volume) is simply described as "a balanced and stable one for the new era, which focuses on defense and coordinates multiple domains." Meanwhile, China's nuclear strategy is "a strategy of self-defense, the goal of which is to maintain national strategic security by deterring other countries from using or threatening to use nuclear weapons against China."

31 See "China's Policies on Asia-Pacific Security Cooperation."

32 US-China Economic and Security Review Commission, *2018 Report to Congress of the US-China Economic and Security Review Commission*, chap. 3, sec. 2.

33 Smith, "China's Bid to Repair its Coronavirus-Hit Image is Backfiring in the West."

34 See, for example, "1 Big Thing: China Takes a Page from Russia's Disinformation Playbook." See also Westcott and Jiang, "Chinese Diplomat Promotes Conspiracy Theory that US Military Brought Coronavirus to Wuhan."

35 It's not clear he does—one can find evidence of debates on either side of the question—although it is generally assumed all Chinese leaders would like that feather in their cap.

36 Some China-watchers speculate that the "dream of great renewal of the Chinese nation" by 2049 likely includes the incorporation of Taiwan into the mainland by that time but Xi has not set this as a timeline. Colonel Liu Mingfu has stated, however, in a May 2019 interview with the *Asahi Shimbun*, that "China cannot become a first-class nation in the world while it remains a divided state. I am confident that President Xi will work actively on the Taiwan issue and achieve ultimate unification of the nation while he is in office." (Minemura, "Interview: Liu Mingfu.")

37 "Highlights of Xi's Speech at Taiwan Message Anniversary Event."

38 See, for example, Buckley and Horton, "Xi Jinping Warns Taiwan That Unification Is the Goal and Force Is an Option."

39 "Highlights of Xi's Speech at Taiwan Message Anniversary Event."

40 "Highlights of Xi's Speech at Taiwan Message Anniversary Event."

41 "Highlights of Xi's Speech at Taiwan Message Anniversary Event."

42 Brown and Churchman, "China-Taiwan Relations." *Comparative Connections* has been tracking China-Taiwan relations on a regular basis since its first edition in July 1999 and thus provides a working archive on the twists and turns in cross-Strait relations.

43 "Highlights of Xi's Speech at Taiwan Message Anniversary Event."

44 Information Office of the State Council, the People's Republic of China, *The Practice of the "One Country, Two Systems" Policy in the Hong Kong Special Administrative Region.*

45 Ing-wen, "A Nation of Resilience, Forward into the World."

46 See, for example, Pomfret and Jim, "Exclusive."

47 Stillwell, "Statement before the Senate Foreign Relations Committee Subcommittee on East Asia, the Pacific, and International Cybersecurity Policy."

48 Over the years, I have participated in a number of National Committee on American Foreign Policy (NCAFP) "shuttle diplomacy" delegations to Taiwan and the PRC. My trip report following the December 2017 visit focused in particular on the revival of the "one country, two systems" formula despite Chinese expectations that it could never be accepted. For details, see Cossa, "A NCAFP Trip to Taipei, Beijing and Seoul."

49 See, for example, Hickey, "What the Latest Opinion Polls Say about Taiwan."

50 According to Hickey, polls show that roughly 70 percent of Taiwanese agree that there is no need to declare independence. Moreover, almost 60 percent oppose independence if it triggers a PRC attack, and the number who believe the PRC threat is credible has jumped: roughly 50 percent now believe Beijing will attack if Taiwan declares independence, compared to 41 percent in 2017.

51 Beijing has poached seven of Taiwan's allies since Tsai came to office. The Republic of China is now only recognized by fifteen small Latin American and Pacific Island states. For details, see, for example, Aspinwall, "Taiwan Loses 2 Diplomatic Allies, Wins US Support ahead of Crucial Presidential Election." For insight into Beijing's broader effort, also see Schmitt and Mazza, "Blinding the Enemy."

52 See, for example, Anwar, "How China Is Using Tourists to Realise Its Geopolitical Goals."

53 See, for example, Chu, "The 'Hong Kong Factor' in the 2020 Taiwanese Presidential Election."

54 One can find dozens, if not hundreds, of military assessments regarding cross-Strait conflict, with widely varying conclusions. The remarks here are my own analysis, based on first-hand assessments of Taiwan, PRC, and US military capabilities over the years. For a wide range of assessments, see, for example, Cole, "China vs. Taiwan"; Greer, "Taiwan Can Win a War with China"; Yeo, "China is Laying the Groundwork for War with Taiwan."

55 For details regarding both approaches and my assessment of the shift, see Cossa, "A NCAFP Trip to Taipei, Beijing and Seoul: December 6–16, 2017."

56 China's Anti-Secession Law, adopted at the Third Session of the Tenth National People's Congress in Beijing on March 14, 2005, while calling for peaceful unification and outlining China's outreach toward Taipei at the time, warns (in full): "In the event that the 'Taiwan independence' secessionist forces should act under any name or by any means to cause the fact of Taiwan's secession from China, or that major incidents entailing Taiwan's secession from China should occur, or that

possibilities for a peaceful reunification should be completely exhausted, the state shall employ non-peaceful means and other necessary measures to protect China's sovereignty and territorial integrity." For the full text, see "Anti-Secession Law (Full Text)."

57 See, for example, "President Urges China to Share Wuhan Virus Information"; Blanchard, "Taiwan Calls China 'Vile' for Limiting WHO Access during Virus Outbreak."

58 See, for example, "WHO: China Sent Its Internet Army to Help Tedros with His Attack on Taiwan."

59 See, for example, Allen-Ebrahimian, "Between the Lines on Chinese Strategy." She argues that "China's handling of the coronavirus has favorably highlighted the capability and transparency of Taiwan."

60 Glaser, "Statement before the US-China Economic and Security Review Commission on 'China's Grand Strategy in Asia.'"

61 Kim, "China's Quest for Influence in Northeast Asia."

62 Kim, "China's Quest for Influence in Northeast Asia.

63 For a two-decade-long running commentary on Japan-China relations, see the appropriate chapter in *Comparative Connections*, which has featured writing chronicling the ups and downs of the relationship since 1999, first by James Przystup and most recently by June Teufel Dreyer. For a recent example, see Dreyer, "Japan-China Relations."

64 Yun, "With Increased Confidence, China and Japan Can Lead on World Stage."

65 Minemura, "Interview: Liu Mingfu."

66 See, for example, Shi, "Could the Coronavirus Help to Improve China's Ties with South Korea, Japan?" See also Silverberg, "Better Ties with China." The latter article, in particular, weighs both the pros and cons of the virus' impact. Both are skeptical regarding any long-term positive impact, as is this author.

67 Fitzpatrick, "How Japan Could Go Nuclear."

68 Japan is the largest investor in China, accounting for 7.3 percent of total cumulative foreign direct investment flows, according to Santander Trade statistics. (The US is second, with 5.8 percent.) Until 2018, Japan was still providing developmental assistance to China as well, in part driven by a lingering guilty conscience over the Second World War, but this has now come to an end. See, for example, "Japan to Discontinue Development Assistance Projects for China."

69 See, for example, Harding and Lewis, "Japan Plans to Tighten Rules on Foreign Investment."

70 For the author's own views on this subject and on the prospects for greater multilateral cooperation in Northeast Asia, please see Cossa, "US-China-Japan-Korea-Russia."

71 *Comparative Connections* provides a running commentary on China's relations with both Seoul and Pyongyang. For example, see Snyder and Byun, "China-Korea Relations."

72 See, for example, "China Adopts the Chaebol."

73 "China, ROK, Japan Vow to Further Enhance Mutual Trust"; "China's Policies on Asia-Pacific Security Cooperation" devotes a full paragraph to condemn the deployment. Kim Sung-han provides an insightful analysis of China's intentions and Moon's response in "The 'Grey Zone' Strategy."

74 See State Council Information Office of the People's Republic of China, *China's National Defense in the New Era*. For a good analysis of the issue, see Panda, "What Is THAAD, What Does It Do, and Why Is China Mad about It?"

75 For example, when Chinese Foreign Minister Wang Yi met with his Japanese and Korean counterparts to promote trilateral economic cooperation, he could not resist complaining about the deployment of US land-based missiles in Asia, noting that "having a Cold War mentality will cause us to go backward in history, and seeking confrontation will result in a double loss." As reported by China Global Television Network in "China, ROK, Japan Vow to Further Enhance Mutual Trust."

76 Snyder and Byun, "China-Korea Relations."

77 For background, see Kang, "Public Anger Swells in South Korea over Coronavirus Outbreak"; Suzuki, "'Hate China Virus' Puts South Korea's Moon under Pressure."

78 Larsen, "South Korea's President Tried to Help China Contain the Coronavirus."

79 "China, 11 More Countries Restrict Travel from S. Korea over Coronavirus Concern."

80 See, for example, Kasulis, "Coronavirus Brings out Anti-Chinese Sentiment in South Korea." Of note, as was the case in Taiwan, South Korea's effective handling once the pandemic struck has been cited as another example of how democracies can effectively deal with such challenges. See, for example, Rogin, "South Korea Shows that Democracies Can Succeed against the Coronavirus."

81 This analysis is derived from an ongoing study involving US and Chinese security specialists. For a discussion on the origins of North Korea as a "buffer state" in Chinese strategic thinking, see Kim, "How China Sees North Korea." For a Chinese assessment, see also "China Won't Give Up N. K. as It Provides 'Strategic Buffer Zone': Expert." *Yonhap*, November 17, 2016. https://en.yna.co.kr.

82 US-China Economic and Security Review Commission, *USCC 2018 Annual Report to Congress*, chap. 3, sec. 5.

83 US-China Economic and Security Review Commission, *USCC 2018 Annual Report to Congress*, chap. 3, sec. 5.

84 US-China Economic and Security Review Commission, *USCC 2018 Annual Report to Congress*, chap. 3, sec. 5.

85 Snyder and Byun, "China-Korea Relations."

86 According to Snyder and Byun, "China-Korea Relations," Chinese ships have engaged in extensive illicit ship-to-ship transfers of oil to North Korea conducted in international waters, as has been comprehensively documented by Washington and others via the UN Panel of Experts.

87 Sang-Hun, "North Korea Bans Foreign Tourists over Coronavirus, Tour Operator Says" discusses the North Korean action, while Kessler, "Trump's Claim That

He Imposed the First 'China Ban'" outlines the timing of China-related travel restrictions.

88 For details, see Stangarone, "North Korea's Exports to China Collapse amid Coronavirus"; Stangarone, "North Korean Coal Smuggling, Still Profitable."

89 Most of these meetings are held under Chatham House rules, which precludes specific references. As an example, in a 2018 meeting involving government representatives and scholars from throughout Northeast Asia, one North Korean speaker accused Beijing of being a false friend and a tool of the US. The senior Chinese delegate was so incensed that he demanded an apology. The head of the North Korean delegation said, in effect, "if the shoe fits, wear it." In another instance, a North Korean representative took great umbrage at the commemoration of "the PLA 'liberation' of the DPRK," arguing that the North had almost single-handedly accomplished this task, even though it had "allowed" some Chinese volunteers to assist in the fighting.

90 This is a quick summation of several years of complicated maneuvering by Beijing, Pyongyang, Washington, and Seoul. For a comprehensive, self-described "look at the often bitter, sometimes bloody, rarely dull modern history of the neighbors," see Kim and Kim, "Key Moments in Relations between North Korea, China." For a running commentary and in-depth analysis, as well as detailed chronologies of events, see the recurring issues of *Comparative Connections*, especially the chapters on China-Korea relations, US-China relations, and my own (with Brad Glosserman) Regional Overview, which has tracked multilateral efforts to deal with the DPRK nuclear challenge.

91 In a series of tweets, President Trump complained that Xi's aid to Kim was "not helpful," implying Xi was undermining progress. See Trump, "Statement from the White House." For an analysis, see "Trump Accuses China of Stalling Progress with North Korea."

92 As noted earlier, this conclusion is based on surveys and ongoing discussions with a group of Chinese and US Asia security specialists. The project's aim is to find common ground between US and Chinese mid- to long-term objectives vis-à-vis the Korean Peninsula. The remainder of this section discusses preliminary findings to date.

93 The stated US policy is to sustain the alliance "as long as the Korean people want us there," but serious questions about it have been raised in both the US and ROK, whether or not President Trump agrees.

BIBLIOGRAPHY

"1 Big Thing: China Takes a Page from Russia's Disinformation Playbook." *Axios-China*, March 25, 2020. www.axios.com.

2018 Annual Report to Congress. US-China Economic and Security Review Commission (USCC), November 2018. www.uscc.gov/.

Allen-Ebrahimian, Bethany. "Between the Lines on Chinese Strategy." *Axios China*, April 8, 2020. www.axios.com.

"Anti-Secession Law (Full Text)." Embassy of the People's Republic of China in the United States. March 15, 2005, www.china-embassy.org.

Anwar, Anu. "How China is Using Tourists to Realise its Geopolitical Goals." *East Asia Forum*. September 19, 2019. www.eastasiaforum.org.

Aspinwall, Nick. "Taiwan Loses 2 Diplomatic Allies, Wins US Support ahead of Crucial Presidential Election." *Diplomat*, September 26, 2019. https://thediplomat.com.

Blanchard, Ben. "Taiwan Calls China 'Vile' for Limiting WHO Access during Virus Outbreak." Reuters. February 3, 2020. www.reuters.com.

Brown, David G., and Kyle Churchman. "China-Taiwan Relations: Hong Kong Impacts Taiwan Elections." *Comparative Connections* 21, no. 2 (September 2019): 65–72. http://cc.pacforum.org.

Brown, David G., and Kyle Churchman. "China-Taiwan Relations: Troubling Tensions." *Comparative Connections* 21, no. 1 (May 2019): 65–74. http://cc.pacforum.org.

Buckley, Chris, and Chris Horton. "Xi Jinping Warns Taiwan That Unification Is the Goal and Force Is an Option." *New York Times,* January 1, 2019. www.nytimes.com.

Chi, Fulin. "Northeast Asia Gateway for Growth." *China Daily Global*, August 22, 2019. www.chinadaily.com.cn.

"China Adopts the Chaebol." *Economist*, June 5, 1997. www.economist.com.

"China and Taiwan." Chap. 3, Sect. 3 of *2018 Annual Report to Congress*. US-China Economic and Security Review Commission (USCC), November 2018. www.uscc.gov.

"China Foreign Investment." *Santander Trade*. https://en.portal.santandertrade.com.

"China Won't Give Up N.K. as it Provides 'Strategic Buffer Zone': Expert." *Yonhap*, November 17, 2016. https://en.yna.co.kr.

"China Won't Give Up N.K. as it Provides 'Strategic Buffer Zone': Expert." *Yonhap*, November 17, 2016. https://en.yna.co.kr.

"China, 11 More Countries Restrict Travel from S. Korea over Coronavirus Concern." *Korea Herald*, February 27, 2020. www.koreaherald.com.

"China, ROK, Japan Vow to Further Enhance Mutual Trust." *China Global Television Network*, August 21, 2019. https://news.cgtn.com.

"China's Evolving North Korea Strategy." Chap. 3, Sect. 5 of *2018 Annual Report to Congress*. US-China Economic and Security Review Commission (USCC), November 2018. www.uscc.gov.

"China's Policies on Asia-Pacific Security Cooperation." Ministry of Foreign Affairs of the People's Republic of China, January 2017. www.fmprc.gov.cn.

"China's Relations with US Allies and Partners." Chap. 3, Sect. 2 of *2018 Annual Report to Congress*. US-China Economic and Security Review Commission (USCC), November 2018. www.uscc.gov.

"China's Xi Allowed to Remain 'President for Life' as Term Limits Removed." *BBC News*, March 11, 2018. www.bbc.com.

"Chinese Ambassador Urges US to Abandon Cold War, Zero-Sum Mentality." *Xinhua*, April 20, 2018. www.xinhuanet.com.

Choe, Sang-Hun. "North Korea Bans Foreign Tourists Over Coronavirus, Tour Operator Says." *New York Times*, January 21, 2020. www.nytimes.com.

Chu, Adrian. "The 'Hong Kong Factor' in the 2020 Taiwanese Presidential Election." *Taiwan Insights*, January 21, 2020. https://taiwaninsight.org.

Clover, Charles. "Xi Jinping Signals Departure from Low-Profile Policy." *Financial Times*, October 19, 2017. www.ft.com.

Cole, Michael J. "China vs. Taiwan: What a War Would Look Like (in a Word: Terrifying)" *National Interest*, June 5, 2019. https://nationalinterest.org

Comparative Connections, with chapters on China-Japan, China-Korea, and China-Taiwan relations, plus a Regional Overview that, three to four times annually, has examined policies and developments among Asia bilateral and multilateral relationships since 1999. http://cc.pacforum.org/.

Cossa, Ralph A. "A NCAFP Trip to Taipei, Beijing and Seoul: December 6–16, 2017." National Committee on American Foreign Policy. December 2017. www.ncafp.org.

Cossa, Ralph A. "US-China-Japan-Korea-Russia: Promoting Multilateral Cooperation," *NCAFP*, May 2019. www.ncafp.org.

Cossa, Ralph A. "US-China-Japan-Korea-Russia: Promoting Multilateral Cooperation," *NCAFP*, May 2019. www.ncafp.org.

Deng, Xiaoping. "Revitalizing the Chinese People." April 7, 1990, *Selected Works of Deng Xiaoping*. Vol. 3. Beijing: Foreign Language Press, 1994.

Dreyer, June Teufel. "Japan-China Relations: External Smiles, Internal Angst." *Comparative Connections* 21, no. 2 (September 2019): 97–104. http://cc.pacforum.org.

Erickson, Andrew. "Full Text of 2019 Defense White Paper: 'China's National Defense in the New Era' (English & Chinese Versions)." Andrew S. Erickson [website]. July 24, 2019. www.andrewerickson.com.

Fitzpatrick, Mark. "How Japan Could Go Nuclear: It Has the Smarts and the Resources, but Does Tokyo Have the Will?" *Foreign Affairs*, October 3, 2019. www.foreignaffairs.com.

Gang, Wu and Yan Shuang. "Xi Jinping Pledges 'Great Renewal of Chinese Nation.'" *Global Times*, November 29, 2012. www.globaltimes.cn.

Glaser, Bonnie. "Statement before the US-China Economic and Security Review Commission on 'China's Grand Strategy in Asia.'" Center for Strategic and International Studies, March 13, 2014. www.csis.org.

Greer, Tanner. "Taiwan Can Win a War with China: Beijing Boasts It Can Seize the Island Easily, the PLA Knows Better." *Foreign Policy*, September 25, 2018. https://foreignpolicy.com.

Harding, Robin, and Leo Lewis, "Japan Plans to Tighten Rules on Foreign Investment." *Financial Times*, September 19, 2019. www.ft.com.

Hickey, Dennis. "What the Latest Opinion Polls Say about Taiwan." *National Interest*, March 5, 2019. https://nationalinterest.org.

"Highlights of Xi's Speech at Taiwan Message Anniversary Event." *China Daily*, January 23, 2019. www.chinadaily.com.cn.

Information Office of the State Council, the People's Republic of China. *The Practice of the "One Country, Two Systems" Policy in the Hong Kong Special Administrative*

Region. The State Council, the People's Republic of China, June 2014. http://english.www.gov.cn.

Ing-wen, Tsai. "A Nation of Resilience, Forward into the World (2019 National Day Address)." *Focus Taiwan*, October 10, 2019. http://focustaiwan.tw.

"Japan to Discontinue Development Assistance Projects for China: Taro Kono." *Japan Times*, October 23, 2018, www.japantimes.co.jp.

Jimin, Chen. "Back to Cold-War Mentality?" *China US Focus*, August 11, 2015. www.chinausfocus.com.

Kang, Tae-jun. "Public Anger Swells in South Korea over Coronavirus Outbreak." *Diplomat*, February 28, 2020. https://thediplomat.com.

Kasulis, Kelly. "Coronavirus Brings out Anti-Chinese Sentiment in South Korea: Racism Witnessed Globally Spreads to South Korea as Panic over New Virus Outbreak Begins to Take Root." *Al Jazeera*, February 21, 2020. www.aljazeera.com.

Kessler, Glen. "Trump's Claim That He Imposed the First 'China Ban.'" *Washington Post*, April 6, 2020. www.washingtonpost.com.

Kim, Patricia M. "China's Quest for Influence in Northeast Asia: The Korean Peninsula, Japan, and the East China Sea." In *Strategic Asia 2019: China's Expanding Strategic Ambitions*, edited by Ashley J. Tellis, Alison Szalwinski, and Michael Wills. Seattle WA: National Bureau of Asian Research, 2019. www.nbr.org.

Kim, Patricia. "How China Sees North Korea: Three Critical Moments in History and Future Directions." *Chicago Council on Global Affairs*, January 17, 2018. www.thechicagocouncil.org.

Kim, Sung-han. "The 'Grey Zone' Strategy." *JoongAng Daily*, November 1, 2019. http://koreajoongangdaily.joins.com.

Kim, Tong-Hyung and Kim Hyung-jin. "Key Moments in Relations between North Korea, China." *AP News*, June 20, 2019. www.apnews.com.

Larsen, Morten Soendergaard. "South Korea's President Tried to Help China Contain the Coronavirus. Now People Want Him Impeached." *Foreign Policy*, March 9, 2020. https://foreignpolicy.com.

Liu, Mingfu. *The China Dream: Great Power Thinking and Strategic Posture in the Post-American Era*. Beijing: PLA National Defense University Press, 2013 [2010]. Kindle edition.

Minemura, Kenji. "Interview: Liu Mingfu: China Dreams of Overtaking US in 30 years." *Asahi Shimbun*, May 28, 2019. www.asahi.com.

Page, Jeremy. "For Xi, a 'China Dream' of Military Power." *Wall Street Journal*, March 13, 2013. www.wsj.com.

Panda, Ankit. "What Is THAAD, What Does It Do, and Why Is China Mad about It?" *Diplomat*, February 25, 2016. https://thediplomat.com.

Pomfret, James, and Clare Jim. "Exclusive: Hong Kongers Support Protester Demands; Minority Wants Independence from China." Reuters. December 31, 2019. www.reuters.com.

"President Urges China to Share Wuhan Virus Information." *Focus Taiwan*, January 22, 2020. https://focustaiwan.tw.

Rogin, Josh. "South Korea Shows that Democracies Can Succeed against the Coronavirus." *Washington Post*, March 11, 2020. www.washingtonpost.com.

Sang-Hun, Choe. "North Korea Bans Foreign Tourists over Coronavirus, Tour Operator Says." *New York Times*, January 21, 2020. www.nytimes.com.

Schmitt, Gary and Michael Mazza. "Blinding the Enemy: CCP Interference in Taiwan's Democracy." Global Taiwan Institute. October 2019. http://globaltaiwan.org.

Shi, Jiangtao. "Could the Coronavirus Help to Improve China's ties with South Korea, Japan?" *South China Morning Post*, February 27, 2020. www.scmp.com.

Silverberg, Elliot. "Better Ties with China: Japan's Coronavirus Silver Lining?" *Japan Times*, April 1, 2020. www.japantimes.co.jp.

Smith, Gerry. "China's Bid to Repair its Coronavirus-Hit Image is Backfiring in the West." *Washington Post*, April 14, 2020. www.washingtonpost.com.

Snyder, Scott, and See-Won Byun. "China-Korea Relations: Post-Hanoi Hopes Trapped in a Sino-Korean Smog." *Comparative Connections* 21, no. 2 (September 2019): 87–96. http://cc.pacforum.org.

Stangarone, Troy. "North Korea's Exports to China Collapse amid Coronavirus." *Diplomat*, March 25, 2020. https://thediplomat.com.

Stangarone, Troy. "North Korean Coal Smuggling, Still Profitable." *Korean Economic Institute*, February 27, 2020. http://blog.keia.org.

State Council Information Office of the People's Republic of China. *China's National Defense in the New Era*. Foreign Languages Press, Beijing, China, 2019. www.andrewerickson.com.

Stillwell, David R. "Statement before the Senate Foreign Relations Committee Subcommittee on East Asia, the Pacific, and International Cybersecurity Policy." US Department of State, October 16, 2019. www.state.gov.

Suzuki, Sotaro. "'Hate China Virus' Puts South Korea's Moon under Pressure." *Nikkei Asian Review*, February 10, 2020. https://asia.nikkei.com.

"The Five Principles of Peaceful Coexistence: The Time-Tested Guideline of China's Policy with Neighbours" (1954). *Chinese Ministry of Foreign Affairs*. www.fmprc.gov.cn.

"Transcript of Ambassador Cui Tiankai's Interview with China-US Focus." *China-US Focus*, January 26, 2019. www.china-embassy.org.

"Trump Accuses China of Stalling Progress with North Korea," *BBC News*, August 30, 2018. www.bbc.com.

Trump, Donald (@realDonaldTrump). "Statement from the White House." Twitter, August 29, 2018. https://twitter.com/realdonaldtrump/status/1034914371099676674?lang=en.

Tsai, Ing-wen. "A Nation of Resilience, Forward into the World (2019 National Day address)." *Focus Taiwan*, October 10, 2019. http://focustaiwan.tw.

US-China Economic and Security Review Commission.. www.uscc.gov.

Wei, Fenghe. "Speech at the 18th Shangri-La Dialogue." China Military (Sponsored by the Chinese People's Liberation Army), June 2, 2019. http://eng.chinamil.com.cn.

Westcott, Ben, and Steven Jiang. "Chinese Diplomat Promotes Conspiracy Theory that US Military Brought Coronavirus to Wuhan." *CNN*, March 13, 2020. www.cnn.com.

"WHO: China Sent Its Internet Army to Help Tedros with His Attack on Taiwan." *Chinascope*, April 11, 2020. http://chinascope.org.

"Xi Jinping: China to Further Friendly Relations with Neighboring Countries." *People's Daily*, October 26, 2013. http://en.people.cn.

Yeo, Mike. "China is Laying the Groundwork for War with Taiwan." *Defense News*, May 3, 2019. www.defensenews.com.

Yun, Zhang. "With Increased Confidence, China and Japan Can Lead on World Stage." *Global Times*, June 26, 2019. www.globaltimes.cn.

5

China's Grand Strategy toward Southeast Asia

Assessing the Response and Efficacy

ANN MARIE MURPHY

China's grand strategy toward Southeast Asia under Xi Jinping is a marked departure from its previous, low-profile strategy of biding time and hiding strength. Xi's adoption of a more assertive policy poses significant threats to the direct interests of certain Southeast Asian states, some of which have pushed back against China. This chapter outlines China's grand strategy toward Southeast Asia and illustrate how it has changed over time. It then discusses key aspects of China's military, economic, and cultural grand strategy under Xi, analyzes the Southeast Asian response, and assesses the extent to which China has achieved its goals.

China's Grand Strategy toward Southeast Asia and the Southeast Asian Response: Changes over Time

During the Cold War, China's export of revolution through local Southeast Asian Communist parties led the governments in countries outside of the three socialist states in Indochina to view China as a revisionist actor and the region's key external threat. Mao's death in 1976 and Deng Xiaoping's 1978 adoption of reforms opened up a new era or "second revolution" in which Deng ushered in economic reforms and a low-profile foreign policy that produced the Chinese economic miracle.[1] Relations between China and Southeast Asia in the 1980s moved from hostility and distrust to an increasingly positive albeit uneasy posture as trade rose and ASEAN and China cooperated to roll back Vietnam's invasion of Cambodia.

China has a complicated security environment because it faces great powers like Russia to the North, Japan to the East, and India to the

South. Comparatively, in Southeast Asia China faces a group of small and medium powers that pose no direct threat outside of their military cooperation with great powers such as the United States. Therefore, as China began to expand its international economic and political ties under Deng, Chinese strategic analysts viewed Southeast Asia as a region where China could focus on cooperative strategies to advance economic interests—in particular, improving access to Southeast Asian markets and resources. Promoting economic cooperation was viewed as way to generate a "win-win" outcome that would result in stable ties with Southeast Asia.[2]

1989 was a pivotal year for Chinese policy toward Southeast Asia, for two key reasons. First, Indonesian President Suharto, who had cut diplomatic ties with China in 1967 due to its complicity in a 1965 coup, agreed to restore relations. Indonesia's decision not only meant that a key Southeast Asian state had put history behind it, but, given Indonesia's leadership role in ASEAN, Suharto's decision also paved the way for greater Chinese ties with the organization. Second, after Western governments responded to the 1989 Tiananmen Massacre by imposing sanctions on China, recalling diplomats and treating it as an international pariah, Southeast Asian states had an opportunity to differentiate themselves from the West. Southeast Asian countries issued carefully worded statements that expressed shock at the events, but their tone was less one of anger than of disappointment and sorrow, according to former Singaporean Foreign Minister George Yeoh.[3] According to Li Mingjiang, "The fact that ASEAN countries didn't make any critical statements on China's domestic politics made it possible for Beijing to view the region positively."[4] These two events accelerated the shift in China's perception of ASEAN from suspicion to receptiveness, reinforcing the positive relationship that had been developing throughout the 1980s.

The Asian financial crisis of 1997–98 created an opportunity for China to support the hardest-hit ASEAN countries. China participated in International Monetary Fund bailouts for the first time to support Thailand and Indonesia. It also refrained from devaluing its currency, which would have made it harder for Southeast Asian states to export their way out of the crisis, and provided other aid. China's economic contributions were minor compared with those of the West, but Southeast Asian leaders expected large contributions from their longstanding Western partners, particularly the US, and were disappointed in the aid they received. In contrast, they had few expectations of China and the Chinese exceeded these. If countries make determinations regarding whether they view rising powers as revisionist according to whether they act in accordance with their narrow self-interests or with more collective ones, then China's actions during the Asian financial crisis demonstrated a willingness to become a responsible stakeholder to many Southeast Asian states.

Beyond China's interest in Southeast Asian resources and markets, Chinese policy makers view Southeast Asia as strategically significant. According to Chinese analysts, since the Opium War, Southeast Asia has been commonly used as a springboard for invasions of China. Many Chinese analysts view Southeast Asia as a site for strategic competition, most notably between the US and China. When China's rise led some strategic analysts, particularly in the US, to view China as a strategic threat, China under Hu Jintao responded by adopting its "peaceful rise" or "peaceful development" strategy. This doctrine was designed to reassure Asia and the US that China's growing economic and military power did not threaten international peace and stability but created opportunities for new forms of cooperation.[5]

China under Hu gave credence to its strategy of peaceful rise in Southeast Asia by becoming an enthusiastic supporter of the ASEAN-based regional architecture. It actively participates in the ASEAN Regional Forum, the ASEAN Plus Three, the East Asian Summit and the ASEAN Defense Ministers Meeting Plus. From China's perspective, joining ASEAN groupings rather than creating new Chinese-led political institutions was a way to demonstrate support for ASEAN and gain acceptance for its policies, while providing important venues to influence regional decisions. From the ASEAN perspective, bringing China into its groups provided an opportunity to socialize China into ASEAN's bedrock norms of nonintervention and peaceful settlement of disputes. Membership in the East Asian Summit requires ascension to the Treaty of Amity and Cooperation, which commits signatories to the settlement of disputes by peaceful means and the "renunciation of the threat or use of force."[6] If ASEAN had a mechanism to ensure Chinese compliance with these norms, then it could ensure that China would be a status-quo rather than a revisionist actor as it rose.

China under Xi has abandoned many Deng-era domestic reforms as well as Deng's low-profile foreign policy posture in favor of a much stronger assertion of Chinese interests in what Elizabeth Economy has called China's "Third Revolution." As Xi has put it, "China has stood up, grown rich, and become strong."[7] As Xi seeks to achieve his goal of becoming a great power by 2049, China now "actively seeks to shape international norms and institutions and forcefully asserts its presence on the global stage."[8]

Within China, Southeast Asia is widely seen as a key target for Xi's foreign policy ambitions. According to Jonathan Stromseth, in 2013 Xi began prioritizing a highly proactive "peripheral" or "neighborhood" diplomacy with the goal of transforming China's neighboring areas into a "community of common destiny."[9] As Stromseth observes, although China frames its concept of "common destiny" in terms of inclusiveness and "win-win cooperation," this seems designed to incorporate neighboring countries into a Sino-centric network of economic, political, security and cultural relations.[10]

China's grand strategy toward Southeast Asia under Xi has been defined by many of its global initiatives, such as the Belt and Road Initiative (BRI) and a soft-power push, which in theory provide opportunities for mutual gains for all parties. Indeed, Chinese analysts often view Southeast Asia as a "good place to learn and practice the ways of becoming a great power."[11] Southeast Asia, however, differs from other regions in important respects. First, geographic proximity means that China has direct national territorial interests in Southeast Asia that it lacks in regions like Europe, Latin America, and Africa. As a result, China's pursuit of these interests has involved the use of hard military power, which it has not typically employed elsewhere, particularly in the South China Sea. China's promotion of its interests in the South China Sea poses a direct threat to Southeast Asian states with competing maritime claims, including Vietnam, the Philippines, Malaysia, Brunei and Indonesia. Second, Southeast Asia is home to the majority of ethnic Chinese living outside China. Xi has increasingly prioritized the importance of the overseas Chinese communities, which provide opportunities for attempts to exert Chinese influence. Outside of Australia, China lacks these mechanisms of influence elsewhere. Finally, Southeast Asia is the region where China's assertion of its national interests most directly conflicts with US interests, causing Sino-American tensions and resultant pressure on regional countries to choose sides. Currently, no Southeast Asian state wants to make a binary choice between the US and China.

This chapter briefly describes China's new policy initiatives under Xi and examines the Southeast Asian response. It proceeds in five parts. First, it reviews China's changing economic relationship with Southeast Asia, focusing on trade ties and the BRI. Second, it discusses Chinese cultural and public diplomacy toward Southeast Asia. Third, it analyzes China's increasingly assertive policy toward the South China Sea. Fourth, it discusses China's changing policy toward ASEAN, focusing on its increasing intervention in ASEAN affairs to pursue its interests. Fifth, it assesses the implications of these actions on Southeast Asian perceptions of China. Finally, a conclusion argues that China has been successful in achieving key national interests to date, particularly in the South China Sea, but that other initiatives have generated resistance, and the future trajectory of Chinese grand strategy in Southeast Asia remains uncertain.

Economic Ties and BRI

China's economic growth and emergence as the world's second largest economy has created significant opportunities as well as significant challenges for Southeast Asia. The Asian financial crisis of 1997–98, which devastated Southeast Asia's major economies, demonstrated the risk of overreliance on Western markets. To hedge against this risk, in 2001 ASEAN began negotiations for the ASEAN-China Free Trade Area (ACFTA), which came into effect in 2010. ASEAN countries hoped that by linking to Chinese production networks, ACFTA would produce economic gains. Whether and how Southeast Asia countries benefited from AFTA, however, depends on the extent to which their economic structure is complementary or competitive with China's. Indonesia provides an illustrative example of the complex mix of costs and benefits associated with increased trade with China. A high degree of economic complementarity exists between Indonesia as a commodity exporter and China as a resource-poor economy, but they compete in low-technology manufacturing areas such as the garment, shoe and electronic industries. In the wake of ACFTA's 2010 implementation, a flood of low-cost Chinese consumer goods hollowed out some domestic Indonesian industries. According to one study, China has a comparative advantage over Indonesia in 77 percent of bilateral trading sectors, primarily in manufacturing.[12]

Beyond comparative advantage, Booth argues that the 2008 global economic slowdown resulted in huge stockpiles of manufactured Chinese goods, which were dumped into countries like Indonesia.[13] Indonesia went from having a trade surplus of $1.1 billion in 2006 to a deficit of $3.2 billion in 2011, and it has only widened since then.[14] According to the Indonesian Ministry of Trade, in 2018 two-way trade between Indonesia and China totaled $52.8 billion but Indonesia ran a trade deficit of $18.4 billion.[15] Indonesia wants to reduce the trade deficit and has called for balanced trade in negotiations with China for years, but no remedies to reduce the deficit have been forthcoming from China.

Indonesian commodity exports soared following the 2010 implementation of ACFTA. In 2011, five raw materials—coal, palm oil, gas, crude petroleum, and rubber—composed approximately 60 percent of Indonesian exports to China.[16] This pattern of trade in which Indonesia exports primary products and imports manufacturing goods has been labeled a "neocolonial" relationship, which has created perceptions of China as an exploitative economic actor.[17] In response, Indonesia has adopted a series of protectionist trade policies to reduce its economic vulnerability to Chinese competition.[18] For example, Indonesia is the world's largest producer of rattan and when its local rattan furniture industry was being decimated by Chinese competition, it banned the export of raw rattan. Indonesia's commodity exports to China have dropped as China's economic growth has slowed, which has reduced the political salience of the "neocolonial" pattern of trade while illustrating the costs of economic dependence on China. It is estimated that for every 1 percent decline in Chinese GDP, Indonesia's GDP declines 0.5 percent.[19]

Today, China is the largest trading partner of every Southeast Asian state, but the nature of the relationship varies across the region. According to a study of China's global economic impact by the McKinsey Global Institute, some Southeast Asian countries have extremely high trade exposure to China, and it has increased over time.[20] In the 2003–07 period, for example, China accounted for 8 percent of Malaysia's exports and 5 percent of its imports. A decade later, in the 2013–17 period, China accounted for 11 percent of Malaysian exports and 11 percent of its imports.[21] Vietnam's dependence on Chinese trade over the same period was sharper: exports to China more than tripled, from 3 percent to 11 percent of total trade, while imports from China more than doubled, from 6 percent to 13 percent.[22] Many Southeast Asian countries are tightly integrated with China in global supply chains, which likely accounts for some of the increased trade in these numbers. As the trade war between the US and China causes disruptions in some of these supply chains, trade between Southeast Asia and China will likely be disrupted as well.

China's most ambitious project is arguably Xi's BRI. Launched in 2013, it now encompasses 900 projects, more than 80 percent of which are contracted to Chinese firms. China has pledged $40 billion for the Silk Road Economic Belt, $25 billion for the Maritime Silk Road, and has also pledged to invest $1.25 trillion worldwide by 2025.[23] Even before the BRI, China had engaged in promoting "connectivity" between China and Southeast Asia. In 2009, China initiated a $10 billion China-ASEAN Fund on Investment Cooperation and once ASEAN developed its Master Plan on ASEAN Connectivity, China offered an additional $10 billion in credit, which included a mix of preferential and commercial loans. A key aspect of China's aim is to build infrastructure like roads, bridges, ports, and dams to connect China to markets, materials, and peoples to enhance not only its prosperity but also its influence. To Southeast Asian countries, where leaders have a keen interest in developing their infrastructure, the BRI offers significant opportunities.

At the same time, the BRI has generated significant pushback in many countries. The practice of importing Chinese workers, including unskilled labor, into countries with high rates of unemployment like Indonesia and Cambodia, is contentious. Chinese construction projects have been criticized for shoddy work; in Indonesia only half of all Chinese-built electrical plants produce at capacity. In Malaysia and elsewhere, corrupt elites have been accused of inflating project costs for their own person gain, leaving the taxpayers to repay the debt without the benefit of revenue-generating assets. Malaysia and Myanmar, among others, have sought to review, renegotiate, cancel, and scale down BRI commitments, citing concerns over cost overruns, erosion of sovereignty, and reports of corruption. After Malaysian Prime Minister Mahathir threatened to cancel the East Coast Rail Link, China reduced the price tag by about a third.[24] In recent elections in Malaysia and Indonesia, politicians successfully used the incumbent's participation in the BRI and perceived acquiescence to China to mobilize voters.

China has also used BRI diplomacy as a tool to punish Southeast Asian counties for not complying with Chinese interests. Thai Prime Minister Prayuth and Singaporean Prime Minister Lee Hsien Loong were both snubbed by being left off the guest list to the first BRI Summit held in Beijing in 2017, which drew twenty-seven heads of state.[25] In the Thai case, China was frustrated by Thailand's opposition to Chinese conditions—including high interest rates, use of Chinese workers, and Chinese land ownership—for a high-speed railway that Beijing views as integral to its hopes of connecting Kunming with Singapore.[26] Singapore, a vocal supporter of the BRI, was denied an invitation for reasons unrelated to BRI, apparently including praise for the US rebalance policy and support for the Permanent Court of Arbitration ruling in favor of the Philippines.[27]

The second BRI Summit in April 2019 was attended by nine of the ten ASEAN heads of state, where they made up a significant percentage of the thirty-seven heads of state who participated.[28] At the 2019 Summit, President Xi acknowledged the criticisms leveled against his signature policy and promised to reform it in a number of ways. China pledged to enhance the transparency of the BRI by working more closely with multilateral development banks on specific projects and to adopt international best practices pertaining to project development, operation, procurement, and tendering and bidding. With the help of Singapore, China is establishing a panel of international mediators from BRI countries to resolve disputes, including cross-border disputes, arising from BRI projects. Whether meaningful change will occur or not remains to be seen. What is clear is that Xi is sufficiently concerned about the BRI detracting from, rather than enhancing, China's image to acknowledge flaws in the strategy.

Critics have accused China of practicing "debt trap diplomacy," in which China lures borrowers into unrepayable debt to gain political leverage over them. Perceptions that China is using the BRI to expand its geopolitical influence were reinforced following Sri Lanka's handover of its strategically located Hambantota port under a 99-year lease to China for an inability to repay debt in 2017. Fears that China was using its economic and diplomatic leverage over Hun Sen's isolated Cambodian regime for similar purposes arose in 2019 when the *Wall Street Journal* reported that the two countries had signed a secret agreement for a Chinese naval base along Cambodia's coast. According to the *Journal*, Cambodia had granted China a 30-year lease on the port and agreed to permit the stationing of troops and the storing of weapons in an installation that includes a pier and a range of other facilities.[29] Satellite images also reveal the construction of a military-grade airport. Being able to operate out of the Cambodian base would significantly enhance China's ability to enforce its claims in the South China Sea, impede the American capacity to come to Taiwan's defense, and help consolidate its "string of pearls" strategy of expanding its naval capacity throughout strategic waterways in Southeast Asia that link the Indian and Pacific Oceans.

Cambodian and Chinese officials have denied the reports. Hun Sen responded to a US request for clarification by claiming that it would be impossible for Cambodia to grant Chinese access because "hosting foreign military bases is against the Cambodian constitution."[30] Neither side, however, has denied the possibility of more flexible arrangements, and it should be remembered that China denied its plans to establish a naval base in Djibouti virtually until the moment the base opened. Moreover, the Chinese navy's interests in ship docking, repair, and fuel replenishment can be accommodated by dual-use commercial port facilities operated by Chinese state-owned enterprises. The revenue from the port's commercial activities lower the costs to China of building and maintaining forward-basing facilities compared with the traditional stand-alone American military model.[31] As of 2017, Chinese state-owned enterprises controlled fifteen strategically located ports around the world. Today, China controls approximately half of Cambodia's coastline and Chinese companies are in the process of dredging deep water ports, and building commercial projects and airfields. Once they are built and manned by Chinese operators, it is difficult to envision scenarios in which Cambodia would have the capacity to deny China use of the facilities regardless of whatever official documentation may or may not exist.

Cultural and Soft Power Diplomacy in China's Grand Strategy toward Southeast Asia

China has made a concerted effort to build its soft power in recent years.[32] Nobody knows for sure how much China spends on "external propaganda" for things such as media, publishing, education, arts, and sports, but David Shambaugh has estimated that it totals $10 billion annually.[33] The Chinese government's State Council Information Office coordinates such activities, and targets "high priority audiences" such as Taiwan, Hong Kong and overseas Chinese communities. Of the estimated fifty million overseas Chinese, most live in Southeast Asia, making the region a key target of Chinese influence efforts.

China promotes cultural diplomacy in a bid to win hearts and minds. In over 120 countries, China has built Confucius Institutes and Confucius classrooms to spread Chinese language and culture but also the secondary objective of promoting local cooperation with Chinese business.[34] Confucius Institutes are non-profit but government-sponsored agencies typically formed in partnership with local universities. In the West, Confucius Institutes have come under criticism for undermining academic freedom, spreading Chinese propaganda, and shutting down freedom of speech with respect to issues sensitive to Beijing, such as Tibet, Taiwan, and the South China Sea, among others. In Southeast Asia, Confucius Institutes have had a mixed reception. They are welcomed in Thailand, which was the second country after South Korea to host a Confucius Institute and today is home to seventeen of them—more than any other country in Southeast Asia. In contrast, there was staunch opposition in Vietnam, where one senior educational official stated that, "in the view of Vietnamese people, Confucius Institutes are nothing but a political organ [of China]" and claimed that the establishment of a Confucius Institute in Vietnam would be "synonymous with the Vietnamese government's confirmation of its subordination to China."[35] A Confucius Institute was, in fact, established in Vietnam in 2014 amid significant criticism by local intellectuals.[36]

China has also increasingly offered scholarships to foreign students to study in China. The number of foreign students studying in China has increased from 85,000 in 2002 to 442,000 in 2016.[37] Nine Southeast Asian countries rank among the top thirteen countries sending students there.[38] Furthermore, recognizing that today's top students will likely be tomorrow's political, business, and educational leaders, China has created a prestigious fellowship program called the Yenching Academy to compete with the Fulbright and Rhodes Scholar programs. China is also experimenting with exchange programs for professionals, such as journalists, politicians, cultural and military leaders, in an effort to socialize them into sympathetic views of China.[39] China has also aggressively purchased media outlets in foreign countries to control the messaging Beijing wants and to engage in debates designed to tilt public opinion in target countries to seeing things China's way.

Promoting Chinese culture in Southeast Asia has generated blowback in some countries, in part because local ethnic Chinese minorities are viewed as potential conduits of China's influence, just as they were perceived as potential "fifth columns" during the Cold War. Blatant attempts by Chinese officials to intervene in domestic politics in Southeast Asian countries (as in the case of China's ambassador to Malaysia making public statements in favor of Sino-Malaysian business groups known to be close to China) have generated strong opposition. Moreover, the Institute of Southeast Asian Studies survey, discussed below, illustrates that most Southeast Asian foreign policy elites do not believe that China is trustworthy or can be depended upon to "do the right thing" and shows Chinese propaganda efforts have failed with this segment of the Southeast Asian public. Whether it has had more of a positive impact on the broader Southeast Asian public is unclear.

The South China Sea Dispute

Policy toward the South China Sea is where China has made the most dramatic shift under Xi away from Deng's mantra of "hide your strength, bide your time." The South China Sea has long been home to numerous territorial disputes over the Paracel and Spratly islands, which are claimed in whole or in part by China, Taiwan, Vietnam, the Philippines, and Brunei. China demonstrated its willingness to use force to seize territory from claimant states in the Paracels against Vietnam in 1974 and in Mischief Reef against the Philippines in 1984. Until 2009, however, the disputes were a largely frozen conflict since China had followed a policy of strategic ambiguity regarding its ultimate goals in the area. China demands that disputes be settled bilaterally since size disparities would enhance its bargaining position over Southeast Asia's smaller states. In contrast, Southeast Asian states prefer multilateral fora. In 2002, China and ASEAN signed a non-binding Declaration on the Conduct of Parties in the South China Sea (DOC). The DOC calls for parties to the South China Sea conflict to resolve disputes peacefully, to exercise restraint in activities that would complicate the disputes such as inhabiting new features, and it enshrines the principles of freedom of navigation in accordance with the United Nations Convention for the Law of the Sea (UNCLOS).[40] China has since violated all of these conditions.

In 2009, China abandoned ambiguity and made its claims clear when it issued its nine-dash-line map and claimed indisputable sovereignty to the waters within it, which account for 90 percent of the South China Sea. China's map does not conform to UNCLOS and threatens the sovereign territory of many Southeast Asian states whose islands fall within the nine-dash line. It also threatens the rights of Southeast Asian states to exploit resources in their Exclusive Economic Zones (EEZs) as granted by UNCLOS. Chinese maritime militia now regularly accompany Chinese fishing boats in disputed waters to deter Southeast Asian attempts to sanction them from fishing in Southeast Asian EEZs. China's claims threaten the principle of the freedom of the high seas, which holds that waters that lie beyond a country's territorial waters are to be treated under international law as international waters open to use by all countries. China's assertions of sovereignty therefore amount to an attempt to privatize the global commons. Southeast Asia's trade-dependent states have a key interest in ensuring that the principle of freedom of the seas is upheld. For archipelagic states such as Indonesia and the Philippines, which gained sovereignty over their internal waterways when UNCLOS came into force, ensuring the sanctity of UNCLOS has traditionally been a key national interest.

China's construction of artificial islands and the weaponization of Chinese occupied island features has been a significant game-changer in the South China Sea. Estimates are that China added over 3,200 acres of land to seven key features in the Spratly Islands. On the Fiery Cross Reef, Subi Reef, and Mischief Reef, China has constructed airfields, port facilities, and water and fuel storage. In 2018, China landed aircraft and moved electronic jamming equipment, surface-to-air missiles, and anti-ship missile systems to its newly built facilities in the region, which many see as a sign that China intends to declare an Air Defense Identification Zone. In a stark statement of the threat China poses, Admiral Davidson, head of the US Indo-Pacific Command, has warned that the People's Liberation Army "will be able to use these bases to challenge the US presence in the region and any forces deployed to the islands would easily overwhelm the military forces of any other South China sea-claimants and squeeze supply lines of smaller claimants. In short, China is now capable of controlling the South China Sea in all scenarios short of war with the United States."[41]

The South China Sea is the place where China's rise most directly impacts US strategic interests. Chinese bases could complicate the US ability to intervene militarily in the defense of Taiwan and to fulfill its obligations to allies such as Japan, the Philippines, and South Korea. The unwillingness of the US to support its allies and maintain its long-standing presence could encourage other Asian countries to reexamine their own defense and foreign policies. Many believe that China is using the South China Sea issue to raise doubts among American allies and partners about US reliability in an effort to drive a wedge between Washington and its partners. If successful, a breach between the US and its Southeast Asian partners would change the balance of power in the region in China's favor—a key goal of Xi's grand strategy.

Southeast Asian states have pushed back against China in a number of ways. All countries with overlapping maritime claims have filed protests against Chinese claims at the United Nations. After China's 2012 seizure of Scarborough Shoal—which lies well within the Philippine EEZ—the Philippines filed a case with the UNCLOS arbitral commission, a process China refused to participate in. In a bid to galvanize global support, the Philippines' then-President Benigno Aquino compared China's assertiveness toward the Philippines to Nazi Germany's demands for Czech land in 1938. Just like Czechoslovakia, Aquino argued that the Philippines was facing demands by a much stronger power to cede territory piece by piece. Aquino called upon the international community to "remember that the Sudetenland was given in an attempt to appease Hitler to prevent World War II."[42] He argued that international community should not fail to support the Philippines in an attempt to appease China the way the West failed to support Czechoslovakia. China punished the Philippines for defying its longstanding demands that the disputes be settled bilaterally rather than "internationalized" by banning imports of Philippine bananas, halting Chinese tourism to the Philippines, and preventing Aquino from attending certain events in China.

The arbitral commission ultimately ruled overwhelmingly in Manilla's favor in July 2016. It declared China's sweeping nine-dash line claim invalid and pronounced China in violation of the Philippines' sovereign rights to fish and explore for resources in the West Philippine Sea, waters within its EEZ. Despite this significant legal victory, Rodrigo Duterte, who had been inaugurated president a few weeks earlier, abandoned Aquino's plans to mobilize global support for the ruling in an effort to constrain China. Instead, Duterte announced that he would "set aside" the ruling. He also announced that he would be "charting a new course" in Philippine foreign policy to make it more "independent" and later announced a strategic shift away from the US and toward China.[43] Lambasting President Obama, Duterte "said goodbye" to the US and embraced China in a bid to secure economic benefits.[44] Under Duterte, the Philippines has officially shifted from one of the most vocal Southeast Asian critics of China to one of its strongest supporters, but many Filipinos have pushed back against the policy. The Philippine military has continued joint exercises with the US despite Duterte's call to suspend them. Duterte responded to critics of his policy shift by announcing that Xi Jinping had threatened war if the Philippines tried to enforce the arbitration ruling or drill for oil in disputed waters.[45] China's outright rejection of the arbitral ruling illustrates that it will not be bound by the rules-based order many of Southeast Asia's small states have long worked to promote.

Chinese Diplomacy toward ASEAN: Increasing Intervention in ASEAN Affairs

China's approach to ASEAN has changed over the past decade. Rather than adhere to ASEAN norms of nonintervention and the amicable settlements of disputes to demonstrate China's intention to rise peacefully, it has violated those norms in the pursuit of hard interests, particularly on the South China Sea. At the 2010 ASEAN Regional Forum meeting in Hanoi, where Vietnam successfully lobbied the US and other ASEAN members for support against China on the South China Sea issue, Chinese Foreign Minister Yang Jiechi reminded his counterparts in an undiplomatic outburst that "China is a big country and other countries are small countries and that is just a fact."[46] At the 2012 ASEAN meeting when the group was debating how strongly to condemn China's takeover of Scarborough Shoal from the Philippines, China used its influence over Cambodia, that year's ASEAN chair, to ensure that ASEAN did not produce a final communique for the first time in its history. Indonesian Foreign Minister Marty Natalegawa pushed back against China by engaging in whirlwind shuttle diplomacy to secure an agreement on a series of principles that were issued in lieu of a statement, thereby "saving ASEAN's face."[47] ASEAN members had hoped that "ASEAN centrality" in the regional architecture would be a mechanism to influence great powers like China to accommodate Southeast Asian interests. Instead, Beijing is increasingly using ASEAN as a conduit to pursue its own interests, unconstrained by ASEAN norms and often with ASEAN's smaller states like Laos and Cambodia acting as its proxies.

China's rising influence in ASEAN can be seen in Beijing's ability to convince ASEAN countries to keep items China disproves of off the agenda of ASEAN meetings and out the final communiques. Keeping items off the agenda means that ASEAN members cannot use their collective leverage on behalf of one member in their disputes with China, as Vietnam did in 2010. ASEAN's consensus decision-making rules give each member an effective veto over the organization's decisions and statements. In 2016, Cambodia used its vote to ensure that the final communique did not mention the arbitral ruling against China's South China Sea claims. During the Philippines chairmanship in 2017, a year that witnessed China assertiveness against Spanish oil company Respol's drilling activities in Vietnamese waters as well as continued militarization and island building, again no mention of these actions was included in the communique. Analysts interpreted this as a bid by Duterte to secure economic benefits by appeasing China. During the 2019 ASEAN meetings, the issue of the alleged Chinese military base in Cambodia, which would permit China to operate much closer to many Southeast Asian countries, was likewise kept off the agenda.

The clearest case of China using ASEAN as a mechanism to pursue its interests in the region are the negotiations over a legally binding ASEAN-China Code of Conduct (COC) to replace ASEAN's non-binding 2002 DOC. Before China's assertiveness over the past decade, many in ASEAN, the US, Japan and elsewhere hoped that a legally binding COC would deter China from future assertiveness in the South China Sea. Negotiations on the COC between China and ASEAN have continued, even as China's actions violate the commitments it made in the DOC. Many believe that the negotiations are simply a part of China "talk and take" strategy of slowing down negotiating processes while quickening the pace of its militarization in the South China Sea. More worrying, however, are reports that the COC single negotiating draft contains provisions inserted by China stating that "signatories must not hold military exercises with parties from outside the region unless other parties to the COC has been notified and express no objection."[48] Such language is clearly an attempt to limit US military activities with its allies and partners.[49] Some ASEAN countries, like Vietnam, have vigorously opposed such provisions, and it is anticipated that Vietnam will use its 2020 ASEAN chairmanship to take a stronger stance on these issues. If a COC is signed with provisions giving signatories veto power over the ability of Southeast Asian states to conduct joint exercises with outside countries, China will have an important new tool to use in its efforts to dislodge the US from Southeast Asia.

China's increasing influence in ASEAN has been facilitated by the decline of US engagement with it under the Trump administration, which has exacerbated longstanding Southeast Asian concerns about the US commitment to the region. Under Obama, the US embraced ASEAN regionalism as a central component of its pivot to Asia and Obama underscored the US commitment by attending seven out of the eight ASEAN summits during his presidency. President Trump attended the 2017 ASEAN summit but skipped the subsequent meetings, sending Vice President Pence in 2018 and newly appointed National Security Advisor Robert O'Brien in 2019. ASEAN leaders understood that domestic political issues including impeachment hearings might keep President Trump in Washington in 2019, but the last-minute announcement that the US delegation would be led by neither the Vice President nor Secretary of State rankled ASEAN. In a tit-for tat-retaliatory move designed to signal their displeasure, seven of the ten ASEAN leaders failed to attend the US-ASEAN Summit, sending lower level officials instead. A US diplomat stated that "We are extremely concerned about the apparent decision [to send lower level officials to the meeting]."[50] The official went on, "A full or partial boycott by ASEAN leaders will be seen as an intentional effort to embarrass the president of the United States of America and this will be very damaging to the substance of the ASEAN-US relations."[51] ASEAN officials retorted that "Trump should at least send a representative who is in the cabinet."[52]

In a surprise announcement that had apparently not been vetted, with Thailand as the ASEAN chair, US National Security Advisor O'Brien read aloud an invitation from President Trump for all ten ASEAN leaders to meet him in the US early in 2020 for a US-ASEAN summit. This put ASEAN leaders in a bind. If the US president is not interested in attending ASEAN's most important meeting, why invite ASEAN as a face-saving measure? The core of ASEAN's dilemma is that ASEAN leaders do not want to march to Trump's drum, but at the same time do not want to turn down an offer from the US in a time of growing Chinese assertiveness. As one Southeast Asian public intellectual observed, "If ASEAN-US relations sour in the near term, China will be a major beneficiary, putting ASEAN at a disadvantage."[53] In the end, the US-ASEAN summit scheduled to be held on March 14, 2020 in Las Vegas was cancelled in late February due to the COVID-19 crisis.[54] The cancellation was a disappointment to countries like Indonesia that had secured private meetings with President Trump to discuss bilateral issues, but was welcome in other ASEAN countries since it kept US-ASEAN relations cordial while avoiding the risk that President Trump might use the occasion to publicly lobby them to counterbalance China.

Southeast Asian Perceptions of China

China's more assertive policy under Xi Jinping has convinced many Southeast Asian elites that it is a threat. According to an Institute of Southeast Asian Studies survey of over one thousand Southeast Asian foreign policy elites conducted in late 2018, 45 percent believed that China will become a revisionist power with the intent to dominate Southeast Asia. At the same time, 68 percent are unsure of, or have little confidence in, US reliability as a security partner and provider of regional security.[55] Therefore, while China's assertiveness in the South China Sea and concerns over BRI have led many Southeast Asians to conclude that China will become a revisionist actor, the lack of credibility of the US under the Trump administration means that Southeast Asian states have not sought to balance as strongly against China as traditional balance-of-power theorists might predict.

Perceptions of China vary across Southeast Asia and within politically polarized countries like Thailand. A 2017 study of 1,800 Thai officials, mainly from the military, illustrated that a majority believed that Chinese influence in Thailand had eclipsed that of the US.[56] Despite unease over increasing Chinese power and of Thailand's status as a major non-NATO ally, more respondents viewed the US as a greater threat to Thailand than China.[57] According to the survey, Thais have a fairly benign view of their external security environment, perceiving no major state-based threat to the country. Therefore, the perception of threat Thai military officials hold is based in part on their opposition to the US response to Thailand's 2014 military coup. Supporters of Prime Minister Prayuth's military-backed government perceived the US response as too harsh and too public, as well as hypocritical because the US did not similarly condemn countries like Egypt when they had coups. The Thai case, therefore, illustrates that despite a concern over Chinese ambitions and actions, opposition to US policy by incumbent elites can facilitate China's influence in the region.

At the same time, China's harsh crackdown on pro-democracy protesters in Hong Kong has highlighted the dramatic differences in the views of China held by the incumbent elite and by more progressive Thais, particularly the younger generation. To the Prayuth government, the Hong Kong protests that shut down wide swaths of the economy triggered memories of the massive May 2010 anti-government Red Shirt protests that took over Bangkok's central business district and were only dispersed with military force. The Hong Kong protests occurred at the same time that the Prayuth government was facing challenges to its authority in both parliament and the streets by supporters of the Future Forward Party, a new party that won 17.65 percent of the vote in the 2019 elections by calling for sweeping political reform. The Prayuth government demonstrated support for China and the Hong

Kong establishment by hosting Chief Executive Carrie Lam in Bangkok.[58] In contrast, many younger, more pro-democratic Thais identified with the Hong Kong protestors. According to Thai China expert Wasana Wongsurawat, "Anti-Beijing sentiment has become a part of Thais' fight against authoritarianism."[59] In February 2020, the Prayuth government used a dubious legal ruling to disband the Future Forward Party, ensuring that its perceptions of China continue to drive Thai foreign policy in the near term. How Thailand's polarized politics play out in the longer term is uncertain, but domestic political change could trigger shifts in Thai policy toward China.

How the COVID-19 pandemic will influence Southeast Asian perceptions of China remains to be seen, in part because China's policy toward Southeast Asia has changed over time and in part because Southeast Asian countries have had varied responses to the pandemic. When the World Health Organization was advising countries against imposing travel restrictions, China strongly lobbied Southeast Asian governments not to follow the US lead and close borders. When countries like Singapore, Vietnam, and Indonesia restricted travel by Chinese citizens in early February 2020, China strongly criticized them. China's ambassador to Indonesia warned that restrictions on Chinese travelers would negatively harm Indonesia's economy and called for a more "rational" policy.[60] At a time when COVID-19 was widespread in China but not in Southeast Asia, China's strongarm response to these governments' attempts to protect their citizens was decidedly unwelcome.

In contrast, Hun Sen used the pandemic as an opportunity to curry favor with China. As other Southeast Asian countries were repatriating their citizens, Hun Sen refused to evacuate Cambodians from the epicenter of the crisis in Wuhan, insisting instead that Cambodians demonstrate solidarity with the Chinese. Hun Sen traveled to Beijing in early February 2020 to meet with Premier Li Keqiang and President Xi Jinping to show his support. Cambodia also permitted the cruise ship Westerdam to land on its territory after it been refused permission to dock in Japan, Guam, the Philippines, Taiwan, and Thailand over fears that someone on board might be carrying the coronavirus.[61] In contrast to other ASEAN states willing to sacrifice goodwill with China to protect their citizens' health, Hun Sen sacrificed the safety of Cambodian citizens to safeguard China's support of his regime.

As China recovered and the pandemic went global, China launched what has been called a "pandemic" or "facemask" diplomacy to portray itself as a global health leader. Chinese government entities, NGOs, and corporations have sent medical teams, personal protective equipment and testing kits to countries across the world in an effort to repair its national image.[62] Southeast Asian countries, particularly those hard hit by the pandemic, like Indonesia and the Philippines, have welcomed the material assistance even as they recognize that its provision is part of a larger strategic public relations effort. As prominent analyst Evan Laksamana has observed, "If this was just about assistance, we wouldn't need press conferences and welcoming ceremonies."[63] China is clearly hoping that its pandemic diplomacy will overcome negative perceptions caused by its early lack of transparency and slow response to COVID-19.

President Trump, however, has sought to deflect criticism of his own uncoordinated response to the crisis by scapegoating China. Trump continually refers to the "China virus," blasts China for playing down early cases, and promotes conspiracy theories that the virus originated in a Wuhan lab, even after they have been debunked by US intelligence officials.[64] With the exception of Cambodia, no Southeast Asian state wants to take sides in the battle of narratives between Trump's America and Xi's China. As the economic toll of the pandemic rises across the region, Southeast Asian states recognize that trade and investment with China will be key to recovery and are unlikely to engage in a public shaming of China at the expense of economic prosperity.

Conclusion

China's grand strategy toward Southeast Asia has changed significantly under Xi Jinping, shifting from the "low-profile, bide time" of Deng and Hu to a much more ambitious and assertive strategy. Xi has accomplished some of China's key objectives, particularly in the South China Sea, where China has changed the balance of power decidedly in its favor. These Chinese gains, however, were accomplished through brute military force, which had led to the perception among Southeast Asian leaders that China is a revisionist actor. This perception of China has helped trigger resistance to other aspects of China's grand strategy under Xi, particularly the BRI. China's success in achieving its connectivity goals under the BRI will depend in part on China's willingness to accommodate Southeast Asian interests through more cooperative strategies, and it is not certain that it will go that route. The future trajectory of Chinese grand strategy and the Southeast Asian response therefore remains unclear.

NOTES

1 Economy, "China's New Revolution."
2 Glosny, "Hedging Toward a Win-Win Future?"
3 Peh, "Friendly Panda, Fiery Dragon."
4 Peh, "Friendly Panda, Fiery Dragon."
5 Glosny, "Hedging Toward a Win-Win Future?"
6 "Treaty of Amity and Cooperation in Southeast Asia Indonesia, February 24, 1976."
7 Economy, "China's New Revolution."
8 Economy, "China's New Revolution."
9 Stromseth, "Don't Make Us Choose."
10 Stromseth, "Don't Make Us Choose," 3.
11 Stromseth, "Don't Make Us Choose," 6.
12 Dizioli et al. "IMF Working Paper."
13 Booth, "China's Economic Relations with Indonesia."
14 Booth, "China's Economic Relations with Indonesia."
15 World Integrated Trade Solution (World Bank Database), updated October 30, 2020. https://wits.worldbank.org.
16 Parameswaran, "Passengers of Westerdam Land after Two Weeks at Sea over Coronavirus Fears."
17 Booth, "China's Economic Relations with Indonesia."
18 Anas, "Indonesia's New Protectionist Trade Policies."
19 Dizioli et al., "IMF Working Paper."
20 Woetzel, China and the World, 53.
21 Woetzel, China and the World, 53.
22 Woetzel, China and the World, 53.
23 Shambaugh, "China's Soft-Power Push."
24 Rana and Ji, "China is Paving a Belt and Road 2.0."
25 Han, "How China Snubbed Singapore at the Belt and Road Summit."
26 Busbarat, "Why was Thailand's Prime Minister Absent in the Belt and Road Initiative Summit?"
27 Han, "How China Snubbed Singapore at the Belt and Road Summit."
28 Indonesia was represented by Vice President Kalla because the official winner of Indonesia's April 17 election had not been announced. Jokowi would have attended otherwise.
29 Heath, "The Ramifications of China's Reported Naval Base in Cambodia."

30 Heath, "The Ramifications of China's Reported Naval Base in Cambodia."
31 Tiezzi, "How China Wins Friends and Influences People." This is an example of China's lower-cost projects.
32 Tiezzi, "How China Wins Friends and Influences People."
33 Shambaugh, "China's Soft-Power Push."
34 Custer et al., "Ties That Bind."
35 Custer et al., "Ties That Bind," 12.
36 Hung, "Intellectuals and Activists Against the Confucius Institute, Beijing's Way to 'Assimilate' Vietnam."
37 Hung, "Intellectuals and Activists Against the Confucius Institute, Beijing's Way to 'Assimilate' Vietnam," 12.
38 Hung, "Intellectuals and Activists Against the Confucius Institute, Beijing's Way to 'Assimilate' Vietnam," 13.
39 Custer et al., "Ties That Bind," 13.
40 "Declaration on the Conduct of Parties in the South China SEA."
41 "Advance Policy Questions for Admiral Philip Davidson, USN Expected Nominee for Commander, U.S. Pacific Command," 18.
42 Bradsher, "Philippine Leader Sounds Alarm on China."
43 Heydarian, "Duterte's Efforts to Align the Philippines with China Face a Backlash."
44 "Philippines President Duterte Says 'Time to Say Goodbye' to America."
45 Mogato, "Duterte Says China's Xi Threatened War If Philippines Drills for Oil."
46 Peh, "Friendly Panda, Fiery Dragon."
47 Emmerson, "How Indonesia Saved ASEAN's Face."
48 Thayer, "A Closer Look at the ASEAN-China Single Draft South China Sea Code of Conduct."
49 Thayer, "A Closer Look at the ASEAN-China Single Draft South China Sea Code of Conduct."
50 Heydarian, "US Loses a March to China in South China Sea."
51 Heydarian, "US Loses a March to China in South China Sea."
52 Pongsudhirak, "Trump Gamesmanship Risks ASEAN Ties."
53 Pongsudhirak, "Trump Gamesmanship Risks ASEAN Ties."
54 Alper and Brunnstrom, "US Postpones Summit with ASEAN Leaders amid Coronavirus Fears."
55 Tang et al., *The State of Southeast Asia Survey Report 2019*.
56 Blaxland and Raymond, *Tipping the Balance in Southeast Asia?*, 5–6.
57 Blaxland and Raymond, *Tipping the Balance in Southeast Asia?*, 7.
58 "Carrie Lam Visit Will Bolster HK Investment."
59 Tanakasempipat, "Young Thais Join 'Milk Tea Alliance' that Angers Beijing."
60 Septiari, "'Don't Overreact.'"
61 Parameswaran, "Passengers of Westerdam Land after Two Weeks at Sea over Coronavirus Fears."

62 Lancaster and Rubin, "Assessing the Early Response to Beijing's Pandemic Diplomacy."

63 Massola, "China's Face-Mask Diplomacy Could Reshape Power in South-East Asia."

64 Tisdall, "Trump Is Playing a Deadly Game in Deflecting Covid-19 Blame to China."

BIBLIOGRAPHY

"Advance Policy Questions for Admiral Philip Davidson, USN Expected Nominee for Commander, US Pacific Command." US Congress. Accessed October 30, 2020. www.armed-services.senate.gov.

Alper, Alexandra, and David Brunnstrom. "US Postpones Summit with ASEAN Leaders amid Coronavirus Fears: Sources." Reuters. February 28, 2020. www.reuters.com.

Anas, Titik. "Indonesia's New Protectionist Trade Policies: A Blast from the Past." East Asia Forum, June 18, 2012. www.eastasiaforum.org.

Blaxland, John, and Greg Raymond, *Tipping the Balance in Southeast Asia? Thailand, the United States and China.* Canberra: Australian National University Strategic and Defence Studies Centre, 2017. http://bellschool.anu.edu.au.

Booth, Anne. "China's Economic Relations with Indonesia: Threats and Opportunities." *Journal of Current Southeast Asian Affairs* 30, no. 2 (2011): 141–60.

Bradsher, Keith. "Philippine Leader Sounds Alarm on China." *New York Times*, February 4, 2014. www.nytimes.com.

Busbarat, Pongphisoot. "Why was Thailand's Prime Minister Absent in the Belt and Road Initiative Summit?" Institute of Southeast Asian Studies—Yusof Ishak Institute. June 9, 2017. www.iseas.edu.sg.

"Carrie Lam Visit Will Bolster HK Investment." *Bangkok Post*, November 27, 2019. www.bangkokpost.com.

Custer, Samantha, Brooke Russell, Matthew DiLorenzo, Mengfan Cheng, Siddhartha Ghose, Harsh Desai, Jacob Sims, and Jennifer Turner. "Ties That Bind: Quantifying China's Public Diplomacy and its 'Good Neighbor' Effect." AidData. June 2018. http://docs.aiddata.org.

"Declaration on the Conduct of Parties in the South China SEA." Association of Southeast Asian Nations. Accessed March 4, 2019. https://asean.org.

Dizioli, Allan, Jaime Guajardo, Vladimir Klyuev, Rui Mano, and Mehdi Raissi. "IMF Working Paper: Spillovers from China's Growth Slowdown and Rebalancing to the ASEAN 5 Economies." International Monetary Fund. August 2016. www.imf.org.

Economy, Elizabeth C. "China's New Revolution." *Foreign Affairs*, March 6, 2019. www.foreignaffairs.com.

Emmerson, Donald K. "How Indonesia Saved ASEAN's Face." *Asia Times*, July 24, 2012.

Glosny, Michael. "Hedging toward a Win-Win Future? Recent Developments in China's Policy toward Southeast Asia, Asian Security." *Asian Security* 2, no. 1 (2006): 24–57.

Han, Angela. "How China Snubbed Singapore at the Belt and Road Summit." *Interpreter* (Lowy Institute). May 18, 2017. www.lowyinstitute.org.

Heath, Timothy R. "The Ramifications of China's Reported Naval Base in Cambodia." *World Politics Review*, August 5, 2019. www.worldpoliticsreview.com.

Heydarian, Richard Javad. "Duterte's Efforts to Align the Philippines With China Face a Backlash." *World Politics Review*, July 19, 2018. www.worldpoliticsreview.com.

Heydarian, Richard Javad. "US Loses a March to China in South China Sea." *Asia Times*, November 5, 2019. www.asiatimes.com.

Hung, Paul N. "Intellectuals and Activists Against the Confucius Institute, Beijing's Way to 'Assimilate' Vietnam." *Asia News*, June 18, 2015. www.asianews.it.

Lancaster, Kirk and Michael Rubin. "Assessing the Early Response to Beijing's Pandemic Diplomacy." Council on Foreign Relations. April 30, 2020. www.cfr.org.

Massola, James. "China's Face-Mask Diplomacy Could Reshape Power in South-East Asia." *Sydney Morning Herald*, April 3, 2020. www.smh.com.au.

Mogato, Manuel. "Duterte Says China's Xi Threatened War If Philippines Drills for Oil." Reuters. May 19, 2017. www.reuters.com.

Parameswaran. "Passengers of Westerdam Land after Two Weeks at Sea over Coronavirus Fears." *Jakarta Post*, February 15, 2020.

Peh, Shing Huei. "Friendly Panda, Fiery Dragon: How China and ASEAN Fell In (and Out) of Love." *South China Morning Post*, December 1, 2018. www.scmp.com.

"Philippines President Duterte Says 'Time to Say Goodbye' to America." *Guardian*, October 20, 2016. www.theguardian.com.

Pongsudhirak, Thitinan. "Trump Gamesmanship Risks ASEAN Ties." *Bangkok Post*, November 15, 2019. www.bangkokpost.com.

Rana, Pradumna B., and Xianbai Ji. "China is Paving a Belt and Road 2.0." East Asia Forum. May 21, 2019. www.eastasiaforum.org.

Septiari, Dian. "'Don't Overreact': Chinese Envoy Responds to Indonesia's Travel Ban amid Virus Fears." *Jakarta Post*, February 4, 2020. www.thejakartapost.com.

Shambaugh, David. "China's Soft-Power Push: The Search for Respect." *Foreign Affairs* 94, no. 4 (Jul/Aug 2015): 99–107.

Stromseth, Jonathan. "Don't Make Us Choose: Southeast Asia in the Throes of US-China Rivalry." Brookings. October 2019. www.brookings.edu.

Tanakasempipat, Patpicha. "Young Thais Join 'Milk Tea Alliance' that Angers Beijing." Reuters. April 15, 2020. www.reuters.com.

Tang, Siew Mun, Moe Thuzar, Hoang Thi Ha, Termsak Chalermpalanupap, Pham Thi Phuong Thao, and Anuthida Saelaow Qian. *The State of Southeast Asia Survey Report 2019*. Institute of Southeast Asian Studies—Yusof Ishak Institute. January 29, 2019. www.iseas.edu.sg.

Thayer, Carl. "A Closer Look at the ASEAN-China Single Draft South China Sea Code of Conduct." *Diplomat*, August 3, 2018. https://thediplomat.com.

Tiezzi, Shannon. "How China Wins Friends and Influences People." *Diplomat*, June 27, 2018. https://thediplomat.com.

Tisdall, Simon. "Trump Is Playing a Deadly Game in Deflecting Covid-19 Blame to China." *Guardian*, April 19, 2020. www.theguardian.com.

"Treaty of Amity and Cooperation in Southeast Asia Indonesia, February 24, 1976." Association of Southeast Asian Nations. Accessed April 1, 2020. https://asean.org.

Woetzel, Jonathan. *China and the World: Inside the Dynamics of a Changing Relationship*. McKinsey Global Institute. July 2019. www.mckinsey.com.

6

China's Current South Asia Strategy

GULSHAN SACHDEVA

In the initial years of the establishment of the People's Republic of China, India was central to the Chinese policy toward South Asia.[1] Despite ideological differences and the emergence of a bipolar world, both China and India fashioned *Panchsheel* (the five principles of peaceful co-existence) for alternative ethics and norms in international relations.[2] The 1959 flight of the Dalai Lama to India and the Sino-Indian conflict of 1962 ended the possibility of collaboration, and a new phase, based on real geopolitics and balance of power, emerged in the South Asian region.

The transfer of military (including nuclear) hardware and technology to Islamabad by China has created a new dynamic, in which Pakistan has played an important role for Beijing by keeping India occupied within the region. Chinese policy has been linked with "military security concerns vis-à-vis that of India and territorial disputes."[3] India shares borders with all South Asian countries. Other than Pakistan and Afghanistan, none of them share borders with each other. Similarly, China also shares borders with five South Asian countries.

Strategic cooperation with China is Pakistan's most important tool for addressing its strategic imbalance with India. As Andrew Small has emphasized, the foundation of the China-Pakistan axis is India. The "secretive ties" between the two run "closer than formal alliances." China provides "diplomatic protection" to Pakistan and is also its main arms supplier. This relationship has survived China's transition to a market economy, the rise of militancy in the region, as well as dynamics of their ties with the United States and India.[4]

The smaller South Asian countries also find their engagement with China useful for keeping Indian hegemonic ambitions in the region under control. Due to the coldness of Sino-Indian relations in the 1970s and early 1980s, China concentrated on other countries in the region. The 1988 visit of Indian Prime Minister Rajiv Gandhi to China normalized relations and both started promoting interactions in various fields. Without compromising their positions, both tried to avoid open confrontation.[5]

India and Pakistan both tested nuclear weapons for the first time in 1988, creating new worries for both China and India. The Sino-Pakistan "all-weather" friendship is important for Beijing because of Pakistan's geopolitical location, China's own war on terrorism/separatism, and its access to the Indian Ocean. Still, India is again becoming more and more important in China's long-term calculations. This is mainly due to the strategic consequences of India's strong economic performance in the last twenty-five years, which has raised India's profile well beyond South Asia.[6] This chapter first looks at current Chinese objectives and strategy toward the South Asian region, including economic linkages and the maritime dimension. Second, it focuses on China's Belt and Road Initiative (BRI) projects in the region and Indian perspectives on them. Third, it looks at the possibility that China can achieve its objectives and the evolving Indian strategy to deal with the challenges posed by neighbor to the north. Finally, the chapter analyzes the dramatic changes taking place in the context of the COVID-19 pandemic in the region.

Current Chinese Objectives and Strategy

Traditionally, Chinese strategy in South Asia has been to maintain a "strategic balance" in the region. In practical terms, this has meant checking India's rise by supporting Pakistan in the context of difficult India-Pakistan relations. In addition to this basic objective, Chinese interests have diversified in the last two decades. China's economic rise, on the one hand, and economic liberalization in South Asia, on the other, opened many new opportunities for Beijing to expand its profile and influence. Beijing is also pursuing strategies to access the Indian Ocean through South Asian ports. Some of the challenges related to separatism, religious extremism, and terrorism, which China faces today, have significant South Asian linkages. To prevent religious extremism spreading into Southern China, security and stability of the Afghanistan-Pakistan region is also becoming important. Through cooperation with South

Asian countries, China also wants to neutralize the US strategy of Chinese containment in the region and beyond.[7]

As these objectives have become more diverse, simple strategic calculations based on the balance of power are not enough to encapsulate current Chinese strategies in South Asia. Beijing has not announced any "South Asia strategy." However, its intensions are reflected in many of its official declarations, speeches, and initiatives. President Xi Jinping asserted a few years ago that South Asia represents a "promising subcontinent with immense potential" and the region has indeed become a new pole of growth in Asia and the world.[8] As already a huge asymmetry has emerged between India and China (the latter enjoying an economy five-times larger and a defense budget three times bigger than the former), there are signs that a confident China is shifting its priorities from strategic calculations to wider economic interests.

China's South Asia strategy is in transition. It previously operated mainly within the regional security complex. China's economic relations, even with Pakistan, were modest. This has changed quite significantly, not just through China-India trade, but also through Chinese investments in various BRI projects, including the China-Pakistan Economic Corridor (CPEC). Though balancing India by supporting Pakistan continues to be China's main objective, the focus is also shifting toward economic interests.[9] The long-term Chinese plan is to integrate the South Asian region into Chinese economic and strategic calculations. Due to China's enormous economic muscle, the difference between the Chinese and Indian economy is widening further. As a result, Beijing feels that it will be difficult for India to continue to be a security challenge to China. In the meanwhile, all South Asian economies, including India, will be integrating more and more into the Chinese economic orbit.

Trade Linkages and Arms Exports

Traditionally, India considered South Asia its exclusive sphere of influence. This was more visible in the economic sphere as Chinese economic linkages with most countries in South Asia were minimal. This has changed dramatically in the last two decades. Since 2005, China has surpassed India in South Asian trade. Even China-India trade, which was only about $3 billion in 2001 surpassed $95 billion in 2018, with a huge surplus of $58 billion in China's favor. Due to a slowdown in growth in the region, trade declined slightly in 2019. Overall, in 2019 China enjoyed a $136 billion trade with South Asia, out of which about $115 billion were exports. It exported products worth about $75 billion to India, $17 billion to Bangladesh, $16 billion to Pakistan and about $4 billion to Sri Lanka. Since South Asian exports were only about $21 billion, China had a surplus of about $95 billion from South Asia (see Tables 6.1 and 6.2). The China-Pakistan free trade agreement also came into effect in 2007.

In 2018, India exported only $25 billion worth of goods to seven South Asian countries compared to Chinese exports of about $41 billion to these countries. These exports further declined to about $22.5 billion in 2019. Still, for countries like Afghanistan, Bhutan, Nepal, the Maldives, and Sri Lanka, the Indian export market was much bigger than China (see Tables 6.3 and 6.4). Chinese investment in South Asian countries has also increased.

In addition to trade, South Asia is also the largest arms exports market for China. According to the SIPRI Arms Transfer Database, between 2000 and 2019, 54 percent of total Chinese arms exports went to South Asia (see Table 6.5).

TABLE 6.1. Chinese Exports to South Asia, 2014–19 (US$ Million)

	2014	2015	2016	2017	2018	2019
Afghanistan	393	364	435	541	670	601
Bangladesh	11,732	13,904	14,694	15,243	17,788	17,335
Bhutan	11	10	5	6	13	11
India	54,237	58,259	59,435	68,143	77,023	74,924
Maldives	104	172	342	300	399	342
Nepal	2,282	829	873	974	1,081	1,483
Pakistan	13,248	16,480	17,697	18,330	16,968	16,183
Sri Lanka	3,794	4,308	4,383	4,110	4,284	4,088
Total South Asia	**85,801**	**94,326**	**97,864**	**107,647**	**118,226**	**114,967**
World	2,343,222	2,280,541	2,136,594	2,280,094	2,501,333	2,498,548
% to South Asia	3.66	4.13	4.58	4.72	4.73	4.60

Source: IMF Direction of Trade Statistics

TABLE 6.2. Chinese Imports from South Asia, 2014–19 (US$ Million)

	2014	2015	2016	2017	2018	2019
Afghanistan	17	12	4	3	24	29
Bangladesh	761	803	858	872	986	1,036
Bhutan	*	*	*	*	*	*
India	16,412	13,395	11,759	16,355	18,847	17,970
Maldives	*	*	*	*	7	34
Nepal	46	21	22	17	22	33
Pakistan	2,760	2,478	1,902	1,831	2,183	1,807
Sri Lanka	248	259	273	309	340	396
Total South Asia	**20,244**	**16,968**	**14,818**	**19,387**	**22,409**	**21,305**
World	1,963,105	1,601,760	1,589,460	1,832,125	2,134,026	2,068,950
% to South Asia	1.03	1.06	0.92	1.06	1.05	1.3

*less than US$1 million
Source: IMF Direction of Trade Statistics

TABLE 6.3. Indian Exports to South Asia, 2014–19 (US$ Million)

	2014	2015	2016	2017	2018	2019
Afghanistan	443	533	473	639	728	869
Bangladesh	6,579	5,727	5,711	7,280	8,826	8,121
Bhutan	303	415	429	417	654	691
Maldives	139	168	181	213	220	228
Nepal	4,405	3,310	4,614	5,567	7,344	7,076
Pakistan	2,181	2,007	1,646	1,795	2,362	1,193
Sri Lanka	6,433	5,526	3,910	4,424	4,662	4,270
South Asia	20,483	17,686	16,964	20,335	24,796	22,448

Source: IMF Direction of Trade Statistics

Chinese arms exports to Pakistan alone amounted to about 40 percent of total Chinese arms exports to the world during this period. Within South Asia, Pakistan was responsible for about three-fourths of arms imports from China. The rest were imported by Bangladesh and Sri Lanka. In 2019, a significant increase in arms exports to Bangladesh and Sri Lanka is visible. In the last two decades, more than half of total Pakistan arms imports have come from China. The rest were from the US, France, Italy, Russia, Sweden, and Ukraine (Table 6.6).

TABLE 6.4. Indian Imports from South Asia, 2014–19 (US$ Million)

	2014	2015	2016	2017	2018	2019
Afghanistan	242	315	282	366	420	492
Bangladesh	556	651	711	570	899	1,219
Bhutan	159	245	220	195	255	244
Maldives	4	5	6	7	20	6
Nepal	602	504	407	374	403	641
Pakistan	529	456	462	431	542	67
Sri Lanka	591	853	631	609	1318	1,040
South Asia	**2,683**	**3,029**	**2,719**	**2,552**	**3,857**	**3,709**

Source: IMF Direction of Trade Statistics

TABLE 6.5. Chinese Arms Exports to South Asian Countries*, 2000–19 (US$ million)

	2000–2012	2013	2014	2015	2016	2017	2018	2019	Total 2000–2019
Afghanistan	0	0	0	0	0	1	0	0	1
Bangladesh	526	488	204	451	261	204	90	644	2,868
Nepal	2	0	0	0	8	1	0	0	11
Pakistan	4,283	744	477	557	727	658	446	421	8,313
Sri Lanka	273	0	0	0	0	0	0	59	332
Total South Asia	**5,084**	**1,232**	**681**	**1,008**	**996**	**864**	**536**	**1124**	**11,525**
Total Chinese Exports	10,004	2,080	1,226	1,799	2,372	1,346	1,140	1,423	21,391
% to South Asia	**50.8**	**59.2**	**55.5**	**56.0**	**41.9**	**64.1**	**47.1**	**78.9**	**53.8**

*No arms exports from China to Bhutan, India, and the Maldives during this period
Source: SIPRI Arms Transfer Database, accessed April 14, 2020, www.sipri.org.

The Maritime Dimension

The Indian Ocean has become increasing significant for China in recent years due to its expanding trade, energy, transport, and investments. Sea lanes of communication running through the Strait of Malacca, the Persian Gulf, the Arabian sea, the Indian Ocean, and the South China Sea are important for China for its increasing need for energy and raw

TABLE 6.6. Arms Imports by Pakistan by Country 2000–18 (US$ million)

	Amount	Percentage
China	7,744	50.1
USA	3,357	21.7
France	1,014	6.6
Italy	6,68	4.3
Russia	5,79	3.7
Sweden	4,27	2.8
Ukraine	359	2.3
Turkey	2,54	1.6
Others	1,036	6.7
Total	15,438	100

Source: SIPRI Arms Transfer Database

materials. Indian Ocean littorals are also becoming important given increasing investments by Chinese companies in the region as well as growing numbers of Chinese citizens and living and working in these areas.[10] For China, maritime expansion is also part of its strategy of economic integration of a range of regions, including South Asia, with the Chinese economy.

As a result, China has been enlarging its footprint in the Indian Ocean. Within South Asia it has made investments in strategic ports, including Chittagong (Bangladesh), Gwadar (Pakistan), and Colombo and Hambantota (Sri Lanka). It is also investing in Kyaukpyu (Myanmar). Pakistani and Sri Lankan authorities have given permission to Chinese companies to manage the ports of Gwadar and Hambantota for forty years and ninety-nine years, respectively. (This is not just a South Asian phenomenon, however. According to Mohan Malik, "nearly two thirds of the world's fifty major ports are either owned by China or have received some Chinese investment."[11]) China is also dispatching increasing number of surface warships and submarines to the Indian Ocean region.[12]

Since commercial ports could be converted to military use, this Chinese "string of pearls" in South Asia has troubled many Indian policy makers and analysts.[13] India considers itself a leading player in the

Indian Ocean and at present has a considerable advantage over China. Although a peaceful maritime environment in South Asia is important for China's economic expansion, it may see increasing competition from India in this area. Many Indian analysts speak of a "Chinese encirclement" that is causing anxiety among policy makers.[14] China, however, would like to portray these investments as purely commercial ventures and perhaps would welcome further Indian investments in South Asian ports, which will improve its own connectivity with the region.

The Chinese challenge, however, has pushed India to formulate its own strategy. It has started fortifying, as Malik has written, its "defences in the Indian Ocean by acquiring privileged access to bases in the Maldives, Mauritius, the Seychelles, Madagascar, Oman, and Iran; conduct joint naval exercises in the East and South China Seas; sign logistics exchange agreements with the US, Singapore, and France to gain access to naval bases in the Indo-Pacific, and launch an ambitious naval expansion program."[15] In addition, it has upgraded its development cooperation programs with the littorals, and, to revive old cultural trade routes in the Indian Ocean, New Delhi has also announced its own doctrine, called Security and Growth for All in the Region. Many in India argue that to a large extent, the upgrade from India's "Look East" policy, initiated in the early 1990s to its more recent "Act East" policy has widened India's engagement with its eastern neighbors mainly in the economic and security domains. Furthermore, its focus has widened from Southeast and Northeast Asia to the Indo-Pacific. Even the acceptance of the concept of the Indo-Pacific means conceiving the Indian and Pacific oceans as a single strategic space and highlights the importance of the maritime dimension of emerging challenges.[16] The current Indian objective of its Act East policy has been aptly summarized by Dhruv Jaishankar as "securing the Indian Ocean, integrating Southeast Asia, deepening strategic partnerships with other balancing powers (the US, Japan, Australia, France, Russia, and others) and managing differences with China."[17]

The Belt and Road Initiative

It is becoming clear that China's ambitious One Belt, One Road or BRI linking Asia and Africa with Europe through a network of various transportation corridors could fundamentally reshape the geo-economics and geopolitics of the whole Eurasian region and beyond. These developments have huge implications for South Asia. Out of China's original proposal of six international corridors,[18] two—the CPEC and the Bangladesh-China-India-Myanmar Economic Cooperation (BCIM) are directed toward South Asia. Another two (the new Eurasia Land Bridge and the China-Central Asia-West Asia Economic Corridor) have an indirect bearing on the subcontinent. Bangladesh, Pakistan, the Maldives, Nepal, and Sri Lanka are already participating, and Afghanistan is keen to be part of the BRI. Of late, there has been some discontent, particularly in the Maldives. Concerns about debt burden have increased, but the BRI's attractiveness in most South Asian countries has not dimmed.

Starting in 2015, and weighing in originally at $44 billion (this was later reported to have increased to $62 billion[19]), CPEC has been a flagship BRI project. In answer to a question in Pakistan's National Assembly on January 9, 2020, the government declared, however, that the actual cost of the project is about $50 billion.[20] A large part of this amount (more than $30 billion) will be spent on energy-related projects. The rest of the projects involve road and railway infrastructure and the port of Gwadar. Details of some of these projects are provided in Tables 6.7 and 6.8. The government of Pakistan expects that CPEC projects will generate more than 17,000 MW of electricity, modernize roads and railways, develop the port of Gwadar, build four urban mass transit projects and nine special economic zones, and connect China and Pakistan with fiber optic cable. The financing is mix of grants, concessional loans, zero-interest loans, partnerships, and foreign direct investment (FDI).

Of these projects in Pakistan, thirteen, worth $11 billion, have been completed; thirteen projects worth $18 billion are under implementation; and additional projects valued at $21 billion are still in pipeline. In the energy sector, completed coal-fired energy projects include Hubco, Port Qasim, Sahiwal, Engro Thar, and the Surfice mine in Block II of the Thar coalfield. Other completed plants are the Dawood wind farm, the Quaid-i-Azam solar complex, the UEP wind farm, the Sachal wind farm, the Port Qasim power plant and the Three Gorges Second and Third wind farms. About 5,000 MW of electricity has been pumped into the national grid so far. As a result of this, Pakistan expects power shortages to soon be a thing of the past.[21]

TABLE 6.7. China-Pakistan Economic Corridor Energy Projects

Sr No.	Project Name	MW	Estimated Cost (US$ M)
Priority Projects			
1	2×660MW Coal-fired Power Plants at Port Qasim Karachi	1,320	1,912
2	Suki Kinari Hydropower Station, Naran, Khyber Pukhtunkhwa	870	1,707
3	Sahiwal 2x660MW Coal-fired Power Plant, Punjab	1,320	1,912
4	Engro Thar Block II 2×330MW Coal-fired Power Plant TEL 1×330MW Mine Mouth Lignite-fired Power Project at Thar Block-II, Sindh, Pakistan ThalNova 1×330MW Mine Mouth Lignite-fired Power Project at Thar Block-II, Sindh, Pakistan	660 330 330	995 498 498
	Surface mine in block II of Thar Coal field, 3.8 million tons/year		1,470
5	Hydro China Dawood Wind Farm (Gharo, Thatta)	49.5	113
6	300MW Imported Coal-based Power Project at Gwadar, Pakistan	300	542
7	Quaid-e-Azam 1000MW Solar Park (Bahawalpur) Quaid-e-Azam	300,600,100	1,302
8	UEP Wind Farm (Jhimpir, Thatta)	99	250
9	Sachal Wind Farm (Jhimpir, Thatta)	49.5	134
10	SSRL Thar Coal Block-I 6.8 mtpa and SEC Mine Mouth Power Plant (2×660MW) (Shinghai)	1,320	1,912 + 1,300
11	Karot Hydropower Station	720	1,698
12	Three Gorges Second Wind Power Project Three Gorges Third Wind Power Project	49.5 49.5	150
13	CPHGC 1,320MW Coal-fired Power Plant, Hub, Balochistan	1,320	1,912
14	Matiari to Lahore ±660kV HVDC Transmission Line Project		1,658
	Matiari (Port Qasim)—Faisalabad Transmission Line Project		1,500
15	Thar Mine Mouth Oracle Power Plant (1320MW) and surface mine	1,320	Yet to be determined
Actively Promoted Projects			
16	Kohala Hydel Project, AJK	1,100	2,364
17	Rahimyar Khan Imported Fuel Power Plant 1320 MW	1,320	1,600
18	Cacho 50MW Wind Power Project	50	
19	Western Energy (Pvt.) Ltd. 50MW Wind Power Project	50	
Potential Projects			
20	Phandar Hydropower Station	80	
21	Gilgit KIU Hydropower	100	

Source: http://cpec.gov.pk

TABLE 6.8. China-Pakistan Economic Corridor Infrastructure Projects

Project Name	Length in kilometers	Estimated Cost in US$ millions and Pakistani Rupees
Roads		
1 KKH Phase II (Thakot-Havelian Section)	118	1,315 US$ m
2 Peshawar-Karachi Motorway (Multan-Sukkur Section)	392	2,889 US$ m
3 Khuzdar-Basima Road N-30	110	19 b Pak. rupees
4 Upgradation of D. I. Khan (Yarik) - Zhob, N-50 Phase-I	210	
5 KKH Thakot-Raikot N35 remaining portion	136	8 b Pak. rupees
Railways		
6 Expansion and reconstruction of existing Line ML-1	1,830	8,172 US$ m
7 Havelian Dry port (450 M. Twenty-Foot Equivalent Units)		65 US$ m
8 Capacity Development of Pakistan Railways		
Ports		
9 Nine projects related to Gwadar port		824 US$ m
Others		
Cross-border Optic Fiber Cable		37 US$ m

Source: http://cpec.gov.pk/

Since 2016, Bangladesh has emerged as the second largest recipient of Chinese BRI investments, after Pakistan. Having staked $38 billion overall in the country, China is already Bangladesh's single largest investor. Various reports indicate that the value of the BRI projects alone may reach $40 billion.[22] Already, about $10 billion worth of infrastructure projects are under construction. These include the Karnaphuli Multi-Channel Tunnel Project, the Chinese Economic and Industrial Zone, the Padma Bridge rail link, Payra Power Plant, the eighth China Bangladesh Friendship Bridge, and the International Exhibition Center. Some of the projects, like the multipurpose Padma bridge or the Rampal coal power plant, which were earlier declined by the World Bank or Western funders because of environmental issues or corruption, are now being undertaken with Chinese money.[23]

In Sri Lanka, China has financed projects worth close to US$8 billion under the BRI. Major projects include the Colombo International Financial Centre, the port of Hambantota, a Colombo port expansion, the Mattala Rajapaksha International Airport (MRIA) in Hambantota, and the Matara Beliatta railway expansion. Critics of the BRI have used the Hambantota port and airport projects as examples of debt trap and failed, white elephant gifts. In 2017 Sri Lanka formally handed over the Hambantota port to Chinese firms for a ninety-nine-year lease.

Nepal signed a framework agreement for the BRI with China in 2017. It identified thirty-five projects under the initiative and expected about $10 billion in investment.[24] Later, a reduced list included nine projects: upgrading the Rasuwagadhi-Kathmandu road; the construction of the Kimathanka-Hile road; road construction from Dipayal to the Chinese southern border; the Tokha-Bidur road; the Galchhi-Rasuwagadhi-Kerung 400 kv transmission line; the Kerung-Kathmandu railway line; the 762MW Tamor hydroelectricity project; the 426 MW Phukot Karnali hydroelectric project; and the Madan Bhandari Technical Institute. Out of these projects, only a feasibility study for the Kurang-Kathmadu railway line has been completed so far. This project was also listed in the new list of projects released at the end of the second BRI Forum.[25]

Over the years, China has gained political and economic influence in Nepal. President Xi Jinping's visit to Kathmandu in October 2019 further reflected the changing dynamic between China, Nepal, and India. The Communist Party's dominance in Nepalese politics has also helped China. It is geo-economics, rather than geopolitics, that is going to decide how Nepal will keep its relations balanced between its two gargantuan neighbors.[26] The political economy of trilateral ties is not simple. It is difficult for Nepal to ignore India, but new economic opportunities from China have also drawn it toward China.

China is funding a few big BRI infrastructure projects in the Maldives. The list includes the Friendship Bridge linking Male to Hulhule Island and a 1,000-apartment housing project on the artificial island Hulhumale.[27] The new government in Male now wants to renegotiate existing debt and some of the projects negotiated under former president Abdulla Yameen.[28]

Although India has not rejected the BRI, the official narrative is quite negative. A broad consensus seems to have emerged in India that the

BRI is primarily a Chinese undertaking with clear Chinese objectives. The initial discussions have focused mainly on two dimensions of the BRI: the geopolitical and developmental implications of the initiative for India. Because of the overwhelming emphasis on the CPEC in Indian discussions, the geopolitical dimensions of the BRI, rather than broader developmental aspects, have mainly shaped perceptions. The major focus has been on the geopolitical impact of infrastructural projects in the neighborhood and in the Indian Ocean region. Assessments of the economic impact of the initiative beyond the CPEC are rather limited. Of late, the political economy dimension of the project has figured prominently in discussions. Here, the emphasis is more on evaluating political, social, environmental, and sustainability issues concerning Chinese-funded projects.

Developments in the broader India-China relationship (the increasing trade deficit, the Dokhlam standoff, etc.) have affected Indian perceptions. India's participation in the Brazil-Russia-India-China-South Africa (BRICS) forum, the Shanghai Cooperation Organization (SCO), and the Asian Infrastructure Investment Bank (AIIB) has had relatively little impact on New Delhi's perception of the BRI. In fact, the BCIM corridor, which was raised to Track I status in 2013, has become something of a victim of the geopolitics of the BRI.

Before the announcement of the BCIM Economic Corridor (BCIM-EC) as an important component of the BRI, the four countries involved had already been working for years to materialize sub-regional cooperation. To integrate eastern and northeastern India with southwestern China along with two of the least developed countries (Bangladesh and Myanmar), a Track II BCIM regional Economic Forum was established in 1999 in Kunming. In 2013, the concept was officially endorsed and participating nations agreed to establish a Joint Study Group to strengthen connectivity, trade, and other linkages through the development of a BCIM-EC.[29] Along with the CPEC, however, when the BCIM-EC was also declared as an important part of the BRI initiative by China, it created difficulties for Indian policy makers.[30] Since the BCIM was conceived well before the BRI, many argue that it should not have been subsumed within the larger BRI strategy.[31] The main Indian objective behind initiating the BCIM-EC was to develop infrastructure and markets for its northeastern region through sub-regional cooperation. In this way, relatively isolated Indian states could take advantage from its Look East/Act East policy. Jointly building missing infrastructural links in the sub-region has been one of the major objectives of the initiative. As the BCIM also became part of larger discourse on the BRI, the progress on this front has also been stalled, though the issue has figured in some formal and informal bilateral meetings.

Although a large number of independent analysts have argued for a selective participation in the BRI, this has hardly been reflected in government policy. As the BRI progresses, the Indian focus is more on pursuing its own connectivity plans (individually or with other partners) and also on showing how some of the BRI projects are creating difficulties for recipient countries. From earlier geopolitical and developmental aspects of the initiative, the focus is now shifting toward a political economy analysis of participating countries. Increasing difficulties faced by BRI projects in terms of debt trap, corruption, political controversies, negative environmental implications, and the overall sustainability of projects are being analyzed.[32]

At the recent BRI-2 meeting, China removed the BCIM-EC from the new list of thirty-five corridors. Instead, the China-Myanmar Economic Corridor and the Nepal-China Multi-dimensional Connectivity Network (including a railway project) are listed. Interestingly, now the International North-South Transport Corridor (INSTC) is also part of the new BRI list. Established well before the BRI, in 2000, India along with Russia and Iran are founding members of the INSTC. India has not formally responded to this new listing. If there were any alternative Indian plan to the BRI, the Chabahar port linked with the INSTC was going to be the central pillar of that strategy. Now the INSTC itself is listed as a BRI project. For India, this is more serious than the BCIM listing. New Delhi will have to work with Moscow and Tehran to resolve this issue. In the current geopolitical framework, however, both of them may not have any problem with listing INSTC as a BRI project.[33]

Overall, India and Pakistan approach the BRI projects mainly through their own geopolitical prisms. The evolving goal of smaller South Asian countries with China is mainly to profit from China's economic rise. As these smaller countries try to balance their relations with New Delhi and Beijing, this may not necessarily translate into major strategic and military gains for China, at least in the short term.[34] Some of the "debt trap" problems in the region could be avoided if an alternative and responsible program for infrastructure development is made available.

The Developing Situation in Jammu and Kashmir

Ever since the Indian government decided to end Jammu and Kashmir's special status, the situation in the Kashmir valley and between India and Pakistan has been tense. Under the new changes, the state of Jammu and Kashmir has now been converted into two Union territories, Jammu and Kashmir and Ladakh, which will be administered directly by the Central government. The government has termed these measures strictly an internal affair of India, which aims mainly to improve governance and economic development. Pakistan has reacted angrily, accusing India of planning a "demographic change" and the further suppression of the Kashmiri people. Since then, both countries have downgraded diplomatic ties and stopped trade as well as bus and train services between the two countries. The situation in the Kashmir valley is still not fully normal.[35] Pakistan, with help from China, raised the issue at a closed door meeting of the UN Security Council.[36] The UN Secretary General has appealed for "maximum restraint" and urged "all parties to refrain from taking steps that could affect the status of Jammu and Kashmir."[37] If India is not able to manage the internal situation in Kashmir properly, Pakistan and China will continue to make efforts in the coming years to involve major powers in the issue. So far, India has been able to manage it at the UN Security Council because of favorable stands taken by France, Russia, and the US. The Kashmir issue, along with the unfolding situation in Afghanistan, will continue to impinge on China-South Asia affairs in the coming years.

Can China Achieve its Objectives?

China's objectives in South Asia are not limited to balancing its interests within the regional security complex. Without compromising its core strategic interests and without raising serious concerns, its challenge is how to integrate growing South Asian economies within the Chinese orbit through trade. The BRI is going to be its main focus for the next five to ten years. Other than India, most South Asian countries are already moving in this direction. Managing its relations with New Delhi is thus going to be crucial.

Indian interests and capacities are now growing far beyond South Asia. Despite the China-Pakistan nexus, India cannot be restricted within South Asia. A certain level of cooperation with India has already developed within the BRICS and the SCO as well as two informal Xi-Modi summits in Wuhan and Chennai. Apart from broad agreements on global and regional issues, reflected in various declarations and statements, New Delhi has participated in the AIIB from the beginning. After China, India is the second largest shareholder in the bank. It is also largest borrower, however. Out of seventy-one projects approved by the AIIB, sixteen are in India. So far, the AIIB has committed about $3.6 billion in investments to India. Another ten projects worth $4 billion are in the pipeline. The most recent approved $500 million loan in May 2020 is to support India's fight against COVID-19.[38]

In the last few years, Chinese companies are also entering the Indian market through venture investments in start-ups. The way FDI is calculated in India,[39] official Chinese FDI is still very limited. However, independent reports indicate that total existing and planned Chinese investments in India are close to $25 billion.[40] A *Gateway House* report shows that Chinese companies have "penetrated the online ecosystem with its popular smartphones and their applications."[41] Chinese companies have invested about $4 billion in Indian start-ups in the last five years. Report suggests that out of thirty leading unicorns, eighteen are Chinese-funded. Unlike investments in physical infrastructure in other countries, the Chinese have concentrated on tech start-ups in India.

In broader Chinese strategy, the CPEC extension will improve the effectiveness and profitability of the Indian economy. Although it is difficult for India to be part of the extended CPEC, participation in other corridors cannot be ruled out in the medium run. The unpredictability of the US commitment to South Asia, particularly after its exit from Afghanistan, may facilitate the success of the Chinese strategy.

With increasing trade difficulties with the US, most Asian countries are likely to concentrate more within Asia itself. This is evident with the recent conclusion of Regional Comprehensive Economic Partnership (RCEP) negotiations. India opting out of the RCEP will have mixed implications for growing Chinese economic clout in Asia. Although China will integrate more within Asia, it still will have to deal separately with a big neighboring economy.

This, however, also shows that the Indian economy is still not fully ready to participate in Asia's economic rise. One of the main reasons seem to be that India has a trade deficit of more than $100 billion with RCEP countries. A slowdown in growth and exports as well as political opposition are possible reasons. Apart from the Indian National Congress, opposition to signing the deal also came from *Swadeshi Jagran Manch* and *Bharatiya Kisan Sangh*, the two affiliates of *Rashtriya Swayamsevak Sangh*, the ideological mentor of the ruling *Bharatiya Janata Party*. The Modi government has been very cautious about trade deals and investment agreements in any case. India has signed hardly any new trade agreements in the last five years. A large number of bilateral investment treaties have also been terminated.[42] As India already has trade agreements with the ASEAN, South Korea and Japan, the real worry has been China.

Despite all strategic calculations and balance-of-power considerations, the influence of economic factors will be a major determining factor in the Indian capacity for dealing with a rising China in the coming years. At the moment, both China and India are facing difficulties at the economic front and economic growth has declined in both.

At the Asian and global levels, China and India have started being noticed (China earlier and India later) not only for their military and strategic strengths. China's three decades of double-digit growth have given it enormous influence. It has provided trade and investment opportunities for all major economic players. Similarly, India has always been a big country and a democracy for more than half a century. But the world started noticing India only when it showed that it could also grow at an average of 7 percent per year for a sustained period of time. Recently, however, even before the economic impact of COVID-19, the economy has been stagnating at about 5 percent growth.

Despite all of the talk of *Made in India* in the past five years, the Indian manufacturing sector has still not taken off. A few years after economic liberalization in the 1990s, three sectors in the economy (information technology, pharmaceuticals, and automobiles) became international and have produced world-class Indian multinationals. This trend changed in the 2010s and many post-liberalization companies are now in difficulty. Some new emerging companies (unicorns) are just cloning Western techniques and lack technological innovation. One of the main reasons is perhaps lack of focus, resources, and lack of direction in the higher education sector.[43]

Economic slowdown and trade tensions with the US have put some pressure on China. However, with an economy five times bigger than India's, the Chinese are still quite relaxed about New Delhi.[44] For Beijing, improvement in trade, investment, and connectivity with India is mutually beneficial. Indian policy makers, however, seem to be uncertain in their responses. Despite a huge current account deficit, India continues to provide a large market for Chinese goods. Still, New Delhi is not confident about Chinese investment in the country. If the Chinese can invest more than $50 billion in BRI projects in Pakistan, they could also easily invest hundreds of billions in Indian infrastructure, including railway modernization and ports. But strategic worries in India have overshadowed economic considerations.

China is also moving up the value chain. Many industries related to textiles, shoes, toys, and the like are already moving into Bangladesh, Cambodia, and Vietnam. The US-China trade war is also pushing many manufactures toward Southeast Asia. Still, very few Chinese companies are looking toward India. With its comparative advantage in certain sectors, Indian IT companies could even participate in technologies like 5G, artificial intelligence, and robotics, where the Chinese are making serious headway. The biggest challenge for India's China policy is to balance its strategic worries with economic opportunities. However, India is not the only country to have to deal with this dilemma. The trouble for India is that an expanding China is also squeezing New Delhi's space in its traditional areas of influence.

The Evolving Indian Strategy

The increased Chinese economic and naval presence in South Asia and the Indian Ocean region has obviously pushed India's policy makers to work on diplomatic, military, and economic strategies to safeguard its interests. A straightforward, realistic assessment based on a balance-of-power approach would suggest that New Delhi should align itself with the US and other countries worried about China's rise in the region. However, as the Indian Foreign Minister has recently outlined, in a world whose dynamics are shifting and where "technology, connectivity and trade are at the heart of new contestations," India is thinking more in terms of "convergences and issue-based arrangements."[45]

Constraints on India's capacities, the complex nature of India-China relations, as well as the unpredictability of US policies are leading it toward multiple strategies for facing the challenge posed by China. These include strategic partnerships with key players worried about China, improving military capabilities, further deepening its ties with the ASEAN, increasing its development partnership engagements within South Asia and the wider region, as well as working with like-minded players (including Japan and the EU) to develop multilateral infrastructural initiatives.

Some analysts have called this approach a limited hard balancing by obtaining asymmetrical military capabilities and as well as soft balancing by forming limited coalitions with US, Japan, Australia, and some ASEAN countries.[46] The upgrade from a "Look-East Policy" to an "Act East" policy; the Security and Growth for All in the Region doctrine, the promotion of the concept of the Indo-Pacific; engagement in the Quadrilateral Security Dialogue, and the launching of an Asia-Africa growth corridor with Japan are all different pieces of this larger strategy of counterbalancing China in South Asia and the Indian Ocean, the areas of traditional Indian influence. In the meantime, India will continue to engage with China for meaningful cooperation on issues concerning trade and climate change, among others. At this point in time, New Delhi may not see any contradiction in participating simultaneously in the Quadrilateral Security Dialogue and the SCO, Japan-America-India, Russia-India-China, or BRICS formats. It has not endorsed the BRI, but has participated in the AIIB. The Indian strategy will therefore be to take advantage of increased Chinese economic capabilities but restrict its strategic footprints in South and Southeast Asia and the Indian Ocean.

The Impact of COVID-19

The COVID-19 pandemic has changed the world dramatically. Millions of people have been infected by the virus and hundreds of thousands have died. The situation is still unfolding as this book goes to press. The geography of the virus is changing and expanding. At one point of time, it was discussed in the context of China and Iran and then Europe and the US. Later it has expanded into Russia, Turkey, Latin America, Middle East and South Asia. At the moment, it is also extremely active in South Asia, particularly in India, Pakistan, and Bangladesh.

It initially appeared that there were two different approaches for dealing with the virus. One was Chinese and the second European (British-French-German). The Chinese approach has been to strictly lock down entire areas, quarantine residents; establish large-scale temporary hospitals; and keep affected areas (or perhaps the entire country) quarantined for a sufficient period. The main focus has been on breaking the transmission. After their initial bungling, Chinese policy makers showed that it is possible to control the epidemic if resources can be mobilized. The European approach, on the other hand, seemed to suggest that very little can be done once the virus enters communities. It will take some time to develop treatment, vaccination, and immunity. Lockdowns and border closures may look attractive at the beginning, but they are not going to be very effective in the medium run. In the process, strict lockdowns will significantly harm economies and societies. So the strategy is to live with the virus carefully and try to minimize the impact. Periodical restrictions and lockdowns may be required mainly to avoid health facilities getting overwhelmed.[47]

After seeing Europe and the US struggling with the situation, South Asian countries, notably India, tried to copy the Chinese approach with a very strict lockdown. The model was appealing because of relatively small initial numbers, the size of its population, an inadequate medical infrastructure, and limited global economic integration.

As numbers continue to increase despite lockdowns, policy makers in South Asia are now talking about learning to live with the virus. As most European countries have also now started lockdowns, there seems to be some convergence between the two different approaches. It is being realized that lockdowns and isolating countries from the outside world may be a good strategy to begin with, but it will have a limited impact if it is not followed by contact tracing, appropriate testing, and the mobilization of resources for improving health systems.

Due to the spread of the virus and the lockdowns, multilateral organizations and international agencies have predicted the worst global economic downturn since the Great Depression.[48] They are almost unanimous in seeing this unprecedented decline, for two main reasons. First, the virus has affected both developed and developing economies simultaneously. Second, it has drastically reduced both demand and supply. Most rich countries have announced huge stimulus packages. However, when the governments themselves have directed industry and services to shut their activities, these stimulus packages may have a limited impact.

The extent of actual decline in the first quarter of 2020 in all major economies has even surpassed these predictions.[49] Since lockdowns started in March 2020 in many countries, the second quarter of 2020 will be even worse. China and South Asia are no exception. China has seen a 6.8 percent decline in the first three months of 2020 from a year ago. This is the first time China has seen this kind of decline since it started recording quarterly data in 1992.[50]

The International Monetary Fund has predicted 1.1 percent GDP growth in China, 1.9 percent in India and negative 1.5 percent in Pakistan in 2020.[51] With this developing global recession, South Asia will be fortunate if it is able to achieve even this level of growth. The Indian economy was already weakening and Pakistan was already facing severe difficulties when the lockdowns started. Still, South Asian economies may perform relatively better. Agriculture and basic food items are the least affected by lockdowns. And a large number of people in these countries still depend on agriculture and spend a significant part of their earnings on food. With its strong pharmaceutical and IT industry, India may also take advantage of new emerging demands in these sectors. When it became clear that COVID-19 is spreading fast in South Asia, Indian Prime Minister Narendra Modi took the initiative to convene a video conference of all South Asian Association for Regional Cooperation nations to work out a joint strategy for the region. Apart from sharing experiences, the leaders also agreed to establish a COVID-19 Emergency Fund for member countries.[52]

COVID-19 has created new suspicions between China and India and brought China-Pakistan still closer. Officially, New Delhi has been careful not to blame China for the virus or its worldwide spread because of

Beijing's lack of initial action. Still, many analysts are blaming China for its lack of transparency and its role in silencing the World Health Organization.[53] This has also led to increased distrust of China among the Indian public.[54] To avoid hostile takeovers amid COVID-19 (mainly targeting China), India has amended its FDI rule. Now all investments from neighboring countries that share borders with India will need government approval.[55] Indian policy makers have been worried not only about data security concerns in new start-ups but also takeovers by Chinese firms during the difficult economic times ahead.

In contrast to India, the Senate in Pakistan passed a unanimous resolution appreciating the leadership of President Xi Jinping for leading "a very successful operation to combat, contain and finally eliminate Corona virus."[56] China has provided some medical support to Pakistan. As internal cases in China are limited, China and Pakistan also plan to collaborate on clinical trials for a COVID-19 vaccine.[57] In an attempt to balance their relations, Afghanistan, Bangladesh, Nepal, and Sri Lanka have engaged both China and India in dealing with the crisis.[58] They have received medical supplies both from China and India.

Conclusion

Traditionally, South Asia was considered to be an Indian area of influence. Its history, geography, religions, languages, and culture are dominated by India. China is trying to counterbalance India through its close strategic ties with Pakistan. With an expanding Chinese economic profile and maritime footprint, India's position is being seriously challenged. China's expansion into South Asia has further accelerated with the BRI. The China-Pakistan nexus has already kept India occupied in the region and has restrained New Delhi's options in South and Central Asia. The US exit from Afghanistan will further strengthen this nexus. With a much larger economy than India's, Beijing has little to fear from New Delhi.

New Delhi is trying to counterbalance Chinese expansion in the region by increasing its own military capabilities and strengthening partnerships with ASEAN, Japan, and the US. In addition to participating in the Quadrilateral Security Dialogue initiative, New Delhi is also raising concerns about various BRI projects. Therefore, the main challenge for China is to expand in the region in such a way that it should not raise serious concerns and push India into major security alignment with the US. This could be achieved by increasing economic linkages within the region and accommodating some of the Indian concerns. India's economic performance in the coming years will determine its role in the evolving Asian security and economic architecture. A stagnating economy will have cause more domestic political difficulties as well as a protectionist and geopolitical attitude toward China. This became evident with India not agreeing to be part of the RCEP and hardening its position on Kashmir.

The COVID-19 pandemic is going to change regional dynamics significantly. Although officially India has not blamed China for the virus or its worldwide spread, concerns are being expressed about its lack of transparency. While China seems to be coming out of the pandemic, South Asian countries are in the throes of the crisis. Economic decline in the region is certain in 2020. However, Chinese and Indian economic performance beyond 2020 will determine regional geopolitics and economic integration. India will also try to woo investors who may be moving away from China. If in 2021 the Indian economy comes back to its earlier growth trajectory of the last twenty-five years, New Delhi may forge economic integration with China and Asia as well as security alignments with the other powers including the US. Overall, India's economic and strategic importance lies mainly in continuing its high economic growth. The Himalayan border clashes between India and China in the summer of 2020 have, for now, been contained but are an indication of major potential conflict in the future. If those border skirmishes are not kept under control, then many of the benefits of economic cooperation will be thwarted.

NOTES

1 South Asia for this chapter refers to all eight countries that belong to the South Asia Association for Regional Cooperation (SAARC)—Afghanistan, Bangladesh, Bhutan, India, Nepal, the Maldives, Pakistan, and Sri Lanka.
2 Acharya, "China and South Asia."
3 Malik, "South Asia in China's Foreign Relations."
4 Small, *China-Pakistan Axis.*
5 Garver, "China and South Asia."
6 See Sachdeva, "The Indian Economy."
7 US-China Economic & Security Review Commission, *2016 Report to Congress of the US-China Economic & Security Review Commission*; US-China Economic & Security Review Commission, *China-South Asia Relations.*
8 Jinping, "In Joint Pursuit of a Dream of National Renewal."

9 Rajan, "China."
10 US-China Economic & Security Review Commission, *US-China Economic & Security Review Commission 2016 Report to the Congress*, 320.
11 Malik, "The China-India Nautical Games in the Indian Ocean."
12 "India Looks for a Strategic Edge in Its Indian Ocean Contest With China."
13 Suri, *China's Expanding Military Maritime Footprints in the Indian Ocean Region*.
14 Prakash, "A Strategic Encirclement."
15 Malik, "The China-India Nautical Games in the Indian Ocean."
16 Jaishankar, *Acting East*.
17 Jaishankar, *Acting East*, 4.
18 See National Development and Reform Commission, "Vision and Actions on Jointly Building Silk Road Economic Belt and 21st-Century Maritime Silk Road"; Organization for Economic Co-operation and Development, *China's Belt and Road Initiative in the Global Trade, Investment and Finance Landscape*.
19 Malik, "News Analysis."
20 Aamir, "Total Value of CPEC Is $50 Billion Not $62 Billion."
21 "Work on 13 Energy Projects under CPEC in Full Swing."
22 See "Belt and Road Initiative"; Brewster, "Bangladesh's Road to the BRI."
23 Ramchandraran, "How Bangladesh Learned to Love the Belt and Road."
24 "Nepal Trims Projects under BRI from 35 to 9 at Chinese Call."
25 "With Just 10 Months Left in BRI Pact, Not a Single Project Has Made Any Real Progress."
26 Mohan, "China's Dramatic Rise in the 21st Century Makes Beijing a Far More Compelling Partner for Kathmandu."
27 Ramchandraran, "The China-Maldives Connection."
28 Munde and Hille, "The Maldives Counts the Cost of its Debts to China."
29 "Joint Statement on the State Visit of Chinese Premier Li Keqiang to India."
30 Patricia Uberoi, "Problems and Prospects of the BCIM Economic Corridor." *China Report* 52, no. 1 (2016): 19–44.
31 Kantha, "Why India Is Cool towards China's Belt and Road."
32 For details see Sachdeva, "Indian Perceptions of the Chinese Belt and Road Initiative."
33 Sachdeva, "The Expansion of China's Belt and Road Initiative Poses New Challenges for India."
34 Samaranayake, *China's Engagement with Smaller South Asian Countries*.
35 Sachdeva, "Implications of the Developing Situation in Kashmir."
36 United Nations, "UN Security Council Discusses Kashmir, China Urges India and Pakistan to Ease Tensions."
37 United Nations, "Statement Attributable to the Spokesman for the Secretary-General on the Situation in Jammu and Kashmir."
38 For details about all of these approved and proposed projects, see "Our Projects."

39 Officially, more than 50 percent of a total of $457 billion FDI into India in the last twenty years has been from Mauritius and Singapore. Due to special bilateral tax treaties, most investors prefer to enter India via these countries. For official FDI data, see "Fact Sheet on Foreign Direct Investment (FDI) from April, 2000 to December, 2019."

40 Krishnan, *Following the Money.*

41 Bhandari, Fernandes, Agarwal, *Chinese Investments in India.*

42 Sachdeva, "Is the Global Trade Conflict a Blessing in Disguise for India?".

43 Aiyer, "2010s."

44 Grant, *India's Response to China's Rise.*

45 Jaishankar, "External Affairs Minister's Speech at the 4th Ramnath Goenka Lecture, 2019."

46 Paul, "How India Will React to the Rise of China."

47 Sachdeva, "Covid-19 Pandemic."

48 International Monetary Fund, *World Economic Outlook, April 2020.*

49 Sachdeva, "Covid-19: Q1 Global Contractions Indicate a Deepening Crisis."

50 "China's Virus-Hit Economy Shrinks for First Time in Decades."

51 International Monetary Fund, *World Economic Outlook, April 2020.*

52 "Prime Minister Interacts with SAARC Leaders to Combat COVID-19 in the Region."

53 See Saran, "Covid19"; Chellaney, "China Must Come Clean on Covid-19."

54 Rajagopalan, "How is COVID-19 Reshaping China-India Relations?"

55 "Government Amends the Extant FDI Policy for Curbing Opportunistic Takeovers/Acquisitions of Indian Companies Due to the Current Covid-19 Pandemic."

56 "Senate of Pakistan Passed the Resolution to Support China's Fight Against COVID-19 Epidemic."

57 "Chinese Pharma Offers to Conduct Clinical Trials of Covid-19 Vaccine in Pakistan.".

58 Aneja, "South Asia Unveils India-China Balancing Act during COVID-19."

BIBLIOGRAPHY

Aamir, Adnan. "Total Value of CPEC Is $50 Billion Not $62 Billion." Balochistan Voices. January 31, 2020. https://balochistanvoices.com.

Acharya, Alka. "China and South Asia." In *China and the Eurasian Region: Geographic and Geopolitical Influences*, edited by C. V. Ranganathan and Sanjeev Kumar, 23–71. New Delhi: Vij Books, 2018.

Aiyer, Swaminathan. "2010s: The Decade is Ending on a Sour Note for Indian Economy." *Times of India*, September 8, 2019. https://timesofindia.indiatimes.com.

Aneja, Atul. "South Asia Unveils India-China Balancing Act during COVID-19." *Hindu*, May 7, 2020. www.thehindu.com.

"Belt and Road Initiative: Perspective from Bangladesh." *Daily Star*, August 7, 2019. www.thedailystar.net.

Bhandari, Amit, Blaise Fernandes, and Aashna Agarwal, *Chinese Investments in India*. Gateway House, February 2020. www.gatewayhouse.in.

Brewster, David. "Bangladesh's Road to the BRI." *Interpreter*, May 30, 2019. www.lowyinstitute.org.

Chellaney, Brahma. "China Must Come Clean on Covid-19." *Hindustan Times*, May 5, 2020. www.hindustantimes.com.

"China's Virus-Hit Economy Shrinks for First Time in Decades." *BBC News*, April 17, 2020, www.bbc.com.

"Chinese Pharma Offers to Conduct Clinical Trials of Covid-19 Vaccine in Pakistan." *Dawn*, April 23, 2020. www.dawn.com.

"Fact Sheet on Foreign Direct Investment (FDI) from April, 2000 to December, 2019." Department for Promotion of Industry and Internal Trade, Government of India, March 5, 2020. https://dipp.gov.in.

Garver, John W. "China and South Asia." *Annals of the American Academy of Political and Social Science* 519 (China's Foreign Relations, January 1992): 67–85.

"Government Amends the Extant FDI Policy for Curbing Opportunistic Takeovers/ Acquisitions of Indian Companies Due to the Current Covid-19 Pandemic." Ministry of Commerce & Industry, Government of India. April 18, 2020. https://pib.gov.in.

Grant, Charles. *India's Response to China's Rise*. London: Centre for European Reform, 2010.

"India Looks for a Strategic Edge in Its Indian Ocean Contest With China." Stratfor, November 23, 2018. https://worldview.stratfor.com.

International Monetary Fund. "Direction of Trade Statistics." Accessed April 30, 2020. https://data.imf.org.

International Monetary Fund. *World Economic Outlook, April 2020: The Great Lockdown*. Washington, DC: International Monetary Fund, April 2020. www.imf.org.

Jaishankar, Dhruv. *Acting East: India in the Indo-Pacific*. New Delhi: Brookings Institution, 2019.

Jaishankar, Subrahmanyam. "External Affairs Minister's Speech at the 4th Ramnath Goenka Lecture, 2019." Ministry of External Affairs. November 14, 2019. https://mea.gov.in.

"Joint Statement on the State Visit of Chinese Premier Li Keqiang to India." Ministry of External Affairs, Government of India. May 20, 2013. https://mea.gov.in.

Kantha, Ashok K. "Why India is Cool towards China's Belt and Road." *South China Morning Post*, May 14, 2017. www.scmp.com.

Krishnan, Ananth. *Following the Money: China Inc's Growing Stake in India-China Relations*. New Delhi: Brookings India, March 2020. www.brookings.edu.

Malik, J. Mohan. "South Asia in China's Foreign Relations." *Pacific Review: Peace, Security & Global Change* 13, no. 1 (2001): 73–90.

Malik, Misbah Saba. "News Analysis: CPEC Not 'Debt-Trap' but Development Schema for Pakistan." *Xinhua*, May 26, 2019. www.xinhuanet.com.

Malik, Mohan. "The China-India Nautical Games in the Indian Ocean: Part One." Macdonald-Laurier Institute. March 15, 2018. www.macdonaldlaurier.ca.

Mohan, C. Raja. "China's Dramatic Rise in the 21st Century Makes Beijing a Far More Compelling Partner for Kathmandu." *Indian Express*, October 22, 2019. https://indianexpress.com.

Munde, Simon, and Kathrin Hille. "The Maldives Counts the Cost of its Debts to China." *Financial Times*, February 11, 2019. www.ft.com.

National Development and Reform Commission, "Vision and Actions on Jointly Building Silk Road Economic Belt and 21st-Century Maritime Silk Road." March 28, 2015. https://en.ndrc.gov.cn.

"Nepal Trims Projects under BRI from 35 to 9 at Chinese Call." *Kathmandu Post*, January 18, 2019. https://kathmandupost.com.

Organization for Economic Co-operation and Development. *China's Belt and Road Initiative in the Global Trade, Investment and Finance Landscape*. Paris: OECD, 2018.

"Our Projects." Asian Infrastructure Investment Bank. Accessed April 30, 2020. www.aiib.org.

Paul, T. V. "How India Will React to the Rise of China: The Soft-Balancing Strategy Reconsidered." War on the Rocks. September 17, 2018. https://warontherocks.com.

Prakash, Arun. "A Strategic Encirclement." *Indian Express*, April 25, 2017. https://indianexpress.com.

"Prime Minister Interacts with SAARC Leaders to Combat COVID-19 in the Region." Ministry of External Affairs, Government of India. March 15, 2020. www.mea.gov.in.

Rajagopalan, Rajeswari Pillai. "How is COVID-19 Reshaping China-India Relations?" *Diplomat*, April 2, 2020. https://thediplomat.com.

Rajan, D. S. "China: President Xi Jinping's South Asia Policy- Implications for India." South Asia Analysis Group. April 27, 2015. www.southasiaanalysis.org.

Ramchandraran, Sudha. "How Bangladesh Learned to Love the Belt and Road." *Diplomat*, July 22, 2019. https://thediplomat.com.

Ramchandraran, Sudha. "The China-Maldives Connection." *Diplomat*, January 25, 2018. https://thediplomat.com.

Sachdeva, Gulshan. "Covid-19 Pandemic: How China and Europe Differ in Tackling the Crisis." Money Control. March 16, 2020. www.moneycontrol.com.

Sachdeva, Gulshan. "Covid-19: Q1 Global Contractions Indicate a Deepening Crisis." Money Control. May 4, 2020. www.moneycontrol.com.

Sachdeva, Gulshan. "Implications of the Developing Situation in Kashmir." Valdai Discussion Group. August 16, 2019. https://valdaiclub.com.

Sachdeva, Gulshan. "Indian Perceptions of the Chinese Belt and Road Initiative." *International Studies* 55, no. 4 (2018): 285–96.

Sachdeva, Gulshan. "Is the Global Trade Conflict a Blessing in Disguise for India?" Money Control. December 31, 2019. www.moneycontrol.com.

Sachdeva, Gulshan. "The Expansion of China's Belt and Road Initiative Poses New Challenges for India." Money Control. May 2, 2019. www.moneycontrol.com.

Sachdeva, Gulshan. "The Indian Economy: Strategic Consequences of Economic Growth." In *La Nouvelle Economie Mondiale: Comparaisons Internationales*, edited by Philippe Clerc, Driss Guerraoui, and Xavier Richet. Paris: Harmattan, 2018.

Samaranayake, Nilanthi. *China's Engagement with Smaller South Asian Countries* (Special Report No. 446). United States Institute of Peace. April 2019. www .usip.org.

Saran, Samir. "Covid-19: Made in China Pandemic." Observer Research Foundation. March 20, 2020. www.orfonline.org.

"Senate of Pakistan Passed the Resolution to Support China's Fight Against COVID-19 Epidemic." Embassy of the People's Republic of China in the Islamic Republic of Pakistan. February 10, 2020. http://pk.chineseembassy.org.

SIPRI Arms Transfer Database. Accessed April 14, 2020. https://www.sipri.org.

Small, Andrew. *China-Pakistan Axis: Asia's New Geopolitics.* New York: Oxford University Press, 2015.

Suri, Gopal. *China's Expanding Military Maritime Footprints in the Indian Ocean Region: India's Response.* New Delhi: Pentagon Press, 2017.

Uberoi, Patricia. "Problems and Prospects of the BCIM Economic Corridor." *China Report* 52, no. 1 (2016): 19–44.

United Nations. "Statement Attributable to the Spokesman for the Secretary-General on the Situation in Jammu and Kashmir." August 8, 2019. www.un.org.

United Nations. "UN Security Council Discusses Kashmir, China Urges India and Pakistan to Ease Tensions." August 16, 2019. https://news.un.org.

US-China Economic & Security Review Commission. *2016 Report to Congress of the US-China Economic & Security Review Commission.* Washington: US Government Publishing House, 2016.

US-China Economic and Security Review Commission. *2018 Report to Congress of the US-China Economic and Security Review Commission.* Washington: US Government Publishing House, 2018.

US-China Economic and Security Review Commission. *China-South Asia Relations: Hearing before the US-China Economic And Security Review Commission,* 114th Congress, 2nd Session. Washington: US Government Publishing House, 2016.

"With Just 10 Months Left in BRI Pact, Not a Single Project Has Made Any Real Progress." *Kathmandu Post,* July 17, 2019. https://kathmandupost.com.

"Work on 13 Energy Projects under CPEC in Full Swing." *News,* October 25, 2019. www.thenews.com.pk.

Xi, Jinping. "In Joint Pursuit of a Dream of National Renewal: Speech by H. E. Xi Jinping, President of the People's Republic of China, at the Indian Council of World Affairs." Ministry of Foreign Affairs of the People's Republic of China. September 18, 2014. www.fmprc.gov.cn.

7

China's Role in Central Asia and Middle East

Geopolitical Vacuum Pragmatist or New International Order Creator?

JOSHUA W. WALKER

China's rise as a global power in the twenty-first century has been most felt in Asia and its near-abroad. The Cold War pitted the United States and the Soviet Union against each other in the aftermath of the Second World War as the two victorious powers. Each had a differing internal political system and they faced off in Europe and created the Iron Curtain that led to the "Communist" and "free" worlds, which were created in parallel.

Now, as the world faces its most significant geopolitical disruption since the Second World War in the form of a pandemic originating from China, the tense rivalry between the US and China is only increasing. Even as the immediate public health crisis abates, the economic and political fallout continues. Unlike the Cold War, which was in many ways an anomaly, pitting a geographically distant US and its "empire by invitation" against Russia with its "empire by force," China has grown directly out of this legacy on the back of its own incredible growth, but also in a broader vacuum in global politics.[1] Initially part of the Communist world, Beijing's own internal dynamics led to an embrace of capitalism "with Chinese characteristics" through the great opening with Washington and an economic integration with the global economy, which was never the case with Moscow.

When the Soviet Union collapsed, the US enjoyed its unipolar moment as China became the natural big brother to the newly independent and "free" nations stretching across Eurasia from Central Asia into the Middle East. This is not to imply that China would have an easy time extending its influence across such an expansive geography, but the opportunity was there to build on its ancient legacy of the Silk Road trade route and to assert its "rightful" place in the world.

Today the geopolitical competition has gone far beyond physical geography to the digital realms and public health. Particularly in the ever-growing competition between the US and China, "geotechnology" that combines geopolitics and technology rather than purely geography has become the name of the game. In the face of COVID-19, China has used its own experience in Wuhan to bolster its own public diplomacy efforts across Eurasia and stretching to Western Europe, offering assistance that is reminiscent of the way the US helped Europe with the Marshall Plan after the Second World War. Yet for Eurasia, the geographies of Central Asia and Middle East still factor largely into perceptions of China's foreign policy ambitions globally thanks to its own efforts.

The liberal international order that has been championed by the West since the end of the Second World War has been under assault, not just from the Arab uprisings in the Middle East or color revolutions across Eurasia, but, in many advanced industrial democracies, it is being challenged from within by populists who undermining the basic assumptions as never before in the aftermath of the coronavirus. For Washington, this has meant a challenge to a foreign policy establishment whose conventional wisdom focused on grand strategies such as the Marshall Plan, the North Atlantic Treaty Organization, and America's alliance systems around the world, which prioritized the Atlantic and Pacific theaters at the expense of the Eurasian landmass that was more geographically distant from Washington.[2]

As evidenced by the Arab uprisings, characterized by popular rebellion and widespread violence, the combination of autocracy and religious extremists has been lethal to the international order and America's role in it, particularly in the Middle East. If such a fate were to extend further eastward from Syria to the countries in the heart of Eurasia, the stability of the corridor between China and Europe would be lost, along with the fragile future of Afghanistan and all of the progress that has been made over a quarter century of independence in Central Asia's fledgling nations. To add fuel to the fire, the nations of the Silk Road are surrounded by a rather looming crowd of countries where globalist Western ideals do not particularly resonate. Destabilizing this area would harken back to the Cold War days and lead down a path that no one has the stomach to face. America's alliance structures in Europe and Asia also depend on stability and pro-Western ideology in the countries bordering the corridor. The levels of investment from China into Eurasia cannot be met by any of its other neighbors. This reality leaves the Eurasian corridor from Central Asia to the Middle East both vulnerable and ripe with opportunity, not only in political and security terms, but perhaps most importantly, in economic ones.

The New Cold War

Competition between the US and China globally is playing out beyond geography, unlike in the Cold War, when the "domino theory" dictated a regional focus on containing the Soviet Union. Beijing and the Silicon Valley are building two distinct online ecosystems driven by very different types of organization, which will have a major economic effect as well. One is state-driven and the other is led by the private sector. The American tech ecosystem, with all of its strengths and shortcomings, is built by the private sector in Silicon Valley and only loosely regulated by the government in Washington. The Chinese system is dominated by the state in Beijing along with its technology allies spread across the country.[3]

The same is true for the Chinese economy, which will soon be the world's largest. Beijing practices state capitalism, a system that allows government officials to ensure that economic growth ultimately serves political and national interests. China's state capitalist system distorts the traditional workings of a market-driven economy by relying heavily on state-owned enterprises and state-backed national champions to ensure economic—and therefore political—stability. It depends on state subsidies that allow political officials to direct enormous amounts of capital and other resources as they choose. The government picks winners and losers. The success of this system for China and the Chinese Communist Party is undeniable. The good news for the rest of the world is that Chinese growth has supported global growth, and nowhere more so than in China's own neighborhood, which makes it difficult for the US to fully compete.

As COVID-19 has demonstrated for all to see, the world economy needs China to remain stable, productive, and increasingly prosperous to fuel global growth. To accomplish this, Beijing must play a constructive international role, even if only a limited one. It must work with other governments to meet the challenges posed by poverty, conflict, public health risks, lack of education, lack of infrastructure, climate change, and the advance of disruptive new technologies. And, of course, the US must do the same.

The threat China poses to the US is smaller than many in Washington believe. China has even less interest in going to war with the US than the US has in going to war with China. China is a regional, but not a global, military power. Economic interdependence will continue, despite concerted efforts on both sides to reduce economic vulnerabilities. The greatest source of US-China conflict comes from technology. Here, China is, today, a true superpower. There is a Cold War-like structure to the relationship that will affect every region of the world and Washington does have an interest in seeing Beijing fail, because China's technological development poses a foundational challenge to the values on which global stability and prosperity depend.

Given that any study of foreign policy is limited by the available information and the accessibility of decision making, particularly in Beijing, as well as the even more difficult task of grouping regions as complex and diverse as Central Asia and the Middle East let alone together, what follows is a nascent attempt to analyze the current state of play. The relatively recent phenomenon of Chinese reengagement in these regions and the beginning of the end of the American-led order means further change is on the way and the pace will only accelerate, rather than stagnate. This chapter highlights the broader trends while acknowledging that far more complexity and challenges lie right beneath the surface—but it is important to start somewhere.

Re-imagining the New Silk Road and the Turkic World

Stretching from the "Adriatic to the Great Wall," the so-called Turkic world is joined by linguistic, cultural, and historical ties that stretch back to Genghis Khan who once united this region into one of the greatest empires of human history. Following the path of the ancient Silk Road that connected the Chinese Middle Kingdom to the European empires of Rome and beyond, the region encompasses Turkey,

Azerbaijan, Mongolia, and the Central Asian Republics of Kazakhstan, Kyrgyzstan, and Turkmenistan. This broad area, home to over 300 million people, also includes parts of Afghanistan, Tajikistan, the Caucasus, Iran, China, and Russia that do not share the "Turkic" element but share other overlapping qualities, at times including significant Sunni and Shia populations. Given the complexity of the region, it is hard to speak of it as a single unit, but for the purposes of this exploration of Chinese foreign policy, I have made an attempt to focus on the "Turkic" and "Muslim" Worlds as broadly conceived. Glimpses of great empires have left the region rich with art, literature, and music even as the outside world misperceives these formerly great societies as poor, undeveloped, and antiquated.

In addition to cultural ties, geographic connections between countries of the Turkic world ensure that the area—which is rich in critical natural resources such as oil, coal, gas, precious metals, and minerals—is connected economically as well. Competing initiatives by the US and China promoting a "New Silk Road" pay homage to historical linkages that, with a little political will and infrastructural investment, could drive economies that have always been stronger when linked together than when separated by their post-Soviet borders.

Since the collapse of the USSR, mixed attention has been paid to these countries, and only those considered most problematic and destabilizing—Iran and Afghanistan—ever occupy the top spot on Western policy agendas. For most, the region is largely viewed more in relation to neighboring superpowers than for its own strategic value. While the post-Soviet Turkic republics have been historically separated from Turkey given the opposite sides they represented during the Cold War, new commonalities are shaping the present reality and perceptions within the region. These predominately pro-Western and secular Turkic states increasingly look toward Europe for international institutional connections while seeing potential in Asia that they could potentially benefit from as Eurasia's natural land bridge.

Traditionally, the Turkic world has been carved up and defined by US policy makers according to each individual nation's relationship to three competing sectors of US foreign policy: Europe, Russia, and China. Within the State Department, the region falls under four separate bureaus—Europe and Eurasian Affairs for Azerbaijan and Turkey, Near

Eastern Affairs for Iran, South and Central Asian Affairs for the post-Soviet "Stans," and East Asian Affairs for China and Mongolia. Outside the State Department, the attempt to form a unified policy based on unified regional challenges and opportunities is further complicated by the frequent parsing out of Afghanistan to be with Pakistan away from other Central Asian states at the White House's National Security Council or, the opposite, lumping in Central Asian states with the whole of the Middle East at the Pentagon's Near East South Asia Center for Strategic Studies.

A framework to fill the void left by the collapse of the USSR is a strategic opportunity no less significant to the US than Eastern Europe's reintegration with the transatlantic community. Yet nearly twenty-five years after independence the lack of coherence of the Turkic world exposes one of the great failings of imagination for leaders in the twenty-first century. Ethnic and linguistic connections have always created a natural base and heritage for cooperation, but have proven weaker than pan-Turkic ideologues had hoped in the wake of the Ottoman Empire's collapse and the rise of the Soviet Union.

After the republics were liberated from the USSR, a half-hearted attempt on the part of Americans and Europeans to engage through an optimistic but woefully underprepared Turkey led to deep disillusionment with Western institutions and rhetoric. Russia's "re-invigorated" Eurasian Union focuses on its near-abroad and China's development of the Shanghai Cooperation Organization and most recent announcements about its "One Belt, One Road" initiative in Central Asia, when paired with its new infrastructure development bank, have never been balanced by a coherent or serious Western plan. Attempts such as the European Union's "Eastern Partnership" or Turkey's "Turkic Peoples" have never been fully supported by the US, while Washington's own "New Silk Road" initiative has never moved beyond rhetoric. Despite the broader geographic challenges and mental blocks often associated with this region of the world, the concept of a coherent and connected Turkic world stretching from the Adriatic to the Great Wall along the ancient Silk Road offers a practical logic and useful framework for partnerships that has never been explored by American policy makers.

Given the unrealized geopolitical potential at the heart of Eurasia, Washington has tended to be reactive rather than proactive in this part of the world to grand initiatives from Moscow and Beijing. Interestingly,

Western companies, particularly defense industrialists and energy groups, have seen potential as they have set up individual sites that are not connected to Moscow but rather to Istanbul or directly to their Western headquarters. Learning from the private sector, government policy could easily re-imagine the region around these existing realities to better serve American interests.

The countries of Central Asia have historically been a corridor connecting the civilizational centers of the Far East in China to the Ancient Mediterranean. Despite thousands of years, essentially it remains a land bridge utilized for land transport of natural resources and various other manufactured products between Europe and the Far East, as the countries rimming the Caspian and Black Sea have facilitated the movement of similar goods via vital sea trade routes. Unlike in the past, when nomadic peoples on the frontiers would be traded between empires, these once-poor, post-Soviet republics have developed into market-adept, resource-rich territories unto themselves. As populations have grown, trade has increased and technology has flourished, local and regional infrastructures have been overwhelmed and incapable of handling the growing economic needs of the population and the market. This has led to a gradual decline in the utilization of trade routes across the Eurasian corridor during the twentieth century. Today, this is not the case, thanks to regional development and the growing geopolitical interest among the great powers, principally economic investment from China and a military embrace from Russia.

As the idea of the "Silk Road" regained popularity globally, economic interest and energy investment in the corridor have begun to see a steady increase. Russia has grand plans for its Eurasian Union, as China mulls its own institutions, such as the Shanghai Cooperation Organization and its "One Belt, One Road" initiative that has been rebranded the Belt and Road Initiative (BRI). The governments of these countries are also heavily involved in promoting regional economic development, especially through the Central Asia Regional Economic Cooperation Program, an initiative of the Western-inspired Asian Development Bank or the various counter projects from the Chinese established Asian Infrastructure and Investment Bank (AIIB). Given the changed nature of geopolitical competition, the "push" of greater power involvement versus the "pull" of regional opportunities is playing out across Central Asia.

The US and its allies, including the Europeans and Japanese, have gotten involved through their respective private sectors, encouraging more local and micro-level small-scale grants, loans, or projects through national agencies, the World Bank, and the United Nations that have not always been closely coordinated and lack the appeal of the grand-scale projects that China and Russia have promised. Western and Japanese interests have funneled into the corridor through non-state actors such as private businesses and various multinational energy corporations, which were mainly interested in the oil and gas pipeline possibilities of this area with little to no initial coordination. This private sector presence has allowed for the diversification of energy supply routes for non-OPEC countries, which has in turn greatly affected the energy market and its policies.

Despite this targeted involvement, particularly under the Obama administration's various "new" Silk Road initiatives, there has yet to be a driving force that can link the many pieces of this puzzle into an overarching plan or program for regional economic development, trade, and investment that engages the Black and Caspian Sea region and Eurasia more broadly. This is largely due to the *de facto* demise of Washington's fatefully named 2011 "New Silk Road Initiative," which regained policy attention under the Trump administration after years of institutional neglect as an easy repackaging for a new administration in Washington.[4] Although Japanese Prime Minister Abe's 2015 Central Asia tour sought to solidify a Central Asian model of engagement in the form of the "C5+1" to complement Washington's "Indo-Pacific" strategy, Washington's lack of interest or significant investment and coordination between American, European, Japanese, and regional leaders led the initiative to remain aimlessly adrift, increasingly creating a vacuum in which Beijing has wielded increasing hegemonic influence in the meantime.[5]

Particularly in comparison to China's BRI, which began with a grand vision under President Xi as a signature initiative and has only been reinforced by the entire weight of Beijing's impressive propaganda efforts behind it, the lack of an alternative has reinforced the importance of China in the region. The ultimate assessment of the BRI is yet to come, but the debates have already begun about the pros and cons. In the absence of a clear alternative, the actual level of investment, debt traps, impacts on Chinese workers, and corruption are all academic, especially in Central Asia, where the majority of the impact of the BRI is profile building and raising awareness. Here Beijing's clever use of summitry, regional visits, and propaganda has already paid dividends in a way that no other power has been able to take advantage of.

Interestingly, China was not the first Asian country to establish a consultative dialogue with all five Central Asian states after the collapse of the Soviet Union in 1991. Rather it was Japan, which launched the "C5+1" dialogue that became the model for all other countries, leading South Korea to establish its own in 2006, the EU in 2009, and the US in 2016. China did not embrace Central Asia as a region, rather launching its own BRI to traverse the Eurasian heartland as a grander vision meant to replace these previous regional piecemeal models. Unlike the US and the EU, China has a unique soft power influence over the region that is free from the kind of political constraints, such as democracy and human rights, that often hamper Western countries there. Yet its own history, with its own Muslim population and region further complicates the picture. As I discuss in the Middle East section of this chapter, China's treatment of its Uighur population in particular has become a flashpoint for protest, but also a way for Central Asia countries to show their value to Beijing and leverage even more investment and "strategic" cooperation.

Beijing from this viewpoint has seen the countries of Central Asia above all as transit territories rather than as ends in themselves, and its use of soft power there has sometimes backfired. Central Asians certainly feel like byproducts, which is reinforced by how they see the Chinese state treating the Uighurs, Tibetans, and all non-Han ethnic communities across China. If there were clearer alternatives, Beijing might pay a price, but, given the strength of the "Chinese model" in comparison to the "American Dream," which seems to be all but abandoned at this point, China is assuming an ever more dominant position in the post-Soviet space. While soft power alone will prove inadequate to protect energy transit routes, Beijing has used this logic to start working more closely with the regimes of the region.

Russian experts have gone so far to suggest that China will inevitably establish a military presence in the region in the form of bases.[6] Given the extreme sensitives of Central Asian states, this would likely undo all of the Chinese efforts up until this point in time. Beijing, for its part, has focused almost all of its efforts on diplomatic and economic efforts, precisely because of the double-edged nature of security cooperation, given its own internal problems in Xinjiang. Taken as a whole, Chinese efforts in the region are, relatively speaking, new. The legacy of President Xi has been seen as more of an outgrowth of a broader grand strategy than a piecemeal approach that is unlike the Western approach, which has been underwhelming throughout the region.

Regional Outlook

Despite being lumped together, the five countries of Central Asia vary widely in terms of size, population, and income. Given their shared heritage from the Soviet Union, they all enjoy a relatively high educational level, but because of their differences in size, Kazakhstan stands out as today's core Eurasian heartland. Control of Kazakhstan would inevitably lead to the status of regional hegemony, a prospect increasingly being realized by China. Although the country remains a *de facto* protectorate under Moscow's security and Beijing's economic influence, the government under first President Nazarbayev has consistently pursued a "multi-vector diplomacy" to maintain regional independence. Kazakhstan's geostrategic significance as the Eurasian pivot point has often led to its self-labeling as the "buckle of the belt," referring to its central role in the Belt and Road Initiative.

More than any other Central Asian Republic, Kazakhstan is and will remain part of a Russian-speaking sphere with a proud legacy from Tsarist Russia and the Soviet Union and has little in common with the culture of the former Middle Kingdom. Yet China's influence in Kazakhstan is unmistakable and, in the long run, inevitable. Russian President Vladimir Putin see this as his Far East, and it is underpopulated compared to the Chinese populations farther south, so when he deals with Chinese President Xi there is a posturing that is unmistakable. Nowhere is the precariousness of Russia's decline and China's rise more directly felt than in Central Asia and specifically Kazakhstan, which was the crown jewel of Russia's empire.

All of the Chinese investment in Kazakhstan, from major infrastructure initiatives like those in Khorgos to hotels in the capital being constructed will serve the interests of the Chinese juggernaut that

Kazakhstan and the region cannot avoid it. All of these projects are encouraged by Beijing's credit, to which strings are attached favoring Chinese companies, products, and labor. At this point, neither local capital nor foreign direct investment from Russia, Japan, or the West can compete with China's scale.[7] The window of opportunity is likely to close very quickly before the Kazakhstani leg of BRI rapidly transforms the country into an "open" market primarily for China's benefit. Once this happens, Kazakhstan will have succumbed to Chinese terms of trade and investment. This not only breaks Moscow's historic grip but also weakens and undermines the US-led international liberal economic order.

Despite being the largest population in Central Asia, Uzbekistan's lack of natural resources in comparison to Kazakhstan and even Turkmenistan has meant that it has punched well below its weight. In particular, its regional disputes with Kazakhstan—until recently, under a new administration—has kept it isolated. With the flourishing of new Kazakh-Uzbek relations and new leaders in all of the Central Asian republics, regional cooperation seems possible once again. However, direct foreign policy outreach still goes through Moscow and Beijing, and has only increased under the BRI.

Including Afghanistan in the Central Asian dialogue has facilitated China's regional connectivity to South Asia and specifically to its ally Pakistan. Beijing's massive investment in the Pakistan and Turkmenistan-China gas pipeline has made both of these countries completely dependent on China, even as Western projects continue to generate more attention. For example, the much-touted but perpetually uncertain Turkmenistan-Afghanistan-Pakistan-India (TAPI) pipeline, a key infrastructure project of Washington's New Silk Road Initiative, currently promoted by Japanese funding, remains the figment of a Western alternative reality compared to a more comprehensive Chinese vision toward this end. TAPI is particularly vulnerable to Beijing's geo-economic opportunism, leading Japan's local infrastructure investment to acquire renewed significance for its regional future. Indeed, China's Machiavellian geo-economics has been on full display in its recent courtship with jihadist militants in TAPI's transit cities, further underscoring Beijing's growing regional clout.[8] Given that Central Asia has historically fallen into either the Chinese or Russian spheres of influences, most of these nations prefer third alternatives like the EU, US, or Japan that have no capability or interest in domination or regional groupings but often fall short.

Perhaps the best example that crystalizes the dynamics in Central Asia comes from the region's first and only World EXPO, which took place in Kazakhstan in the summer of 2017. Over a hundred countries were represented, but the US was among the last countries to sign up despite its importance to the Kazakhs, who made the case that if the US was not present the entire event would fail. While the numbers are not public, the clear difference in scale of the Russia pavilion—which featured a literal iceberg shipped in from the artic and President Putin's favorite Siberian tiger—and China's pavilion—which featured several major theaters and a high-speed rail exhibit—in comparison with the empty US pavilion, was telling. The USA Pavilion tried to make up the difference with its student ambassadors, but the sheer amount of money spent, staff brought in, and volunteers recruited by the Chinese and Russian efforts dwarfed all others at the EXPO. This level of commitment from Central Asia's northern and eastern neighbors calls for a coherent and sustained grand strategy from the West, which does exist and is not likely to appear in the next decade given the state of our collective democracies, which are focusing their energies on the home front.

Ultimately, as seen at the region's first World's Fair, the countries of Central Asia would appreciate more, not less international engagement. Given the attention and investment they have received from China as a neighbor and rising international power, the trend lines are clear. As part of its backyard and near-abroad, Central Asia's place in Chinese foreign-policy thinking will only grow. The global ascendancy of the Chinese brand of state capitalism and authoritarian regime is only heightened in Central Asia, where stability is the name of the game. Mutual interest in combatting Islamic extremism will only drive Central Asia into China's orbit rather than become a divisive issue, even as China continues to crack down on its own Muslim population. Washington's own lack of serious initiative in the region and further distraction from domestic politics means that rather than replicating its "Indo-Pacific" strategy, which Australia, India, and Japan all jointly own with the US, in their region in Central Asia, there will be a power vacuum that China will continue to fill for the foreseeable future.

Middle East: Balancing Western Asia's Dynamics through
Far Eastern Pragmaticism

In the Middle East, unlike in Central Asia, China benefits from not having the kind of historic baggage that the US and other Western powers
are burdened with. Given China's almost exclusively economic focus
in the region, Beijing has been able to maintain good relations with
regional players even throughout the Syrian Civil War and the split
between Saudi Arabia and Qatar. China's ability to balance its relations
with all of the major players in the region while avoiding strategic entanglements has been based on realpolitik. Particularly in relation to Iran,
China has tried to avoid getting involved in the Sunni-Shia schism in
favor of more pragmatic economic deals.

Especially in light of President Trump's withdrawal from the Iran
deal (the Joint Comprehensive Plan of Action) and the assassination of
General Suleimani, Beijing has more room to maneuver in the Middle
East geopolitically. Particularly in the area of energy and infrastructure
investment, China has been proactive across the Silk Road, of which
Tehran was always a critical component, even before the Iran sanctions,
and particularly now that regular rail service has been established all the
way to Beijing. With the US pullback from the Middle East, China holds
a unique place as an economic power that is more pragmatically focused
on economic cooperation, investment, and regional stability.

As the Soviet Union's collapse created a vacuum for China in Central Asia, Washington's withdrawal and lack of coherent strategy in the
Middle East has created new opportunities for Beijing, which has now
replaced the UAE as the main investor in the region. Having declared its
BRI—which is far more ambitious than the Marshall Plan ever was, and
does not have the same limited time horizons or constraints—China is
uniquely situated in a more ambitious and independent-minded Middle
East.

China has already built strategic partnerships across the region, taking advantage of whatever opportunities have arisen, from Algeria to
Saudi Arabia to Iran. Having targeted major OPEC and Gulf Cooperation Council members and even US allies such as Egypt, Israel, Jordan,
Qatar, and Turkey, China is in a position to reap the geopolitical re-
wards of its diplomatic and economic investment.[9] Especially given an

increasingly isolated Washington that is estranged from Europe on Iran and seen as too dependent on Israel and Saudi Arabia, the challenge for Beijing is less Washington than avoiding the traditional pitfalls of domestic and regional Middle East politics, which is why China has taken a more detached approach to Syria than Russia, which has been using it to further its own interests and drive further wedges against American interests.

The establishment of an annual BRI review conference has created yet another global platform and regional incentive structure to attract the attention of Central Asian and Middle Eastern countries that are looking for non-Western alternatives. China's role on the UN Security Council and its economic clout have made it an attractive partner for all of these countries. However, one of the biggest challenges for China in the Muslim world is to maintain good relations with both Shia and Sunni states at the same time.

China's noninterference policy has played well throughout the region and its hands-off approach to the security conflicts that the US and Russia have competed over is particularly important in this regard. By focusing its efforts on diplomatic and economic initiatives, China has avoided many of the landmines that confront external powers in the region.

Given the lack of understanding in China of the Middle East and its problems with its own Muslim population, the challenges are far more significant in this region than in Central Asia. Without the same historic or geographic connection that Central Asia shares with China, the Middle East and the Muslim world more broadly is a difficult space for Beijing to navigate. Especially given the collective memory of the Turkic world, which has always viewed the Uighur population as one of its own, China's treatment of this indigenous Muslim population with significant connections to Kazakhs, Kyrgyz, and Turks is a flash point that has been used by countries like Turkey to stir up Middle Eastern politics as a way of distracting from domestic problems. However, like the Israel-Palestine conflict, the geopolitics of the region have necessitated a more realist approach to foreign policy, which is increasingly putting Beijing in the driver's seat.[10]

Turkey has traditionally been one of China's biggest detractors and problems given the large dissident Uighur population that calls Ankara home. President Erdogan labeled Beijing's treatment of the Uighurs a "genocide" which is a particularly loaded term, coming from Turkey. However, after careful Chinese outreach and deteriorating Western relations, Turkey's tune began to change and today it is one of the most important countries to engage with China's BRI, with subsequent visits by President Erdogan to Beijing and President Xi to Ankara. The warmth of the relations between these two rivals bodes well for greater Chinese engagement in the Middle East and throughout the Muslim world.

Beijing has been particularly present in Turkey and Iran during the fight against COVID-19, offering medical advice, equipment, and expertise that has not been available from the US or Europe as they have battled their own public health crisis. Meanwhile, especially in such resource-rich states as Saudi Arabia and Qatar, China's increasing energy demands mean that relations remain on a strong footing. Even in Israel, America's closest Middle Eastern ally, China has been expanding its relationships, particularly in the port of Haifa and through its investments in 5G and as the technology partner of choice, while using its current public health diplomacy to its advantage. Using its newfound clout has paid significant dividends for China, but not in the same controversial ways that it has in Africa, where it has generated a backlash.

Ultimately Chinese management and projects throughout the region will be judged on the merits of their outcomes, but Middle Eastern states increasingly have an incentive to turn to China as the kind of partner they have long considered the US and the EU. Managing regional dynamics without being dragged into intractable conflicts and a civilizational conflict with the Middle East independent of Sunni-Shia-Turkic concerns will remain a top priority for Beijing. Further cooperation with Europe in Middle East using the BRI as a framework makes a lot of sense for China, which can access its investments there along both land and sea routes in its re-imagined attempts to connect Europe with Asia.

Conclusion

China's engagement in Central Asia and the Middle East are emblematic of a rising power, though one that is reasserting itself rather than emerging as a new entrant.[11] Its focus on diplomatic, economic, and technological cooperation will pay significant dividends in the future even as it competes directly with Washington. Time is on China's side and its long view of history positions it well. Yet ultimately China's success will be determined at home by the growth rates it is able to maintain along with its ability to recreate America's postwar formula of empire by invitation rather than force. Beijing is well-positioned across Eurasia in this regard, from Eastern Europe to the Middle East through Central Asia. How China chooses to deal with Hong Kong, its own Muslim population, Tibet, Taiwan and beyond will have ripple effects, especially if the US continues its more aggressive posture against China.

While the future is far from certain, China's involvement in Central Asia and the Middle East is sure to grow and will be a harbinger of the coming changes in the international order that already are beginning to upend these regions in Beijing's favor. Yet China's harsh treatment of its Uighur minority poses an ongoing problem that will limit Beijing's diplomatic success among many Central Asian and Middle Eastern states.

NOTES

1 For more on these distinctions and history, see John Lewis Gaddis' seminal work, *The Cold War*.

2 See Jon B. Alterman's more recent statement before the House Foreign Affairs Subcommittee on the Middle East, North Africa, and International Terrorism, "Chinese and Russian Influence in the Middle East."

3 For more, see Ian Bremmer's speech at the GZERO Summit, "The End of the American Order."

4 For further specifics, see "US Revives Silk Road Projects to Counter China's 'Soft Power.'"

5 See Miyake, "China as a Middle East Power."

6 See Goble, "China Will Have Military Bases in Central Asia within Five Years, Russian Expert Says."

7 See Kirişci and Le Corre, "The New Geopolitics of Central Asia: China Vies for Influence in Russia's Backyard: What Will It Mean for Kazakhstan?"

8 "China Woos Baloch Separatists to Secure Belt and Road Initiative."

9 See Cohen, "Will China Replace the US as the Middle East Hegemon?"

10 For more, see Ibrahim, "China's Uighur Strategy and South Asian Risk."

11 For further context, see James M. Dorsey's working paper, "China and the Middle East: Venturing into the Maelstrom."

BIBLIOGRAPHY

Alterman, Jon B. "Chinese and Russian Influence in the Middle East." Statement before the House Foreign Affairs Subcommittee on the Middle East, North Africa, and International Terrorism. *Middle East Policy* 26, no. 2 (Summer 2019): 129–36.

Bremmer, Ian. "The End of the American Order: Ian Bremmer Speech at 2019 GZERO Summit." Eurasia Group. November 18, 2019. www.eurasiagroup.net.

Calabrese, John. "Fate of the Dragon in the Year of the Red Fire Monkey: China and the Middle East 2016." Middle East Institute, February 3, 2016. www.mei.edu.

Chang, I-Wei. "The Middle East in China's Silk Road Visions: Business as Usual?" Middle East Institute, April 14, 2015. www.mei.edu.

"China in the Middle East." *Middle East Report*, no. 270 (Spring 2014). Tacoma, WA: Middle East Research and Information Project.

"China Woos Baloch Separatists to Secure Belt and Road Initiative." *Financial Times*, February 19, 2018. www.ft.com.

Cohen, Ariel. "Will China Replace the US as the Middle East Hegemon?" *Forbes*, February 14, 2019. www.forbes.com.

Dorsey, James M. "China and the Middle East: Venturing into the Maelstrom." RSIS Working Paper No. 296. S. Rajaratnam School of International Studies. March 18, 2016. www.rsis.edu.sg.

Gaddis, John Lewis. *The Cold War: A New History*. New York: Penguin, 2005.

Goble, Paul. "China Will Have Military Bases in Central Asia within Five Years, Russian Expert Says." *Eurasia Daily Monitor* 16, no. 48 (April 4, 2019). https://jamestown.org.

Houlden, Gordon, and Noureddin Zaamout. *A New Great Power Engages with the Middle East: China's Middle East Balancing Approach*. China Institute, University of Alberta, January 2019. https://era.library.ualberta.ca.

Hughes, Lindsay. "China in the Middle East: The Overarching Imperatives." Future Directions International, September 25, 2018. www.futuredirections.org.au.

Ibrahim, Samah. "China's Uighur Strategy and South Asian Risk." Future Directions International. January 29, 2019. www.futuredirections.org.au.

Kirişci, Kemal, and Philippe Le Corre. "The New Geopolitics of Central Asia: China Vies for Influence in Russia's Backyard: What Will It Mean for Kazakhstan?" Brookings. January 2, 2018. www.brookings.edu.

Lons, Camille, Jonathan Fulton, Degang Sun, Naser Al-Tamimi. "China's Great Game in the Middle East." European Council on Foreign Relations, October 2019. www.ecfr.eu.

Miyake, Kuni. "China as a Middle East Power: The Pros and Cons of a More Assertive and Capable China in the Gulf and Beyond." Center for a New American Security (CNAS). March 2017. https://css.ethz.ch.

Payne, Jeffrey S. "The GCC and China's One Belt, One Road: Risk or Opportunity?" Middle East Institute, August 11, 2016. www.mei.edu.

"US Revives Silk Road Projects to Counter China's 'Soft Power.'" Eurasia Business Briefing, May 26, 2017. www.eurasianbusinessbriefing.com.

8

China's Policy toward Russia and Europe

The Eurasian Hookup

ANDREW C. KUCHINS

China's policy toward Russia and Europe must be viewed through two prisms: (1) the broader expansion of Chinese economic and political power across the Eurasian supercontinent; and (2) its ties with China-US relations. As the first view is more significant for the subject at hand, and the US-China relationship is covered elsewhere in this volume, this chapter[1] mainly focuses more strictly on China's relations with Russia and Europe in and of themselves. This puts much of the focus on the BRI, but much of what is now consolidated under that umbrella has roots in a multitude of economic initiatives that predate the BRI's formal institutionalization in the fall of 2013.

It is the dramatic growth of Chinese economic engagement and influence across the Eurasian supercontinent that empirically leads to broader hypotheses about Chinese strategy. In a sense, the methodology can be reduced almost to "follow the money." Historically, the growth of many great powers and empires involves a process in which commercial engagement is followed by the "flag," or military security.[2] Wittingly or unwittingly, the rapid expansion of Chinese economic power is calling into play a greater need for the Chinese government to protect its investments, which will lead to more complicated political relations with the relevant states. In Central Asia, for example, China has for now been willing to cede management of political stability and military security to Russia, but as these investments increase, if China becomes less confident that Russia is capable of these tasks, we will likely see an increased engagement of Chinese military and security forces.

Chinese Policy toward Russia

The essence of Chinese policy toward Russia may be still formulated as the "three nos": (1) no alliance; (2) no bilateral conflict; and (3) no uncontrolled border.[3] While some in Chinese military circles would advocate an alliance with Russia, the policy remains opposed to one. The experience of the Sino-Soviet alliance of the 1950s is viewed negatively in both Beijing and Moscow, and the majority view in China is that there is no need for a military alliance at present. In fact, China and Russia rhetorically trumpet the contemporary Sino-Russian relationship as a new and superior form of great power relations in contrast to the US security alliances in Europe and Asia.

China (and Russia) also view the Sino-Soviet split that emerged into the open in 1960 as a major mistake that only benefited the United States. Given the qualitative improvement in Sino-Russian relations since the Ukraine crisis in 2014 and the further deterioration in US relations with Russia and China since the advent of the Trump administration, realistically it is hard to imagine now how and why China and Russia could rupture their bilateral relations, and recent calls for the Trump administration to attract Russia away from China are not grounded in reality.[4]

For centuries, management of the border between Russia and China has been a highly conflicted issue. The Russians certainly have not forgotten Mao's demands for about 1.5 million square kilometers of Soviet/Russian territory acquired through allegedly "unfair" treaties going back to the seventeenth century. Vladimir Putin has publicly stated many times that he views the Sino-Russian border treaty of 2004 as among his greatest achievements. Although Russians are naturally nervous about the dramatic demographic and economic imbalances on each side of the border, there is no reason for China now to upset the status quo through military action. Chinese strategy today leads with economic investment and political engagement—not so much in border regions but rather through the personal relationship between Xi Jinping and Vladimir Putin and some investments controlled by figures who have close relations with Mr. Putin.[5]

Chinese companies are not overly eager to invest in Russia because of the challenging investment environment there. Since 2014 the increasing risk that Chinese investments may be viewed as violations of

US economic sanctions has further dampened enthusiasm. China has a far larger economic relationship with the US, and so it is understandable the Chinese would approach Russia with caution in this sanctions environment. While Moscow had high hopes that Chinese and other Asian and Middle Eastern capital would replace their lost access to Western financial markets, they have been bitterly disappointed. Chinese investment in Russia has actually fallen since 2014. What major investments the Chinese have made are shrewdly targeted at Russian oligarchs closely tied to Putin, such as Gennady Timchenko who in 2016 was anointed the "go-to guy" for Chinese investment when he was appointed head of the Russian-Chinese Business Council. Timchenko's company SIBUR then sold a 10-percent stake to SINOPEC, a much-needed infusion of cash for SIBUR. The Chinese have also purchased a 20-percent stake in the high-profile Yamal LNG project,[6] a signature project for Putin.

A critical and telling moment in the Sino-Russian economic relationship came in May 2014 when Putin travelled to China for discussions that would feature a huge agreement for the development of Russian gas and its shipment to China over thirty years. At the end of two days of tense negotiations, the blockbuster $400 billion deal was announced, but the terms of that deal have never been made public. What we do know is that the Chinese refused to make an up-front payment of $25 billion for the development of gas fields and the building of the Power of Siberia pipeline. These negotiations had been dragging on for more than ten years. President Xi understood that it was extremely important for Putin to be seen closing a major deal with China at a time when Russia was being increasingly ostracized from the West. But it was also clear that he and the Chinese negotiation team took advantage of the weak and highly leveraged Russian financial position at the time to make the most commercially advantageous deal.

The first nearly quarter-century of post-Soviet Russian-Chinese relations can be described as steady and incremental improvement through economic ties that have notably included Russian arms sales to China and a deepening and broadening of political interactions. In 2014, the relationship made a qualitative leap, but mainly at the initiative of Russia, which found itself alienated from the West because of its activities in Ukraine. Indicators include Russian willingness to sell more advanced military systems to Beijing, the conclusion of a major gas deal in 2014 that had been under negotiation for more than a decade, and an agreement in May 2015 for cooperation between China's BRI (or as it was termed at that time, the Silk Road Economic Belt) and Putin's pet multilateral integration project, the Eurasian Economic Union. But a further look into the latter two agreements points to the significant increase in Chinese leverage in bilateral relations as well as Beijing's willingness to help Putin save face while under pressure from the West. For the past fifteen years, the Chinese has been willing to provide Moscow with significant financial resources during periods of economic duress for Russia in 2004, 2009, and 2014. But these interventions on Beijing's part came with the price for Moscow of greater economic indebtedness and dependence on China, which must ultimately have political implications for bilateral relations. Russia's corporate indebtedness to China has grown greatly, and it is very closely tied to its political relationship. Before 2014 and the Ukraine crisis, Russian debt to China already exceeded $36 billion.[7] It has since grown two to four times since then, reaching between 5 and 10 percent of Russian GDP.[8] Because of Chinese non-transparency it is difficult to put an exact figure on what Russia and many other countries owe China.[9]

The Chinese view of Russia's role in the BRI also appears to be rather ambiguous at best.[10] In its initial formulation, Russia appeared to be a minor player with few potential projects. This changed somewhat after the 2015 Silk Road Economic Belt (SREB)/Eurasian Economic Union (EAEU) agreement, but negotiations on some projects have been very slow, and it appears that one of the flagship endeavors, a high-speed railway between Kazan and Moscow, has been tabled for now. The noted 2015 SREB-EAEU agreement was even more of a face-saving gift from Beijing to Moscow than the gas deal of 2014. It was important from the Chinese standpoint as it symbolized that Russia would not thwart the Chinese project in Central Asia and the South Caucasus. From the Russian standpoint, this deal represented Chinese recognition of the EAEU, but it was and remains hardly clear how these two very different projects would work together. The principal feature of the EAEU is a customs union that increases tariffs to outsiders to protect local industries. The SREB/BRI is an instrument to gain larger access to markets for China throughout Eurasia.

The legality of the May 2015 agreement was highly dubious in that it did not appear that other members of the EAEU (Armenia, Belarus, Kazakhstan, and Kyrgyzstan) had given Putin the responsibility to negotiate bilaterally on their behalf with China. This point was clarified in a discussion in November 2015 at a meeting of the Astana Club with then Kazakh Prime Minister Massimov. He was very clear that Kazakhstan would prioritize bilateral negotiations with Beijing over multilateral negotiations involving the EAEU, an institution dominated by Moscow.[11]

It is fair to say that Moscow and Beijing approach each other very carefully regarding the BRI. Moscow's initial lack of enthusiasm was reflected by its being a late joiner to the Asian Infrastructure and Investment Bank in 2015. This wariness of the dominating role of Chinese capital in its neighborhood existed just a few years earlier when Moscow was reluctant to agree on the terms of a new development bank for the Shanghai Cooperation Organization (SCO). In fact, Moscow's general lack of interest in promoting a broader economic role for the SCO was a significant frustration for Beijing that likely contributed somewhat to the decision to consolidate what became the BRI starting in 2013. In its relationship with the EAEU, what China really seeks is a free trade zone with the organization, since this would provide a low tariff transit corridor for shipping Chinese products all the way to Europe. But Russia and the other members fear being swamped with Chinese goods if a free trade zone is concluded. And, as noted above, China does not view Moscow as a great investment environment and is principally concerned that Moscow will not take measures to subvert Chinese projects and goals in neighboring countries.

It is true that some of Russia's worst fears of the BRI swamping Russian interests in Central Asia and elsewhere were assuaged when the Chinese stock market crashed and Chinese foreign exchange reserves plummeted by more than $700 billion in a short period of time. Also, Moscow has increasingly understood that China was not ready to throw money at projects willy-nilly simply to buy political interest without a reasonable hope of some return on capital.[12] Also, the political backlash in places like Malaysia, Sri Lanka, Pakistan, and elsewhere that has increased anti-Chinese sentiments and has contributed to political losses of leaders tied to corrupt and poorly negotiated deals with China was a relief for Moscow. But these developments hardly influenced the Chinese to be more forthcoming in making investments in Russia either.

Another interesting case showing the deep ambivalence between these two continental rivals and partners relates to the Artic. Putin has taken a deep interest in developing oil and gas resources in Russia's Arctic as well as expanding Arctic shipping through what the Russians term the Northern Sea Route.[13] As Russia controls the majority of the territory adjacent to the Arctic, it has been covetous of protecting this status and preventing other non-Arctic countries from gaining a voice in the governance of the Arctic. The country of greatest concern for Russia in this regard is China. In 2013, when the Arctic Council (members: Canada, Denmark, Finland, Iceland, Norway, Russia, Sweden, US) was considering a number of countries for a newly designated observer status in 2013, it was striking that Russia supported Japan and Korea's candidacies, but not that of China. Given the dramatic deterioration of Moscow's ties with the West over Ukraine in 2014, it is unimaginable that if this question of Arctic Council membership was put forward in 2015 or later that Moscow would have voted against China gaining status. In fact, in 2017, Russia proposed to cooperate on the development of the Northern Sea Route, and very tellingly each side agreed to refer to it as the Polar Silk Road.[14] For China, the route's economic viability is a serious question, and its perspective is that it will still be significant in the future when the transit route makes more commercial sense. The financial needs are enormous. And just because ice is melting and large pieces of glaciers are breaking off does not mean that the route is getting dramatically safer now. Remember the fate of the Titanic and the floating glacier that took it down. Nor could the Chinese have not forgotten the cold shoulder Russia gave to China on the Arctic just six years ago. And while Moscow is now open to negotiate on the route, Beijing views Moscow's position as insufficiently accommodating to justify major expenditures now.

Looking to the future, perhaps the most intriguing economic opportunity involves Russian supplies of fresh water to China. A memorandum of understanding between Russia and China was signed in December 2018 for a project that would deliver Russian water from Southern Siberia to water-starved Western China by canal through

Kazakhstan. The target date for completion of the project was 2030, with a price tag of $82 billion. The complementarity on this natural commodity is even greater for the two countries than hydrocarbons, since there are fewer competing suppliers. Russia holds the largest freshwater resources of water in the world, and much of it is in Eastern and Southern Siberia, relatively close to China. Two other neighboring supply sources for China are the small, mountainous Central Asian States of Kyrgyzstan and Tajikistan. China has made major economic inroads in each country, but Russia remains the security guarantor and holds greater political and cultural influence. The political economy of water between Russia, China, and Central Asia will be a growing topic of significance in the coming decade.

Arms Sales, Security Cooperation, and Global Governance

Sale of Russian arms to China has been a key factor in the relationship since the collapse of the Soviet Union in 1991. Since 1989, both the US and European allies have boycotted sales of arms to China in response to the tragic events on Tiananmen Square in June of that year. For Russia, arms sales to China, and later to India, were critical for maintaining part of the massive Soviet military industrial complex in the 1990s when domestic orders dried up as well as those from the members of the defunct Warsaw Pact. For China, these sales were very important for the development of its air and naval capabilities as well anti-air defense and more broadly to increase the risk to the US Seventh Fleet from operating in close proximity to defend Taiwan. The arms sales relationship slipped somewhat in the middle of the previous decade for a number of years as the Chinese indigenous capabilities increased and the Russians were more reluctant to deliver more advanced systems for fear of Chinese violations of copyrights through reverse engineering and then essentially producing Russian models in Chinese factories.

After the crisis with the West over Ukraine in 2014, however, the Russian leadership became much more willing to sell its most advanced systems to the Chinese. For one, this represented a broader qualitative deepening of the Sino-Russian relationship. But it was also due to areas in which Chinese military enterprises could not match Russian quality as well as greater Russian confidence in the technical difficulty of reverse-engineering more complex systems. Key areas of interest for China include submarines, helicopters, armored vehicles, warships, aircraft engines, and anti-air defense, to name a few. A signature deal was the Russian agreement to sell China the vaunted S-400 anti-air system. This system significantly complicates the US ability to control air space over Taiwan, for example.

Joint research and development in the arms field has also grown in recent years. There is clearly complementarity in technological areas in which each side has some advantages, and China has a lot of capital to support this work. But the issue of trust, which has increased greatly in the last five years, may still constrain each side from revealing some of their most advanced technologies. The larger challenge for their analyst, however, is access to information, whether classified or open source.

Russian and Chinese military forces have been conducting joint military exercises under the auspices of the Shanghai Cooperation Organization since 2005. In September of 2018 this aspect of the relationship took a major step forward when Chinese forces joined Russian forces essentially on a bilateral basis (some Mongolian forces participated, as well) in the huge "Vostok" [East] exercises that combined air, ground, and naval force engagement. Coming on the heels of Xi Jinping's participation in the Russian Far Eastern Economic Forum in Vladivostok, together these events sent strong signals to Washington about the deepening of Sino-Russian ties. Previously, the Chinese had been more reluctant to trumpet the strategic significance of the relationship with Moscow, but with the Trump administration's growing trade war with Beijing coupled with clearer rhetoric identifying China as a military rival, Beijing has more incentive to emphasize Russia as a key strategic partner, although not an ally.

China also views Russia as an ideological ally against US-led liberal interventionist economic, political, and military policies. On global governance, each are stalwart supporters of nonintervention in the domestic affairs of sovereign states.[15] They have cooperated numerous times with double vetoes on the United Nations Security Council to thwart US and Western–led resolutions over the last decade, perhaps most prominently regarding Syria, to punish authoritarian states and human rights violations. Each have been increasingly vocal about the anachronistic nature of many of the Bretton Woods institutions set up at the end of the

Second World War. For the most part, however, China has not appeared as critical as Russia, recognizing that existing institutions need reform rather than revolution.[16]

In sum, Russia has been consistently a highly valued relationship for China since the collapse of the Soviet Union for reasons of border security and significant economic complementarities, especially in energy and arms sales. But relations with the US, for both security and economic reasons, is an even higher priority for Beijing. The more bellicose trade and military policy of the Trump administration, however, has pushed China to tilt more closely to Moscow. But for now, those wary of a full embrace including a security alliance relationship with Moscow remain the more powerful faction in Chinese domestic politics.[17]

China and Europe

Chinese policy toward Europe mirrors Russian policy toward Europe in three critical ways: (1) the strong preference to focus on bilateral relations rather than ties with the EU, (2) the focus on economic relations, and (3) the focus on investments in states, such as Greece, that are most vulnerable to being picked off from the EU. For China, the emphasis is transit infrastructure in the context of the BRI, and for Russia it is hydrocarbon sales to European states and pipeline politics.

While the EU shares many US concerns about China, it also shares some of China's concerns about the US. In particular, both China and Europe oppose US isolationism and protectionism and support a multilateral global order based on institutional rules. In accordance with liberalism, Europe has always believed that international institutions can facilitate cooperation between countries and promote multipolarity. China shares the same belief and has joined many international institutions, though it prioritizes its national interests and has thus rejected some of the more binding features such as international law.[18] When a conflict emerges, China and Europe will first resort to dialogue rather than direct confrontation. Hence, compared to the US, Europe is less willing to use sanctions against China.

One cannot view Chinese infrastructure investments in Europe, especially growing control of major port facilities, outside of its broader Maritime Silk Road investments, including in South East Asia, South

Asia, and the greater Middle East. Looking at the map of these investments reveals a broad strategic design on the part of Beijing to contest
US hegemony on the open seas and support freedom of navigation.[19] It
appears that the way the Chinese are countering US naval strategy may
be to constrain access to ports in a large containment maneuver from
the Indo-Pacific to the Atlantic.

Like Russia, China also seeks to split the North American alliance,
both by taking advantage of Washington's miscues and by developing
stronger economic and thus political leverage with European states.
Here, Beijing has benefited greatly from the Trump administration's
toughening of US trade policy toward Europe as well as his instinctive
disdain for NATO. Naturally Europe's geographic distance from China
means that it lags behind on BRI investments compared to countries in
closer proximity to China.

The European Union and Washington have grown increasingly skeptical of what some interpret as Chinese efforts to dilute EU solidarity
through bilateral economic deal making as Russia operates but China
has also disrupted consensus in Europe through its multilateral efforts
toward Europe. Notwithstanding Europe's concern about China using
the "16+1" Initiative to play divide-and-rule with the EU, China has always stressed that it has no such intention, that "16+1" was developed
based on mutual demand rather than geopolitical interests, and that Europe's sensitivity to "16+1" is caused by its internal disunity. China believes that many Eastern European countries joined the "16+1" after the
European debt crisis because they felt that they were not suited to the
model of Western European countries and that their national interests
do not always align with the policies of the EU and the US. It is thus only
natural that many Eastern European countries that do not perceive any
threat from China chose to cooperate with it. Indeed, "16+1" has now
ceased to exist, as it has expanded to include Greece in 2019 and has thus
become "17+1." Joint projects between China and countries in "17+1" include the construction of a variety of key infrastructure projects such as
railways, highways, ports, and canals. China thinks that in the future the
only obstacle to "17+1" will be Washington, which has repeatedly warned
about China's desire to weaken European solidarity.

The other area in which China is actively seeking greater support
from Europe is countering US unilateralism and ultimately revising the

terms of global governance established at the conclusion of the Second World War. Here, China positions itself as the responsible global stakeholder as opposed to the US that is increasingly withdrawing from key multilateral institutions and agreements. Of greatest relevance for Europe in this regard is the US withdrawal from the Kyoto Protocol and opposition to measures to curtail and manage climate change and the P5+1 agreement to contain the Iranian nuclear weapons program. China continues to support both of these landmark multilateral agreements.

An Alternative Strategic Triangle: China-Europe-United States

For nearly the last fifty years, since the US opening to China in 1972, most discussions of a "strategic triangle" have focused on China-USSR/Russia-US. But the China-Europe-US triangular relationship is emerging as both fluid and of increasing significance.[20] As economic entities, the three are quite close in size, far more so than the China-Russia-US triangle whose strategic significance far outweighs its economic significance. And although nuclear weapons give Russia added strategic power, from the standpoint of military spending, China, Europe, and the US are also more closely balanced. While the NATO alliance brings Europe and the US far closer together than any "bilateral" tie in the China-Russia-US triangle, Europe is quite economically independent from both China and the US, although trade and investment ties with both are large.

In comparing Chinese policy toward Russia and Europe, I would argue that China is more proactive in its Europe policy than in its Russia policy. With Russia, in the past five years, China has been more reactive to Russia's alienation from the West. China pursues some initiatives with Russia and its partners, such as establishing a Free Trade Zone with the EAEU. Beijing would be pleased if Russia were to take a less neutral position on China's territorial disputes with its neighbors, but does not push this with much energy. China had been disappointed with the slow pace of building an energy partnership with Russia for at least fifteen years, and decided to hedge its imports through relations with other suppliers.[21] And since 2014, it is decidedly Russia that appears to be more of the *demandeur* in the relationship. For the most part, China is rather satisfied with the status quo in relations with Russia: oil and gas supplies have grown; the border is settled and peaceful; and Russia is unlikely to take actions to thwart the BRI. And while many, especially in Washington, focus on the potential clash of interests in Central Asia, for both countries this is a tertiary theatre at best in which both share interests in stability rather than competing for hegemony.

Europe's approach to China is a different matter. It is more of a *greenfield* as China's policy has both globalized and, through the BRI. developed more strategic goals for expanding ties on the Eurasian super-continent. Let's start with security issues. First, China deeply opposes a larger European military presence in the Asia-Pacific to support the US and its allies.[22] Unlike Russia, China is not so concerned about NATO, unless it were to strengthen its ties with Central Asian states close to the Chinese border. Chinese military and civilian analysts were deeply skeptical, for example, that the US was spending so much blood and treasure in Afghanistan for so long merely to eliminate Al Qaeda, other radical Islamists, and contain the Taliban. Their view was that the US wanted to establish permanently based troops on China's strategic rear close to most of China's Muslim population in Xinjiang Province.[23] China most definitely would like to see the Europeans act more independently from their American allies. For example, Beijing has continually tried to coax European arms-producing states to defect from the US-led boycott on arms sales to China since 1989. But the sanctions question is more likely to get more complicated for China with the concurrent crackdown in Hong Kong and the brutal displacement of more than one million Chinese Muslims in Xinjiang into "reeducation camps." So far, these issues have not received the political attention they might because politicians in the US and Europe have been awaiting the results of the trade negotiations that have been going on for more than a year between China and the Trump administration.

On the US trade dispute with China, hopes in Beijing at the outset were that the Europeans would be more opposed to Trump's policies since the American president was taking much harder positions against Europe. as well, early in his administration. But since some US pressure on trade with Europe has eased, Europeans have realized that they share many of the same grievances as the Americans on issues like access to the Chinese market and respect for intellectual property rights. As a recent paper put it, many Europeans would agree with the substance of the accusations that the US makes to China, but not with the confrontational approach adopted by the Trump administration.[24]

Europe also finds itself in an awkward position regarding the Trump administration's increased concern about Chinese high technology development, which competes with US products in the European market. The most high-profile case is that of Huawei and its development of 5G technology, which also has security implications as well as market concerns for Washington.

The main issue faced by the US, EU, and the UK is that, while the Swedish Ericsson and Finnish Nokia are competitors of Huawei and are able to produce 5G technology, it will be difficult for the West to rely solely on Ericsson and Nokia due to their price, which is much higher than that of Huawei because Huawei receives subsidies from the Chinese government. Europe, of course, understands the danger of Huawei. Nonetheless, so far, most European countries have hesitated to impose restrictions on Huawei due to fear of Chinese retaliation as well as the challenge of producing an equally high-performing and low-cost alternative to Huawei. Indeed, even the US still needs to develop an alternative to Huawei, which is why in January 2020 the Senate proposed to invest $1.2 billion to do just that. Some countries, like the UK, however, refuse to wait until an alternative is found and judge that it is safe to import Huawei's technology so long as the use of Huawei is limited. Currently, the UK has allowed Huawei to supply 35 percent of its 5G network equipment, all of which will be used in the peripheral radio network rather than the more sensitive areas such as the core routes traffic. UK's willingness to deal with Huawei probably would not have happened if it remained in the EU, so we can expect China to continue to use Brexit to its advantage.

China and the BRI

From the standpoint of the BRI, Europe finds itself on the Western end of both the Silk Road Economic Belt (overland) and the Maritime Road. There are two major strategic and economic justifications for the Belt: (1) modernizing overland transit corridors between Asia and Europe that are faster than sea trade; and (2) creating an overland route for access to Middle Eastern energy resources that can avoid interdiction by the US or another hostile navy in the event of conflict. The Maritime Road that links the Asia-Pacific with the Indian Ocean and then the Atlantic, like the SREB, finds its historic precedent going back more than 2,000 years in history. The key feature of the Road is the series of ports along the way that China has acquired and/or invested heavily in. Some, like Gwadar in Pakistan would appear to have little commercial potential and greater military use. Note that China has already established an overseas military base in Djibouti. As we earlier noted from the map of these bases, one can find both commercial and military rationales behind the strategy. On the commercial side is the possible profits simply from operating the ports as well as potentially the preferred treatment of Chinese commercial ships or those carrying primarily Chinese goods seeking access to the ports.

Strategically, Chinese control of more ports might be construed as a counter to the US Navy's domination of the seas. Provision of the common good of freedom of the seas benefits everyone economically, but reducing the vulnerability of a great trading nation like China to being constrained on the seas by the US Navy and its allies must be a major long-term goal of Beijing. Having greater control of port access along the Maritime Road can begin to address this problem. Ultimately, the best solution for all along the Maritime Road would be for the US and China to start to jointly take responsibility with partners to ensure freedom of the seas. China has already been active in peacekeeping missions that have extended the projection of the Chinese navy. The base in Djibouti, as well as the port/base in Gwadar also serve the purpose of facilitating evacuation of Chinese workers under threat in Pakistan and the Middle East. But this latter rationale would hardly apply to Chinese companies owned and operated in Europe.

Latter day followers of the great British geopolitician Halford MacKinder may be inclined to view China's goals in Russia and Europe, and the BRI more broadly, as an effort to one day become the hegemonic power on the "World Island," or, in more contemporary terms, the Eurasian supercontinent. This is an unlikely outcome, but one that will at least take several decades to be realized. It would be dependent on China achieving a quite extraordinary set of geopolitical and geo-economic goals, starting with the ejection of US naval power from disputed territories in the South China Sea and Taiwan. US Asian allies Japan and South Korea would have to decide to bandwagon with the regional hegemon rather than balance against it in alliance with the US. It would depend on major transformation in the China-India relationship and then replacing the US as the guarantor of freedom of the seas around the Persian Gulf. Finally, it would require wooing Europe away from US security ties while extending further leverage over Russia and its neighbors. Frankly, the required economic, military, and especially diplomatic resources to execute these tasks seem beyond the scope of any state or political entity in Eurasia, including China. One key requirement for such a scenario to transpire would be a retrenchment of the US away from being the global power it has been since the nineteenth century. Also, China would face the dilemma of whether its advance would inspire states to bandwagon or balance Chinese power.[25] To be successful, China would need to exercise a deft touch such as has never been seen before in world history, as well continue a pace of economic growth over decades that has also never been witnessed. The remarkable Chinese transition from a low income to a high middle-income country over the past four decades is a terrific achievement, but as economists know, further development to becoming a high-income country is the hardest part, as many states get caught in the "middle-income trap."

A New Wildcard: The Coronavirus Pandemic

The emergence of the novel coronavirus initially in Wuhan City, Hubei Province, in December 2019 and its rapid growth to global pandemic in the Spring of 2020 has focused world attention away from most of the issues discussed in this chapter. At this time of writing in early May 2020, there is no clear end of the spread of the virus in sight. Some countries, notably China, Japan, and South Korea, appear to have managed through the peak of the virus; the US and then Europe have been by far the hardest hit; and at the moment of writing the focus is on Russia as it struggles with a very rapid infection rate.

China's relations with Russia as well as Europe have experienced ups and downs since the emergence of the virus. Initially the Chinese were unhappy that Russia quickly closed its border in January, but in the spring it was the Chinese who were unhappy with infected Russians crossing the border after China had appeared to have contained the virus.[26] Russia's largest trading relationship, $110 trillion in 2019, is with China, and the fasting growing part of that growth since 2015 was growing numbers of Chinese tourists coming to Russia, China's third largest tourist destination.[27] Russian demand for Chinese consumer goods has declined, as have Chinese imports of oil and gas. The virus, combined with the steep drop in the price of oil, is battering the Russian economy, and Putin's ratings are lower than they have ever been in twenty years.

But the larger issue at hand from China's strategic standpoint is the degree to which the brand "made in China" is tarnished, and secondly how the BRI's policy of enhancing connectivity between nations and peoples will be viewed. The ultimate impact of the pandemic crisis will depend to a great extent on how long it lasts and the degree of economic fallout that results. There is also the distinct possibility that the crisis will return in the fall/winter of 2020–21 as a second wave. Students of the largest global pandemic since the misnamed Spanish Flu of 1918–19 know that it was far greater when it returned in 1919 after seeming to be contained in 1918. Nobody knows what will happen as a result of claims by US Secretary of State Mike Pompeo that the virus was produced in a lab in Wuhan Province and accidentally exposed to the public. The damage for the "made in China" brand could be crushing for Chinese relations with virtually all of the countries that have been hard hit by COVID, which is virtually everyone.[28]

We do know, however, that COVID-19 is the third major epidemic that has originated in China in the last twenty years: SARS in 2002 and Avian Flu in 2008 preceded it. China's economic growth had already slowed to about 6 percent in 2019, there will be huge decreases in consumer demand in 2020 and perhaps longer, and likely looming questions for domestic and foreign investors in China for the foreseeable future, which is hardly foreseeable at this moment. For the time being, global focus will be on containing and ultimately stopping the virus and managing what is at least now a global recession, but with the strong potential to become a global depression. Will China, Europe, Russia, and the US lean toward greater cooperation over health and economic challenges or will a more competitive dynamic emerge as we saw between the great powers in the 1930s?

Conclusion

The Belt and Road Initiative is a project of grand strategic magnitude, but its end goal is hardly clear. Its place in the history of the People's Republic of China has been magnified since the Chinese Communist Party has elevated Xi Jinping to its "Mount Rushmore" of leaders along with Mao Zedong and Deng Xiaoping. The BRI, formerly launched in 2013, is scheduled to be concluded in 2049, the one-hundredth anniversary of the founding of the People's Republic. Domestically, the goal is that by 2049 China will have joined the ranks of the most developed countries as judged by per capita GDP, a global economic powerhouse the likes of which find no comparison in world history. To use the terminology prevalent fifteen years ago, China's "peaceful rise" will be completed. The role of global hegemon will have passed from the US to China peacefully, as Great Britain one hundred years ago started to pass the baton to the US. China will continue to pay lip service to the ideology of multipolarity until its unilateral dominance is *de facto* clear to all.

The role of Russia will continue primarily to serve as a source of critical natural resources and commodities for China. If climate change makes more Russian territory north of the Chinese border viable for agricultural development, then expect the Chinese to be the largest investor, possibly sending Chinese workers. As long as the Russian economy is stagnant, as it has been for the past twelve years, the role of Chinese capital will continue to grow, especially if Russia's access to Western financial markets is constrained by sanctions. It is unlikely that China will desire an alliance with Moscow, but Russian sovereignty will continue its current trend of being bought by China.

China will continue to look for opportunities to split Europe from the US; Chinese-European economic integration will continue to deepen. The future of political and security relations between China and Europe is harder to foresee, since the crucial variable is the future of US-European relations. As memories of the US role in tipping the balance in two world wars in the first half of the twentieth century and the crucial security alliance during most of the second half of the twentieth century fades further in the past, the underpinnings of NATO and the trans-Atlantic will continue to weaken. Donald Trump's campaign promise to refrain from using US military power to topple odious governments in far-off places definitely resonates with the majority of Americans. The US commitment to defend wealthy Europeans most likely will continue to ebb. The long war in Afghanistan and the senseless decision to invade Iraq were never popular with most Europeans, and national publics will likely continue to balk at raising defense spending, as Washington wants them to, when no clear enemy exists. Present-day Russia is a weak shadow of the Soviet Union.

Time should be on the side of China to continue to expand its economic and political influence across Eurasia. China's policies themselves, however, will probably mostly determine how successful China's rise will be in the next thirty years, including its goals with Russia and Europe. There are already significant warning signs of self-imposed errors. Xi Jinping's anti-market inclinations and preference for strong Chinese Communist Party control of the political economy and extremely inefficient state-owned enterprises will slow growth and make it more difficult for China to escape the middle-income trap. Many of us are old enough to remember the 1980s, when the US felt threatened by the rapid rise of Japan until the Japanese economy went into a multi-decade stagnation starting with a banking system burdened with too many non-performing loans. The balance sheets of contemporary Chinese banks must be much more vulnerable. The Chinese leadership has been obsessed with studying the errors of the Soviet Union that led to its collapse, but I fear they have learned the wrong lessons.

It is very hard to see how China's horrendous treatment of their Muslim minorities will not backfire badly by attracting greater attention of foreign Jihadists as well as further radicalizing the local Muslim population. If China is too aggressive with its neighbors, as it certainly was at the beginning of this decade, their inclination to counterbalance Chinese power rather than bandwagon with it will increase, imposing further security and economic costs on China. Security costs for continental powers like China and Russia are naturally higher than for island or sea powers because of demands for border defense and beyond. It is not surprising that the two most successful hegemonic global powers of the past two centuries have been island powers (or virtually so), Great Britain and the US. Finally, how the COVID-19 crisis plays out holds enormous importance for China's future and the rest of the world, including China's relations with Russia and Europe. How much of this analysis will remain valid is an open question.

NOTES

1 The author is deeply grateful for the superb and indispensable efforts of Sabrina Sui in assisting with the research and preparation of this chapter. Sabrina Sui is a junior at the School of Foreign Service at Georgetown University majoring in Regional and Comparative Studies with a focus on Russia and China. She is a research assistant for Dr. Kuchins.

2 Frankopan, *The Silk Roads.*

3 Lukin, *China and Russia*, 42.

4 Kuchins, "US Policy Goals With Russia in a Broader Asian Context."

5 Gabuev, "China's Pivot to Putin's Friends."

6 Gabuev, "China's Pivot to Putin's Friends."

7 Hass, "The Politics of Chinese Loans in Russia."

8 Buchholz, "The Countries Most in Debt to China."

9 Horn, Reinhart, and Trebesch, "How Much Money Does the World Owe China?"

10 Gabuev, "China's Pivot to Putin's Friends."

11 The author was a participant in this first gathering of the Astana Club. More broadly, there was a very striking difference between Russian participants' exuberant praise of the importance of the Sino-Russian relations with the studied aloof posture on this topic from Chinese participants.

12 Gabuev, "Russia's Policy towards China."

13 The founding of the Northern Sea Route goes back to 1932 under the leadership of Josef Stalin. It reached a peak high of shipping in 1987, but this was facilitated by the fact that Soviet shippers were not obligated to make commercial profits. As there was no spare money to support commercially non-viable shipping for the next twenty years, the Northern Sea Route was a backwater, so to speak. Since, in the last ten years, this route has become more operational thanks to rising sea temperatures and glacial melting, the issue has again emerged as a significant goal for Putin.

14 Sun, "The Northern Sea Route."

15 Rozman, *The Sino-Russian Challenge to the World Order.*

16 Salzman, *Russia, BRICS, and the Disruption of the Global Order.*

17 Lukin, *China and Russia.*

18 Telò, "European and Chinese Multilateralism at Stake."

19 Image from Kakissis, "Chinese Firms Now Hold Stakes in over a Dozen European Ports."

20 Erickson and Strange, "Scalene Perspectives, Isosceles Ideas and Equilateral Dependence."

21 Itoh and Kuchins, "The Energy Factor in Russia's Asia Pivot."
22 Erickson and Strange, "Scalene Perspectives, Isosceles Ideas and Equilateral Dependence."
23 Kuchins, "What is Eurasia to US (the US)?"
24 Telò, "European and Chinese Multilateralism at Stake."
25 Walt, *The Origins of Alliances.*
26 For China-Europe, see Brattberg and Le Corre "No, COVID-19 Isn't Turning Europe Pro-China (Yet)."
27 Foy, "Coronavirus."
28 Bredemeier, "China Accuses Pompeo of Lying about Origin of Coronavirus."

BIBLIOGRAPHY

Brattberg, Erik, and Philippe Le Corre. "No, COVID-19 Isn't Turning Europe Pro-China (Yet)." *Diplomat.* April 15, 2020. https://thediplomat.com.

Bredemeier, Ken. "China Accuses Pompeo of Lying about Origin of Coronavirus." *VOA News,* May 4, 2020. www.voanews.com.

Buchholz, Katharina. "The Countries Most in Debt to China." Statista. October 14, 2019. www.statista.com.

Erickson, Andrew S., and Austin M. Strange. "Scalene Perspectives, Isosceles Ideas and Equilateral Dependence: The US-Europe-China 'Strategic Triangle' and Transatlantic Policy." *China International Strategy Review* (2016): 337–61.

Foy, Henry. "Coronavirus: Closure of Russia-China Border Sparks Trade Fears." *Financial Times,* January 30, 2020. www.ft.com.

Frankopan, Peter. *The Silk Roads: A New History of the World.* London: Bloomsbury, 2015.

Gabuev, Alexander. "China's Pivot to Putin's Friends." *Foreign Policy,* June 25, 2016. https://foreignpolicy.com.

Gabuev, Alexander. "Russia's Policy towards China: Key Players and the Decision-making Process." Asan Forum, March 5, 2015. www.theasanforum.org.

Hass, Maximilian. "The Politics of Chinese Loans in Russia." Riddle. July 12, 2019. www.ridl.io.

Horn, Sebastian, Carmen M. Reinhart, and Christoph Trebesch. "How Much Money Does the World Owe China?" *Harvard Business Review.* February 26, 2020. https://hbr.org.

Itoh, Shoichi, and Andrew Kuchins. "The Energy Factor in Russia's Asia Pivot." In *Energy Security in Asia and Eurasia,* edited by Mike Mochizuki and Deepa Olapoly, 140–62. Florence: Taylor and Francis, 2016.

Kakissis, Joanna. "Chinese Firms Now Hold Stakes in over A Dozen European Ports." *NPR,* October 9, 2018. www.npr.org.

Kuchins, Andrew. "US Policy Goals with Russia in a Broader Asian Context." In *Change and Continuity in Japan-Russia Relations: Implications for the United States,* edited by Paul J. Saunders and John S. Van Oudenaren, 37–48. Washington, DC: Center for the National Interest, 2019.

Kuchins, Andrew. "What is Eurasia to US (the US)?" *Journal of Eurasian Studies* 9, no. 2 (July 2018): 125–33.

Lukin, Alexander. *China and Russia: The New Rapprochement.* Cambridge, UK: Polity Press, 2018.

Rozman, Gilbert. *The Sino-Russian Challenge to the World Order: National Identities, Bilateral Relations, and East versus West in the 2010s.* Washington, DC: Woodrow Wilson Center Press, 2014.

Salzman, Rachel. *Russia, BRICS, and the Disruption of the Global Order.* Washington, DC: Georgetown University Press, 2019.

Sun, Yun. "The Northern Sea Route: The Myth of Sino-Russian Cooperation." The Stimson Center. December 5, 2018. www.stimson.org.

Telò, Mario. "European and Chinese Multilateralism at Stake: Political and Theoretical Implications." In *Deepening the EU-China Partnership in an Unstable World: Bridging Institutional and Ideational Differences,* edited by Mario Telò, Ding Chun and Zhang Xiaotong, 28-42. London: Routledge, 2017.

Walt, Stephen M. *The Origins of Alliances.* Ithaca, NY: Cornell University Press, 1988.

9

China's Grand Strategy toward North America

ZHIQUN ZHU

This chapter addresses the following questions: What are China's fundamental objectives and strategies in North America? What mix of policies is China currently pursuing in North America? How successful have China's strategies been so far? And given the presumptions about China's continued economic growth and future capabilities, can China plausibly achieve its objectives in there?

As expected, China's strategic focus in North America is to manage its complex relations with the United States. However, both Canada and Mexico are valuable diplomatic and economic partners for China amid growing US-China rivalry.

What Are China's Interests and Strategies in North America?

There seems to be a coalescing consensus among many Western governments and observers that China's rise portends a mortal threat to the modern liberal order led by the US. Whether such an assessment is true depends largely on what China's intentions are. A thorough examination of China's foreign policy objectives and fundamental national interests is required in order to fully understand what China's rise means for the world, and for the US in particular.

Chinese strategies toward the West, particularly the US, are profoundly shaped by several factors: the history of the so-called "century of humiliation," the persistent pursuit of wealth and power or national rejuvenation, a deep sense of insecurity due to mounting challenges at home and perceived hostile forces outside, and the preferences of the political leadership. China's policies toward North American countries have been consistent, with the same goals as its policies toward other regions: maximizing its national interests by expanding cooperation in various fields while vigorously defending its sovereignty and domestic stability.

The major objectives of the leaders of the People's Republic of China (PRC) have of course evolved since 1949. The first generation of PRC leaders were able to unify the nation, expel foreign influences and establish an independent "New China." In Mao Zedong's words, "the Chinese people have stood up!" Following Mao's death, the second generation of PRC leaders, led by Deng Xiaoping, spearheaded reform and opening-up in order to bring China out of poverty and integrate into the global system. Deng's successors Jiang Zemin and Hu Jintao continued with his policy of keeping a low profile in international affairs while focusing on domestic development throughout the 1990s and 2000s.

By the time Xi Jinping became general secretary of the Communist Party at the Eighteenth Party Congress in November 2012 and president of the PRC in March 2013, China had already overtaken Japan to be the second largest economy in the world. Xi's ambition is to turn China into a wealthy and powerful nation by the mid-twenty-first century as part of the "Chinese Dream."

From Mao's "*zhan qilai*" (standing up) to Deng/Jiang/Hu's "*fu qilai*" (getting rich) and to Xi's "*qiang qilai*" (wealthy and powerful), the PRC has come a long way. China's foreign policy under President Xi has been summarized by Chinese Foreign Minister Wang Yi as "big power diplomacy with Chinese characteristics, which promotes the construction of a new type of international relations and the formation of a community of shared future for mankind" (中国特色大国外交就是要推动建设新型国际关系，推动构建人类命运共同体。)[1]

It is generally understood that President Xi has gradually abandoned Deng's "*taoguang yanghui*" (keeping a low profile) strategy and has shifted to "*you suo zuo wei*" (getting some things done) to reflect China's current status as a major player in international politics and economics. In the official narrative, China is moving close to the center stage of global affairs.

China's fundamental interests since the Deng era have been to maintain a stable and peaceful regional and international environment so as to focus on continued domestic development. A Chinese "Defense White Paper" published in July 2019 stated that

> China will remain committed to peaceful development and work with people of all countries to safeguard world peace and promote common development. . . . The development of China's national defense aims to meet its rightful security needs and contribute to the growth of the world's peaceful forces. . . . China will never follow the beaten track of big powers in seeking hegemony. No matter how it might develop, China will never threaten any other country or seek any sphere of influence.[2]

The white paper "China and the World in the New Era," published in September 2019 just before the seventieth anniversary of the PRC, stated that "Peace and development remain the underlying themes of our times" and "Rather than a threat or challenge, China's development is an opportunity for the world."[3]

In North America, China's primary foreign policy objectives have been to develop friendly relationships with the US, Canada, and Mexico, promote cooperation, and avoid conflict. China invariably emphasizes its "core interests" of sovereignty and territorial integrity in its foreign policy, and as far as the US is concerned, the Taiwan issue is one of the "core interests." China is not happy that the US has maintained a special "unofficial" relationship with Taiwan since 1979 when it established diplomatic ties with Beijing.

As part of its "going global" policy, China has significantly increased investments in the US and Canada since 2010 and expanded trade with Mexico. A major global strategy under President Xi's leadership is the massive Belt and Road Initiative (BRI), which involves some 170 countries and international organizations in trade, investment, and infrastructure building.[4] China has been working hard to get support for the BRI from the three North American countries. As of this writing, the US and Canada remain critical of the BRI, but Mexico has affirmed it is interested in working with China as "a friend and a partner."[5]

Judging from official statements, China does not seem interested in attempting to replace the US as the dominant global power. At the China Institutes of Contemporary International Relations Forum 2019 held in Beijing, Chinese Vice Foreign Minister Le Yucheng pointed out that it was wrong to assert that US hegemony would be handed over to China amid the global power shift. China "believes in a multipolar world and supports multilateralism and free trade." China has never "intended to rival for hegemony with the US, and we are not interested in power games."[6] Repeated statements and clarifications about China's national interests by Chinese officials notwithstanding, many in the West still feel uncertain about China's true global intentions.

The United States in China's Grand Strategy

China's Conflicting Identities

As China has become a major force in international political economy, how does the country identify itself? Officially, China still considers itself a developing nation or a rising power, not a superpower. On the other hand, President Xi seems highly ambitious about China's role in world affairs. In a national security conference in 2017, he used the "two guides"—guiding the international community to jointly form a more just and more reasonable new international order, and guiding the international community to jointly maintain international security (引导国际社会共同塑造更加公正合理的国际新秩序，引导国际社会共同维护国际安全)—to indicate China's leadership ambition in the world today. This dual identity—a large developing nation and an aspiring great power—has triggered various, sometimes opposite, reactions from the international community to China's foreign policy initiatives. China continues to enjoy developing-nation status at many international organizations, such as the World Trade Organization, but global expectations are high for China to take on more responsibilities in international affairs as its power continues to grow.

Is China a status quo or a revisionist power? Since the time Deng launched his reforms, China has benefited enormously from the US-led international system. There is no reason for China to overthrow it and replace it with something different. Yet China is not a status quo power either, since it is not completely satisfied with the current international order built and maintained by the West. Instead, China is a reformist power and has become more active in global governance; it desires more say in shaping global affairs, from climate change to international trade. It has developed the Asian Infrastructure Investment Bank (AIIB) to complement, not replace, the Asian Development Bank and the World Bank. It has worked with other BRICS countries and established the New Development Bank with its headquarters in Shanghai. It is also a proponent of reforms of major international institutions, including the United Nations and the World Trade Organization. At a time when the US, under President Donald Trump, is more inward-looking and has withdrawn from many international institutions and regimes, China has projected itself as a major defender of international rules. All of this suggests that China intends to play a leadership role in maintaining and reforming, rather than completely changing, the multilateral international system so that it better reflects the interests of developing nations.

What Does China Want from the United States?

China has a long tradition of admiring and looking up to the US as a model of modernization. Generations of Chinese, since the mid-nineteenth century, have been inspired by the "city upon a hill." For most Chinese, the US represents democracy, freedom, power and prosperity—exactly what the Chinese have pursued since the first Opium War, or the beginning of the so-called "century of humiliation." Despite ups and downs in the relationship, ordinary Chinese have never changed their positive views of the US, which remains the number one destination of Chinese students pursuing better education overseas. By 2019, Chinese students had accounted for over one third of all international students in the US.

Deng Xiaoping famously remarked that those countries that followed the US were all wealthy, so China should befriend America—a key reason that he decided to normalize relations with the US. In January 1979, shortly after the two countries established diplomatic ties, Deng visited the US to strengthen relations and to learn from the US. In addition to Washington, DC, he toured Atlanta, Houston, and Seattle, where he expressed deep interest in America's scientific prowess and encouraged American businesses such as Boeing and Coca Cola to invest in China.

Now that China has become the second largest economy, does it feel that it no longer needs to learn from the US? Will the trade war launched by President Donald Trump harden China's resolve to beat the US in science and technology? Or will China be happy to be part of the "G2," with the two powers co-existing and co-managing global and regional affairs? The answers to such questions are not entirely clear to an outside observer based on China's words and deeds.

Despite hyperbolic rhetoric by nationalistic media outlets like the *Global Times*, most Chinese are fully aware that China still lags far behind the US in many aspects. China has a long way to go to catch up with the US in science and technology, education, soft power, and comprehensive development. It still needs to learn from the US and other Western countries. On many occasions, Chinese leaders have noted that the Pacific Ocean is big enough to accommodate both the US and China.[7] Though China has neither the intention nor the capability to replace the US as the dominant global power, it expects recognition and the respect of its "core interests" by the US and other nations. Such "core interests" include China's sovereignty, territorial integrity, and political and economic stability.

In managing relations with other big powers, especially the US, Xi has proposed a new model to avoid the so-called "Thucydides's trap" associated with the global power shift. During his visit to the US as vice president in 2012, Xi first uttered the concept of a "new type of great power relations." At his first meeting with President Barack Obama in 2013, Xi remarked that the US and China must work together to build "a new model of major country relationship based on mutual respect and win-win cooperation for the benefit of the Chinese and American peoples, and people elsewhere in the world." China has since attempted to use the "new model of major country relationship" to define its relations with the US. The US response to the Chinese proposal, however, has been lukewarm at best.

A benign view of China's rise would propose that China does not intend to replace the US as the dominant global power or drive the US out of the Asia-Pacific. However, many Americans tend to see China's rapid development in a negative light. Michael Pillsbury of the Hudson Institute claims in his *The Hundred-Year Marathon* that it has been China's long-standing intention to replace the US to be the dominant power in the world.[8] Some US analysts assert that China's pivot to high tech represents an "existential threat"[9] and the US intelligence community warned in June 2018 that Chinese recruitment of foreign scientists and its targeted acquisition of US firms constitute an "unprecedented threat" to

America's industrial base.[10] Some scholars suggest that the international system is returning to a bipolarity. Øystein Tunsjø of the Norwegian Defence University College argues that for geo-structural reasons, the US and China will be preoccupied with rivalry and conflict in East Asia, and that the risk of limited war between the two superpowers is likely to be higher in the new bipolarity.[11]

Cui Tiankai, Chinese ambassador to the US, said China has no interest in global dominance because it is a costly role and China's top priorities are domestic: "Our goals for the next few decades are mainly for China's own development and modernization. We still have close to twenty million people living under the poverty line. We still have to deal with the serious threat of environmental degradation. We still have to guard against any economic or financial turbulence in the world that could affect the Chinese economy." Meanwhile, China really intends to "build a strong and stable relationship with the United States."[12] Contrary to the inflated view that China is getting closer to the center of the global stage, Cui's comments are sober and reflect priorities and challenges of the Chinese government.

Despite the trade war he launched with China, President Trump has established a strong and cordial working relationship with President Xi. As Vice President Mike Pence stated in his China policy speech on October 24, 2019, the US will not take a confrontational approach toward China. Economic decoupling is not possible and is not the US policy. Instead, the US will continue to engage and work with China to build a peaceful future together.[13] Clearly, the two countries have many differences and are rivals in many ways, but they both intend to continue cooperation on bilateral, regional, and global issues where they can. It is unlikely that the world will be splitting into two opposite poles, with the US and China each heading a camp.

Key Challenges from the United States

There will be twists and turns in the relationship, and the so-called US-China trade war will end sooner or later. In fact, after thirteen rounds of negotiations, on October 11, 2019 both sides announced that they had reached a "Phase I" trade agreement. With the outbreak of the corona-virus in 2020, however, the full implementation of the agreement was thrown into doubt. Trade agreements notwithstanding, structural conflicts in the relationship will remain.

China is sometimes perceived in the West as a revisionist power bent on changing the international order. Singaporean diplomat Kishore Mahbubani argues that, on the contrary, China has been one of the biggest beneficiaries of the current international system. Even as Donald Trump's US turns inward, China, by comparison, has cast itself as a key supporter of international commerce and a pillar against climate change, while committing itself to reforming the World Trade Organization. In Mahbubani's view, China is actually a status quo power globally, and it is now the US that is the biggest threat to the multilateral rules-based order.[14]

Inconsistency and lack of consensus in US policy toward China will affect China's reactive strategy toward the US. The National Security Strategy issued by the White House in December 2017 stated that the US was re-entering an era of great power competition, in which China and Russia "want to shape a world antithetical to US values and interests."[15] Some also argue that China, rather than Russia, is the long-term threat to US security and global dominance. In other words, China is the biggest potential enemy. Yet, during a G-20 news conference in Osaka, Japan in late June 2019, Trump suggested that the US and China "are going to be strategic partners." This is a sharp turnaround from the "strategic competitors" label identified in various US government documents during his presidency. Trump's announcement that US companies could continue to sell products to Huawei while it is blacklisted by the US is also perplexing.

Kiron Skinner, former Director of Policy Planning for the US Department of State, has described today's US-China conflict as "a fight with a really different civilization and a different ideology, and the United States hasn't had that before." She claimed US rivalry with China represented "the first time that we will have a great power competitor that is not Caucasian."[16] Talk of civilizational conflict and racial rivalry added a new dimension to already complex US-China relations.

In the ongoing trade war, China has been bewildered about US intentions and objectives. In China, people ask, what does the US want? If the US just wants China's money (钱)—meaning a reduction of the trade deficit and a level playing field for US businesses, the problem will be easy to resolve and China appears willing to work with the US. But if the

US wants China's life (命)—meaning blockage of China's technological advance and containment of China's continued growth, as in the case of Huawei, then the two countries are on a collision course.

As protests in Hong Kong dragged on in 2019, US politicians, especially some members of Congress, became more critical of the Hong Kong government's handling of the protests and of Beijing's "one country, two systems" policy while not condemning the violence by a small group of radical protestors. It serves as a reminder that the two countries have divergent differences in political cultures and political systems. Taiwan, Tibet, Xinjiang, together with the South China Sea, are just some of the other sources of contention down the road.

Most notably, the Trump administration upgraded relations with Taiwan by enacting a series of legislation to expand US-Taiwan exchanges, over strong opposition from Beijing. The Taiwan Travel Act, for example, passed by Congress and signed into law by President Trump in March 2018, allows officials "at all levels of the United States government" to travel to Taiwan to meet their Taiwanese counterparts, and vice versa. In March 2020, when both China and the US were busy combating the novel coronavirus, President Trump signed into law the Taiwan Allies International Protection and Enhancement Initiative (TAIPEI Act) to help Taiwan maintain its fifteen remaining diplomatic allies. In Beijing's view, such legislation is clearly provocative and violates Washington's commitment to maintaining unofficial relations with Taiwan. Many observers believe that Taiwan remains the most explosive issue between the two powers and perhaps the only issue that may drag the US into war with China.

The "new normal" in US-China relations will probably include more conflicts than cooperation, but direct military confrontation remains a low likelihood. The new Chinese strategy seems to be "fight but not break" (斗而不破). In the words of Chinese Foreign Ministry spokesman Geng Shuang, China does not want to fight a trade war, but is not afraid of fighting a trade war, and if the US wants to escalate trade frictions, China will "resolutely respond and fight to the end."[17] Neither side will emerge from trade conflicts as the winner and many other countries will also be negatively affected due to the interdependent nature of the global economy today. It is imperative that the two countries find a better way to resolve their differences.

The Chinese Dream versus the American Dream

According to Xi, the Chinese Dream means to "make China prosperous and strong, rejuvenate the nation and bring happiness to the Chinese people. . . . The Chinese Dream is the dream of the country and the nation, but also of every ordinary Chinese. . . . It is a dream of peace, development, cooperation, and mutual benefit. It has many things in common with all the beautiful dreams, including the American Dream, of people all over the world."[18] Americans may not share such a rosy perspective and will continue to take China to task as long as the Chinese do not fully enjoy individual freedom.

Looking ahead, the US and China need to manage several key areas in their relations: trade (economic rivalry), Tibet and Xinjiang (human rights), Taiwan and Hong Kong (democracy and freedom), the South China Sea and North Korea (international security), and technology (future dominance). US sanctions again Huawei suggest that what the US is really concerned about is the eclipse of its technological edge by China. Indeed, according to artificial intelligence expert and venture capitalist Kai-Fu Lee, US-China competition in high tech will intensify in the years ahead.[19] Phase II trade negotiations will be more difficult as they touch on areas of competition beyond trade, including high technologies.

Both countries have changed as the global power structure shifts. The US is demonstrating signs of anxiety, insecurity, and lack of confidence; China, on the other hand, shows growing confidence, rising nationalism, and insensitivity to others. Both countries need to adjust to the changing power structure and conditions in the international system. China considers its relations with the US to be of the utmost importance in its foreign affairs. In the short term, China needs to counter the revived "China threat" discourse in Washington and to work with an unpredictable president in the White House.

The outbreak of the coronavirus in 2020 added mutual distrust to the relationship as a Chinese foreign ministry official hinted that the virus might have been brought to Wuhan by US military athletes when attending an international military game in the city in 2019 and as US officials called it "Chinese virus" or "Wuhan virus." The blame game between China and the US disappointed other countries that were expecting the two powers to play a leadership role during the global health crisis.

With the likelihood of Xi staying in power through the 2020s, Tsai Ing-wen's re-election in Taiwan in January 2020, and American politicians' now generally anti-China sentiment, the US-China relationship will enter a period of uncertainty and potential confrontation. China has had to deal with a combative and irate Trump and his hawkish aides like Peter Navarro, Mike Pompeo, and Christopher Wray. But a Democratic president may make no major difference. It is often said that these days Republicans and Democrats only agree on one thing: to be tough on China. Indeed, no matter who is in the White House, the US-China relationship will not be smooth in the years ahead.

Canada and Mexico in China's Foreign Policy

Neither Canada nor Mexico are key players on the Chinese diplomatic chessboard. Obviously, China does not treat Canada and Mexico the same way as it does the US. China's strategies toward Canada and Mexico focus on economic, social, and cultural dimensions, but the two countries could also become valuable diplomatic partners for China in its competition with the US.

Canada

The Chinese have always had a special fond feeling toward Canada, largely due to Norman Bethune, a Canadian physician who served with the Eighth Route Army during the Chinese war against Japan in the 1930s and treated wounded soldiers and villagers in Northern China. In 1970, under Prime Minister Pierre Trudeau (father of current Prime Minister Justin Trudeau), Canada became one of the first Western countries to recognize the PRC. Canada is home to a large Chinese diaspora, which affects diplomatic, cultural and other dimensions of the bilateral relationship. According to the 2016 census, Canadians of Chinese descent make up about 5 percent of the Canadian population, or about 1.76 million people.

China has been Canada's largest trading partner in Asia for many years; it is Canada's top export market and Canada's top import supplier in Asia. In March 2017, Canada officially joined the China-led AIIB, representing a diplomatic win for China and a blow to the US. All major

US allies (except Japan) became members of the new bank despite US pressures. It is in China's interest to maintain strong diplomatic, economic, and cultural ties with Canada. The recently strained relationship is hurting both countries.

According to the Spring 2017 Global Attitudes Survey by the Pew Research Center, 48 percent of Canadians had a favorable view of China, while 40 percent had a negative view. An October 2017 survey indicated that close to 70 percent of Canadians supported a free trade agreement between the two countries, in spite of concerns about the latter's growing world power and China's record on human rights.[20] However, as bilateral relations deteriorated since the end of 2018, following Huawei CFO Meng Wanzhou's arrest by Canadian authorities, the September 2019 Pew survey showed that the proportion of Canadians holding negative views of China had jumped to 67 percent.

As China expands its economic and cultural exchanges with Canada, some Canadians have become worried that the Chinese Communist Party (CCP) is turning Canada into a battleground on which it seeks to terrorize, humiliate, and neuter its opponents, grossly encroaching upon Canada's rule of law and freedom of speech. A new book by a Canadian journalist offers a detailed description of the CCP's campaign to embed agents of influence in Canadian business, politics, media, and academia. According to John Manthorpe's book *Claws of the Panda: Beijing's Campaign of Influence and Intimidation in Canada*, Canadian leaders have constantly misjudged the reality and potential of the relationship, while the CCP and its agents have benefited from Canadian naiveté.[21] Just like in the US, growing China-Canada relations and increasing Chinese activities in Canada have raised security concerns among Canadians who believe that the CCP seeks to influence Canada's domestic politics.

China-Canada relations have experienced ups and downs in the past. Most recently, they have suffered as a result of Canada's arrest of Meng Wanzhou at the request of the US government and the ensuing arrest of two Canadians by the Chinese government. Meng was arrested ostensibly for defrauding multiple financial institutions in breach of US-imposed bans on dealing with Iran, but the case highlights the US distrust of Huawei and growing technological rivalry between the US and China; it has also seriously damaged China-Canada relations. In the eyes of many Chinese, Canada acted like a sycophant of the US, following orders from Washington at the expense of its relations with China.

China swiftly took revenge in December 2018, detaining Michael Kovrig, a former Canadian diplomat and an analyst with the International Crisis Group, and Michael Spavor, a Canadian businessman who ran tours and promotes investment in North Korea. On May 16, 2019, Kovrig was formally charged with gathering state secrets while Spavor was charged with stealing and providing secrets for overseas forces. On January 14, 2019, Canadian Robert Lloyd Schellenberg had his 15-year drug smuggling prison sentence escalated to a death sentence, resulting in Canada issuing a travel warning to China on "the risk of arbitrary enforcement of local laws." China in turn issued its own travel advisory, citing "arbitrary detention" at the request of a "third-party country."[22] China also suspended pork, beef, soybean, and canola oil imports from Canada as part of the retaliation. Economic cooperation has suffered as political tensions increase between the two countries.

Canada has become embroiled in the US-China rivalry, as the Meng case suggests. In early 2019, Canada's then-ambassador to China John McCallum was quoted after Meng's detention as saying that it "would be great for Canada" if the US extradition request were dropped, conditional on release of Canadians detained in China.[23] On January 29, 2019, McCallum submitted his resignation as ambassador to China, at the request of Prime Minister Trudeau. Trudeau did not disclose the reasoning behind his decision, but it was widely believed that he was unhappy with McCallum's "politically incorrect" comment on the Meng case. The Meng case may take some time to be resolved as the US sought her extradition while China sought her release. It will be a big challenge for China and Canada to de-escalate from recent tensions in the relationship and resume normal political and economic interactions. It's obviously not in China's interest to have problematic relations with two powers in North America at the same time. It's encouraging that many Chinese businesses, including Huawei, have donated face masks and other medical supplies to Canada and the US as these countries were combating the coronavirus in 2020. When government-to-government relations are strained, such informal diplomacy often helps smooth the tensions.

Mexico

China and Mexico, which established diplomatic relations in 1972, are two large emerging economies with no territorial, historical, political or economic disputes. China is Mexico's second-largest trading partner and Mexico is China's second-largest trading partner in Latin America after Brazil. The two countries have a cooperative relationship as members of the Asia-Pacific Economic Cooperation and the G20. In 2013, the two countries upgraded their relationship into a "comprehensive strategic partnership." A statement published on the website of China's Foreign Ministry following Foreign Minister Wang Yi's October 2018 phone conversation with his Mexican counterpart Luis Videgaray said Wang described China and Mexico as "all-round strategic partners," and noted that both countries consistently supported, understood, and trusted each other on major issues.

However, in economic and trade arenas, their relationship tends to be more competitive. Both have thrived on cheap labor and the assembly of products sold to the US and other wealthy nations. Mexico is also a key port of entry for Chinese products to the US market. As both China and Mexico depend heavily on the US market, there has been an intense export rivalry, with the Mexican government having accused the Chinese of impinging on its key export territory by flooding the US with cheap goods manufactured in low-wage factories.[24] The US-China trade war and the 2019 US-Mexico-Canada (USMCA) trade agreement will have a deep impact on both China's and Mexico's exports to the US, and China-Mexico competition for the US market may intensify.

China's main policy goal toward Mexico is to seek more access to the Mexico market and widen economic cooperation and cultural exchanges. Several Chinese multinational companies operate in Mexico, including Hisense, Huawei, JAC Motors, Lenovo, and ZTE. At the same time, several Mexican multinational companies operate in China, including Gruma, Grupo Bimbo, Nemak, and Softtek.[25] The Industrial and Commercial Bank of China, the world's largest bank, began operations in Mexico in 2015, providing a platform that further facilitates trade and investment between the two countries.

China's relationship with Mexico ran into trouble briefly under President Enrique Pena Nieto. In 2014, Mexico awarded a $4.3 billion contract to a consortium led by a Chinese company for a high-speed rail line. It was cancelled three days later, just before journalists revealed that Pena Nieto's wife had agreed to buy a luxury home from a unit of another consortium member.[26] President Pena Nieto attended the Dialogue of Emerging Markets and Developing Countries on the sidelines of the BRICS summit in Xiamen, China in September 2015, meeting with President Xi to boost bilateral relations. He also penned an opinion piece titled "Stronger China Relations Underline Mexico's Look-East Policy" for the *South China Morning Post* before the visit.[27]

President Trump's aggressive policies provide a new opportunity for China and Mexico to deepen their relationship. As Mexico faces hostile immigration policies and a tariffs threat from Trump and as the US-China trade war drags on, China and Mexico are both looking to diversify exports to the US. Mexico and China agreed to bolster their economic and cultural ties under President Andres Manuel Lopez Obrador who took office in December 2018.

There is also a potential for Mexico to be part of the BRI as China expands its global reach to Latin America. The BRI did not originally include Latin America. In January 2018 China announced its plans to expand it at a meeting with the Community of Latin American and Caribbean States. Chinese loans to Latin America multiplied by more than twenty times between 2007 and 2017, and approximately 88 percent of this lending went to infrastructure projects. Of Latin America's six major markets for infrastructure (Brazil, Mexico, Colombia, Argentina, Peru, and Chile), Peru and Chile have formally signed on to the BRI so far, while the others continue to accept significant Chinese investment without formal BRI agreements.[28]

With impediments in the developed West, Chinese investment to developing countries including Mexico is likely to grow. According to Luz Maria de la Mora, Undersecretary of Foreign Trade from the Mexican Ministry of Economy, China's investment in Mexico represented a mere 1 percent of the total flow that Mexico received between 1999 to 2018, which was about US$ 1 billion. Both nations are pushing for an enlarged Chinese presence in Mexican markets.[29]

Cultural exchanges and tourism between China and Mexico are expected to increase in the years ahead as Chinese tourists and students diversify their destinations. Aeromexico, Mexico's global airline, is the only airline in Latin America that offers regular and direct flights to Chinese cities. China Southern also has direct flights linking the two countries.

As an indication of close China-Mexico relations, Mexico was one of the seventeen countries that were invited to participate in a military parade in Beijing in September 2015 that marked the seventieth anniversary of the end of the Second World War. Despite competition for the US market, China-Mexico relations have a lot of potential for further development.

Conclusions

China's overall strategy of maintaining a peaceful regional and global environment, developing a "new type of major power relationship" with the US, and strengthening economic cooperation with Canada and Mexico has largely succeeded despite recent challenges in China's relations with the US and Canada. Looking forward, whether such a strategy will continue to work depends to a great extent on whether China will fundamentally change its foreign policy and how China and the US will interact in the future. US policy toward China will also shape China's relations with all three North American countries.

According to Australian strategic expert Hugh White, the US has three choices in dealing with a rising China: it can compete, share power, or concede leadership in Asia.[30] The choice is momentous—China is already more formidable than any country the US has faced before—and if the US does not want to find itself facing China as an enemy, it may have to accept it as an equal partner. Weighing the huge difficulties of accepting China as an equal with the immense cost and risks of making it an enemy, the choice is simple, even if it is not easy. China is likely to continue to grow and its influence will continue to expand. The US simply must share power with China in Asia and co-exist with China in other parts of the world. The alternative is too dreadful to contemplate.

White's recommendation does not resonate with the prevailing mood in Washington now, where suggestions about developing a positive relationship with China are often viewed as politically incorrect. The US-China relationship has become more conflictual, reflecting deep-rooted structural problems associated with the global power transition and ideological differences. How China and the US adjust to a changing power structure and conditions in the international system and whether they can engage in a smart competition will not only define the future of their bilateral relationship but also have consequential impact on the global politics and economics of the twenty-first century.

One should not see US-China competition as a zero-sum game. So long as the US does not treat China as an enemy, the foundation for cooperation will always be present. Canada and Mexico will remain important partners in China's overall diplomacy. The main challenge for China is how to overcome difficulties, build trust, maintain friendly relations, and promote economic, social, and cultural exchanges with these countries.

While its bilateral relations with the three North American countries are important to handle, China must continue to promote multilateral cooperation in dealing with global challenges. Indeed, in this highly interdependent world, isolation and retreat from globalization are not the right answers to global problems. The COVID-19 pandemic that ravaged the world in 2020 is yet another example of why multilateral cooperation is critical in addressing global challenges.

NOTES

1 "王毅谈新时代中国特色大国外交总目标：推动构建人类命运共同体."
2 "China's National Defense in the New Era."
3 "China and the World in the New Era."
4 According to the official BRI website, by the end of January 2020, China had signed 200 documents for BRI cooperation with 138 countries and thirty international organizations. See "已同中国签订共建 "一带一路" 合作文件的国家一览."
5 "Mexico and China Can Be Stronger Together."
6 "Le Yucheng."
7 For example, in a joint press conference during President Donald Trump's visit to China on November 9, 2017, President Xi Jinping remarked: "The Pacific Ocean is big enough to accommodate both China and the United States. The two sides need to step up communication and cooperation on Asia Pacific affairs, foster common friends, build constructive interactions, and jointly maintain and promote peace and stability and prosperity in the region." See "Remarks by President Trump and President Xi of China in Joint Press Statement | Beijing."
8 Pillsbury, *Hundred-Year Marathon*.
9 Araya, "China's Grand Strategy."
10 Capaccio, "US Faces 'Unprecedented Threat' from China on Tech Takeover."

11 Tunsjø, *The Return of Bipolarity in World Politics*.
12 "Q&A: China has 'No Interest in Global Domination.'"
13 Pence, "Remarks by Vice President Pence at the Frederic V. Malek Memorial Lecture."
14 Vanderklippe, "Munk Debates."
15 "National Security Strategy of the United States of America."
16 Pei, "Is Trump's Trade War with China a Civilizational Conflict?"
17 Quoted in Huang and Jeong-ho, "US Wanted to 'Rewrite China's Laws' for Deal."
18 Jinping, *Governance of China*.
19 Kai-fu, *AI Superpowers*.
20 Smith, "More than Two Thirds of Canadians Support a Free Trade Deal with China."
21 Manthorpe, *Claws of the Panda*.
22 "China Issues Travel Advisory for Canada after 'Arbitrary Detention' of Chinese National."
23 "McCallum Says Dropping Meng Extradition Would Be 'Great' for Canada."
24 "Flu Spat Cools Budding Mexico-China Relationship."
25 "Relación Económica."
26 Martin, "China and Mexico Lay Out Broad Plans to Strengthen Relations."
27 Nieto, "Stronger China Relations Underline Mexico's Look-East Policy."
28 Dabus, Basu, and Yao, "China's Belt and Road Reaches Latin America."
29 "Mexico and China Can Be Stronger Together."
30 White, *The China Choice*.

BIBLIOGRAPHY

Araya, Daniel. "China's Grand Strategy." *Forbes*, January 14, 2019. www.forbes.com.
Buckley, Chris. "Xi Jinping Thought Explained: A New Ideology for a New Era." *The New York Times*, February 26, 2018. www.nytimes.com.
Capaccio, Anthony. "US Faces 'Unprecedented Threat' From China on Tech Takeover." *Bloomberg*, June 22, 2018. www.bloomberg.com.
Carey, Glen, and Philip Heijmans. "Singapore Urges U.S. to Accept China's Rise, Spare Other Nations." *Bloomberg*, May 16, 2019. www.bloomberg.com.
"China and the World in the New Era." The State Council Information Office of the People's Republic of China. Updated September 27, 2019. http://english.www.gov.cn.
"China Issues Travel Advisory for Canada after 'Arbitrary Detention' of Chinese National." Reuters. January 15, 2019. www.reuters.com.
"China's National Defense in the New Era." The State Council Information Office of the People's Republic of China. Updated July 24, 2019. http://english.www.gov.cn.
Dabus, Andre, Meghna Basu, and Leon Yao. "China's Belt and Road Reaches Latin America." *Brinknews*, May 27, 2019. www.brinknews.com.
Danner, Lukas. *China's Grand Strategy: Contradictory Foreign Policy?* New York: Palgrave Macmillan, 2018.
Denoon, David, ed. *China, the U.S. and the Future of Latin America*. New York, NY: New York University Press, 2017.

Economy, Elizabeth C. *The Third Revolution: Xi Jinping and the New Chinese State*. Oxford: Oxford University Press, 2018.

"Flu Spat Cools Budding Mexico-China Relationship." Reuters. May 4, 2009. www.reuters.com.

Friedman, Uri. "America Is Alone in Its Cold War with China." *Atlantic*, February 17, 2020. www.theatlantic.com.

Gan, Nectar, and Owen Churchill. "FBI Director Christopher Wray Making His Mark as a Loud and Insistent China Critic." *South China Morning Post*, May 3, 2019. www.scmp.com.

Gehrke, Joel. "State Department Preparing for Clash of Civilizations with China." *Washington Examiner*, April 30, 2019. www.washingtonexaminer.com.

Huang, Kristin, and Lee Jeong-ho. "US Wanted to 'Rewrite China's Laws' for Deal." *South China Morning Post*, June 12, 2019.

Johnston, Alastair Iain. "The Failures of the 'Failure of Engagement' with China." *Washington Quarterly* 42, no. 2 (Summer 2019): 99–114.

Kashmeri, Sarwar A. *China's Grand Strategy: Weaving a New Silk Road to Global Primacy*. Santa Barbara, CA: Praeger, 2019.

Khan, Sulmaan Wasif. *Haunted by Chaos: China's Grand Strategy from Mao Zedong to Xi Jinping*. Cambridge, MA: Harvard University Press, 2018.

Le Corre, Philippe, "Addressing China's Global Strategy." Carnegie Endowment for International Peace, April 10, 2019. https://carnegieendowment.org.

"Le Yucheng: China Has No Interest in Hegemony or Power Games." Ministry of Foreign Affairs of the People's Republic of China, October 24, 2019. www.fmprc.gov.cn.

Lee, Kai-Fu. *AI Superpowers: China, Silicon Valley, and the New World Order*. Boston, MA: Houghton Mifflin Harcourt, 2018.

Li, Cheng, and Lucy Xu. "Chinese Enthusiasm and American Cynicism Over the 'New Type of Great Power Relations'." Brookings Institution, December 4, 2014. www.brookings.edu

Lyle J. Goldstein. *Meeting China Halfway: How to Defuse the Emerging US-China Rivalry*. Washington, DC: Georgetown University Press, 2015.

Maçães, Bruno. *Belt and Road: A Chinese World Order*. London: Hurst, 2019.

Manthorpe, John. *Claws of the Panda: Beijing's Campaign of Influence and Intimidation in Canada*. Toronto: Cormorant Books, 2019.

Martin, Eric. "China and Mexico Lay Out Broad Plans to Strengthen Relations." Bloomberg. July 2, 2019. www.bloomberg.com.

"McCallum Says Dropping Meng Extradition Would Be "Great" for Canada: Report." *Canadian Press*, January 23, 2019. www.ctvnews.ca.

"Mexico and China Can Be Stronger Together: Mexican Gov't." *Belt & Road News*, June 7, 2019. www.beltandroad.news.

"National Security Strategy of the United States of America." The White House. December 2017. www.whitehouse.gov.

Nieto, Enrique Pena. "Stronger China Relations Underline Mexico's Look-East Policy." *South China Morning Post*, September 5, 2017. www.scmp.com.

Office of the Leading Group for Promoting the Belt and Road Initiative. *The Belt and Road Initiative Progress, Contribution and Prospects.* Beijing: Foreign Language Press, 2019. www.beltandroad.news.

Pei, Minxin. "Is Trump's Trade War with China a Civilizational Conflict?" *Project Syndicate*, May 14, 2019. www.project-syndicate.org.

Pence, Mike. "Remarks by Vice President Pence at the Frederic V. Malek Memorial Lecture." The White House. October 24, 2019. www.whitehouse.gov.

Pillsbury, Michael. *The Hundred-Year Marathon: China's Secret Strategy to Replace America as the Global Superpower.* New York: Henry Holt, 2015.

"Q&A: China Has 'No Interest in Global Domination.'" *USA Today*, January 29, 2018. www.usatoday.com.

"Relación Económica" [Economic Relationship]. Embassy of Mexico in China. Accessed May 17, 2019. https://embamex.sre.gob.mx.

"Remarks by President Trump and President Xi of China in Joint Press Statement | Beijing." US Embassy and Consulates in China, November 9, 2017. https://china.usembassy-china.org.cn.

Roach, Stephen. "America's False Narrative on China." *Project Syndicate*, April 26, 2019. www.project-syndicate.org.

Rubio, Luis. "On Mexico-China Relations." Pacific Council on International Policy, September 27, 2018. www.pacificcouncil.org.

Sands, Christopher. "China Testing Trump in Canada." CSIS, February 1, 2019. https://www.csis.org/analysis/china-testing-trump-canada.

Smith, Marie-Danielle. "More than Two Thirds of Canadians Support a Free Trade Deal with China." *National Post*, October 23, 2017. https://nationalpost.com.

Tunsjø, Øystein. *The Return of Bipolarity in World Politics: China, the United States, and Geostructural Realism.* New York: Columbia University Press, 2018.

Vanderklippe, Nathan. "Munk Debates: Former UN Security Council President Kishore Mahbubani Details Why China Stands to Lose If Rules-Based Order Evaporates." *Globe and Mail*, May 8, 2019. www.theglobeandmail.com.

White, Hugh. *The China Choice: Why America Should Share Power?* Carlton, Australia: Black Inc. 2013.

Xi, Jinping. *The Governance of China.* Beijing: Foreign Languages Press, 2014.

Xu, Yanran. *China's Strategic Partnerships in Latin America: Case Studies of China's Oil Diplomacy in Argentina, Brazil, Mexico, and Venezuela, 1991–2015.* Lanham, MD: Lexington Books, 2016.

Zhong, Feiteng. "China's Grand Strategy in a New Era." *East Asia Forum*, March 5, 2018. https://www.eastasiaforum.org.

Zhu, Zhiqun. "An Insecure America and An Assertive China." *The Hill*, March 27, 2020. https://thehill.com.

"已同中国签订共建"一带一路"合作文件的国家一览" [List of Countries that Have Signed Cooperation Documents with China on the Belt and Road Initiative]. The website of Belt and Road Portal. Accessed on February 20, 2020. www.yidaiyilu.gov.cn.

"王毅谈新时代中国特色大国外交总目标：推动构建人类命运共同体" [Wang Yi on the Overall Objective of Big Power Diplomacy with Chinese Characteristics: Promoting Formation of a Community of Shared Future for Mankind]. Ministry of Foreign Affairs of the People's Republic of China. October 19, 2017. www.fmprc .gov.cn.

Conclusion

DAVID B. H. DENOON

Is there a concise statement of China's grand strategy that guides all major Chinese policies? We don't know if one exists, but there is enough coherence in China's major foreign policy initiatives that we can assume there is at least agreement among the top leadership on the basic directions of policy.

How Do We Know Whether There Is Agreement on Basic Objectives?

We know this because each of the major elements of national policy fit together for the purpose of enhancing Chinese power and influence. In this volume, we have divided policy into three functional categories (military, economic and scientific, and diplomatic). There is little doubt that the Chinese try to integrate these elements when seeking objectives like GDP growth, power projection, and undermining the influence of outside powers.

What Are the Key Features of China's Grand Strategy?

First and foremost, China intends to become the preeminent global power and has set a target date of 2049 for achieving that goal. The Chinese leadership does not think war is necessary to attain preeminence, but coercion and limited forms of force are considered acceptable means to that end. Beijing's leaders think steady, incremental improvements in military, economic, and scientific capabilities will present most potential challengers with a *fait accompli*. At present, the United States can match China in each of these functional areas, but Beijing is counting on the US losing resilience over time and being unwilling to sustain the rivalry indefinitely.

If China could become preeminent without a military conflict, that would be its preferred outcome. Yet isolating weaker states and presenting them with overwhelming force is China's standard approach. This tactic has been used with the Association of Southeast Asian Nations (ASEAN) states for dealing with territorial disputes in the South China Sea. If coercion doesn't work, however, China is willing to prosecute limited wars, as it did with India in 1962 and with Vietnam in 1979. Since war with the US risks escalation to a major conflict, China will, initially, just seek concessions from Washington as acknowledgement of its growing stature.

As long as China has a rapidly growing economy and can devote ample resources to challenging its competitors, the Chinese intend to present their opponents with "an opportunity they cannot refuse." Hence, the gradual accretion of Chinese power and influence is designed to get former challengers to accept a subordinate status.

Can China's Strategy Be Plausibly Implemented?

The Chinese grand strategy requires a buoyant economy for a sustained period of several more decades, the hesitancy of smaller powers to challenge Beijing's plans, and the unwillingness or inability of other major powers to form an effective balancing coalition.

In the two decades since China joined the World Trade Organization, Japan, South Korea, the European Union, and many in the US have been unwilling to counter China's rise. If that pattern continues for another two decades, it would require a massive "catch-up" effort on their part to form an effective balancing coalition against China. That is the situation China hopes to create.

A coalition of Japan, South Korea, India, Australia, the European Union, and the US would be economically and technologically capable of counterbalancing China. The question is whether these states have the political will to make that happen.

What Are the Odds That China Can Implement Its Strategy?

The Chinese grand strategy requires that its economy continue to grow rapidly and steadily. China's economy is now slowing considerably from a 7 to 8 percent annual rate to one of 5 to 6 percent, and, according to the International Monetary Fund, it is probably slowing to 1 to 2 percent in 2020 due to the global recession. Thus, Beijing will need to focus on developing new internal sources of economic dynamism and find policy measures to ensure consistent, steady growth.

The current political leadership is counting on continuing an authoritarian political system. If there is any major internal challenge to that political model, economic growth will be disrupted and China's aspirations for supremacy will be postponed. Nevertheless, China's military position of rising strength can be maintained as long as growth is not completely interrupted.

The essence of China's grand strategy is thus a steady rise to prominence with a commitment to maintaining both a high growth profile and internal political restraints. Only an internal political upheaval or a major interruption of economic growth would derail this strategy.

Northeast Asia

This is the most critical and complex region for China's strategy. Japan and South Korea are potential adversaries if they stay allied with the US. Russia is a sometime ally but could just as easily become an opponent, and North Korea is a troublesome ally but ever willing to abandon China if it could strike a security deal with the US.

For China, the ideal arrangements in Northeast Asia are secure alliances with Russia and North Korea and enough friction in the US ties with South Korea and Japan to give Beijing room to offer various inducements for its neighbors to weaken links with Washington. Russia and North Korea are by no means certain allies for China, but they are "allies of convenience" who are more likely to side with Beijing than with the Western countries.

Western Pacific

China's ambition to encircle and eventually absorb Taiwan makes the Western Pacific a vital and diplomatically delicate sub-region. At the moment, China's focus is on broadening its ties east of Taiwan, as in the Solomon Islands. If China were to succeed at broadening its influence in the Western Pacific, then, in the longer-run future, it might be able to cut off US access to Taiwan. The question would then become: how would the US and Taiwanese public respond?

Southeast Asia

China's goal in Southeast Asia is to maintain and enhance its links with the "northern tier" countries in the region (Myanmar, Laos, Cambodia, Thailand), to isolate Vietnam, and to keep Singapore, Malaysia, and Indonesia from allying with the US. Since most of China's imported oil still moves through the Strait of Malacca, China cannot afford to openly antagonize Malaysia, Singapore, or Indonesia. Beijing is thus using its Belt and Road Initiative (BRI) funds as an inducement for closer ties with Malaysia and Indonesia.[1] Since ASEAN has not been successful at creating a tightly integrated political or security grouping, all China needs to do is to keep the friction going within the region so that it can deal with individual ASEAN countries and prevent any potential group from counterbalancing Chinese influence.

South Asia

Other than Russia and Japan, India is the only country in Asia that could potentially pose a strategic challenge to China. At present India's GDP is only about one third of China's and India is avoiding directly taking its northern neighbor on. Yet New Delhi sends out a relatively steady set of signals to Beijing that it is not part of China's orbit. India is tenacious, for example, in defending its northern border claims; repeatedly opposes China's massive aid program to Pakistan (the China-Pakistan Economic Corridor, CPEC), refuses to join the BRI, and has withdrawn from the negotiations to create a trade pact among Asian states (the RCEP). These are low-key but clear indications by India that it intends to maintain an independent foreign policy and that it does not welcome Chinese influence in South Asia.[2]

Nevertheless, China is proceeding rapidly with attempts to encircle India by forging military and economic ties to its direct neighbors. The Chinese funds committed are substantial: $62 billion for CPEC plus a major port and military complex on Gwadar Island for Pakistan; debt write-offs for Sri Lanka in the Hambantota port complex; major port improvements for Dacca in Bangladesh, and a new commitment to build a tunnel through the Himalayas to connect Nepal to China. India views all of these Chinese initiatives as malign and will certainly do what it can to weaken Chinese influence in South Asia.

Central Asia

China and Russia compete for influence in Central Asia. Although China has the upper hand on economic issues, Russia still has very close security ties with most of the Central Asian states. Central Asian elites still go to Russia for higher education; the Russian intelligence and security services have widespread influence; and family ties are close as there is continuing inter-marriage between Central Asians and Russians. Since the Central Asian states are predominantly Muslim and China does not want additional sectarian problems (beyond its current issues in Xinjiang), Beijing has been content to let Russia take the lead on security concerns in Central Asia.

If there were to be political turmoil or religious friction emanating from Central Asia, China would have to decide whether to intervene. For example, if NATO forces permanently leave Afghanistan and greater violence results, China may choose to act, particularly to prevent India from developing a sphere of influence there.

Europe

The EU is the area of the globe where China has its greatest concentration of foreign investment and the leadership in Beijing has made a major play for influence there. BRI projects have been approved in Greece and Italy, and China is actively looking to expand investments in Eastern Europe. However, the EU has a strong commitment to human rights advocacy and this is a source of friction with China, particularly with the protest movement in Hong Kong. Nevertheless, commercial ties are very extensive between the EU and China and neither side wants to lose the trade and investment links.

Russia

China's most important potential ally is Russia. The two countries have a long mutual border, a complicated history of both alliance and friction, and, at present, both are in a tense relationship with the US. If Moscow and Beijing could agree on coordinating policy, that would be a troubling development for Washington. If China and Russia were to go further and recreate their alliance of the 1950s, that would be a very adverse development for the US. The prior history of friction between Russia and China makes a close alliance unlikely, however.

If Russia had not invaded Crimea and did not have troops and special forces in Eastern Ukraine, the West might be able to form some kind of entente with Moscow that could be used to balance China. Yet, because President Putin is unwilling to compromise on Russia's recent ventures, it is engaged in a stand-off with the West that is driving Russia and China together. This means that, on a number of issues (Libya, Iraq, Syria, Iran, and UN governance) China is siding with Russia, which makes it harder to achieve Sino-Western cooperation.

The United States

China's ties with the US are its single most important relationship. Yet, in the past eighteen months, friction over trade and investment issues (discussed in Chapter 3) has been so severe that neither state has been willing to compromise on other issues. We thus see a widening gap between Washington and Beijing plus the possibility of further tension ahead. If protests in Hong Kong continue after the COVID-19 crisis is over, and if the Democratic Progressive Party's win in the January 2020 Taiwan presidential elections leads to a more outspoken Taiwanese government, Beijing's leaders may think their aspirations for consolidating their hold on the region are at risk. Moreover, if the US were to make progress in negotiations with North Korea, China would see this as a sign of further erosion of its sphere of influence in Northeast Asia. In the end, although many trends favor China's expansion of power and influence, it is worth noting that China has some important vulnerabilities close to home.

Factors that Could Fundamentally Alter the Strategic Balance between China and the United States

Most of the discussion in this chapter has assumed that the US has both an economic and military advantage over China. The US economy is substantially larger and more diverse, and the US military is more versatile and capable of projecting power in more parts of the world. Yet, because the US has chosen to allow tight integration of the two economies, it would be costly and disruptive for the US to continue to impose tariffs or sanctions on China to change Beijing's behavior.

Similarly, in the military arena, though the US probably has "escalation dominance"—meaning that it could impose unacceptable costs on China if war breaks out between the two states, Beijing has enough retaliatory ability to inflict unacceptable costs on the US, as well. As the 2019–20 "trade war" has proceeded, China has incurred the greater costs, but the US has also suffered. Fortunately, both states have refrained from the use of force.

China and the US are thus both capable of inflicting considerable harm on each other, but neither state can be confident of being able to impose its will on the other. Although the US has certain key advantages over China, it must be mindful of China's retaliatory capability and the interaction between the two can best be described as a series of jousts where neither side always wins.

Nevertheless, there are many fast-changing arenas in which the US and China compete and there is a possibility of a breakthrough that would fundamentally change the strategic balance between them. Several areas of competition and potential developments that warrant our attention are: (1) internet development, (2) applications of artificial intelligence, (3) a possible "decoupling" of the two economies, (4) China's efforts to sway public opinion inside the US, and (5) China's efforts at shaping international institutions.

Internet Development

For the past three decades, the US has been the unquestioned world leader in internet development. The US has led in hardware, software, and conceptual design for almost all major areas of internet evolution.

This has meant that US firms designed and supervised the manufacture of most of the key internet advances. Hence, US firms have led in chip design (Intel, AMD), chip equipment manufacturing (Micron Technology), software development (Microsoft) internet search (Google), internet advertising (Facebook), and internet marketing (Amazon).[3]

In the past decade, however, China has caught up: Alibaba is now bigger than Amazon; Weibo and Wechat are bigger than several of the US messaging firms, and Baidu completely dominates the search market inside China. Now, with the rapid acceptance of Tik Tok in Western countries, China is beginning to be a formidable competitor in the messaging and image transferring fields.[4]

Since the Chinese government controls and tightly censors its internet, there is at least the possibility that Beijing may be able to impose its standards and protocols on countries that use its internet products. As it appears that Huawei's Fifth Generation telecommunications equipment is ahead of that produced by American firms, countries are now having to make a choice about whether to use Chinese or American equipment.

The US government is trying to convince other countries to avoid using Huawei's Fifth Generation equipment on the grounds that Chinese intelligence may gain access through Huawei's products. The US has forbidden American telecommunications firms (except in under-served rural areas) to use Huawei's routers and switches. Yet Huawei claims it intends to provide Fifth Generation equipment to 480 million households in the next five years.[5] The market for these products is enormous.

Because the Chinese government is subsidizing the cost of Huawei equipment, many countries may select Huawei as their telecom vendor. Not only would this facilitate Chinese access to massive amounts of consumer information but it may also allow China to impose its technical protocols on millions of users. This could split the global internet into two systems: American and Chinese.[6]

Artificial Intelligence

Like the internet, the US has led in artificial intelligence (AI) development for the past three decades, but China is rapidly catching up. Because China is an authoritarian state willing to coerce its own citizens, major expenditures have been made by the government to develop facial recognition software. China now has a functioning AI system that can recognize hundreds of millions of its citizens. This technical capacity is linked with a "social credit" monitoring system that keeps records on all citizens, noting whether they pay their taxes, have good credit ratings, have any criminal records, and whether they participate in activities that support the Chinese Communist Party (CCP).

This effort to develop a comprehensive facial recognition system has stimulated Chinese research and development efforts in other areas of AI. Robotics, computer monitoring of manufacturing, autonomous driving, language translation, and pharmaceutical research are all areas where China is making significant advances in AI.[7] In addition, the Chinese government has used national identity cards to monitor its citizens during the COVID-19 pandemic.

Like the progress in internet development, AI research has applications in both the commercial and military arenas. Capabilities for real-time identification, improved targeting, and assorted types of cyber attacks can all be used to address China's desire to challenge the US.[8]

Decoupling

In addition to China's own research and development efforts, there are three ways that China can acquire foreign technology: (1) direct purchases, (2) requiring foreign firms to give up their technology as the price for entering he Chinese market, and (3) through theft. Sadly, much of China's technology acquisition has been accomplished by either coercion or theft. Specialists in this area estimate that the technology that China has stolen is worth billions of dollars per year.[9]

This raises the question: should the US limit its interaction with China in critical high-tech fields?[10] The Trump administration has already argued that American multinational corporations should reduce manufacturing in China and move their operations to other countries or bring them back to the continental US. Obviously, this would raise the costs of manufacturing, but it could help the US regain control over its technology. Some American multinationals have already begun the process of moving their operations out of China to lower cost locations (notably Vietnam).

Nevertheless, a widespread American shift of manufacturing out of China or a ban on Sino-US high-tech transactions would affect hundreds of billions of current US investment. This may be the only definitive solution to the "technology coercion or theft" problem, but it is an extremely costly one.[11] If the "Phase Two" US-China trade negotiations (the ones following the 2020 round) are successful in resolving deep structural issues, decoupling may be unnecessary. Yet it may occur anyway as a result of normal business decision making as corporations decide that manufacturing in China is just too complex and yields insufficient returns.

Public Diplomacy

As noted in Chapter 3, in the past decade China has made a major effort to influence public opinion in Western countries. This has included programs to shape university faculties, students, think tanks, and the Western press. Dozens of Confucius Institutes have been set up to teach Chinese language skills and to promote Beijing's position on various foreign policy issues. Similarly, Chinese intelligence operatives pay frequent calls on opinion makers in the West to make sure that Beijing's stance is well understood.[12]

Shaping International Institutions

China has also made a sophisticated attempt to promote its interests through: (1) influencing current international organizations and (2) creating new institutions that it controls. For example, it was only after the World Health Organization had put out misleading information on COVID-19 that it became clear that China had used its influence to help select a director who would follow Beijing's line. In addition to influencing current international organizations, China has also set up a range of institutions that it completely controls, like the New Development Bank and the Asian Infrastructure Investment Bank. The US followed a similar pattern after the Second World War but, recently, has been slow to recognize that China has gained a great deal of political favor by creating new institutions outside of Western control.

Aspects of the COVID-19 Controversy

As COVID-19 spread from Wuhan to the rest of China and then to the rest of the world, China's international status has been seriously damaged. As the crisis developed, the reaction of the Chinese government leadership was particularly distressing and counterproductive. Its first move, in November and December 2019, was to attempt to cut off discussion of the issue entirely.[13] Doctors in Wuhan were reporting a new kind of pneumonia, but government authorities censored them and threatened them with penalties if they continued discussing their findings. The Wuhan government did this despite the country having an emergency disease reporting system.[14] One especially brave physician, Dr. Li Wenliang, continued to comment. He was summoned to the Public Security Bureau and forced to retract his comments and required to do self-criticism. Dr. LI continued to treat his patients, and, sadly, died from the effects of COVID-19. When the Chinese public found out the details of Dr. Li's experience, there was widespread criticism of the CCP leadership inside China.

Between November 17, 2019, when the first COVID-19 case appeared in Hubei province and January 23, 2020, when the government declared a lockdown on the city of Wuhan, government authorities failed to alert the public or other countries to the problem. This meant that several million workers left Wuhan to return home for Lunar New Year celebrations and tens of thousands of Chinese tourists traveled overseas, including to the US and Europe. This enabled the virus to spread worldwide before most people even knew about the problem. In a further questionable act, the Chinese Foreign Ministry Spokesman Zhao Lijian implied, on March 14, 2020, without any evidence, that, "It might be that the US Army brought the epidemic to Wuhan."[15] Zhao further commented, "No conclusion has been reached yet on the origins of the virus." Zhao did not acknowledge that the Wuhan government had forced scientists to destroy early samples of the virus and had refused offers of foreign epidemiologists to come to Wuhan to help analyze its origins.

Since then the Chinese government has begun a global effort to portray its actions regarding COVID-19 in a positive light. China has sent surgical masks to Japan and offered various medical supplies to Serbia and Italy.[16] China has also been criticized for supplying faulty virus test kits to Spain and Italy.

Since then, the US government has openly referred to COVID-19 as the "Wuhan virus" and has repeatedly called for the Chinese government to permit outside researchers to examine on-site evidence regarding the spread of the virus. The state of Missouri has even passed a bill to strip China of its "sovereign immunity" and make it subject to litigation over its failure to warn other nations about COVID-19's contagiousness. It is obvious that intensive sparring has begun between China and the US regarding responsibility for the current epidemic. We now turn to the effects of the pandemic and other recent issues on China's long-term strategy.[17]

The Deteriorating US-China Relationship

Negotiating Change in the Trade Sector

The Phase I Agreement signed on January 15, 2020 between the US and China has essentially three parts: (1) a Chinese commitment to increase purchases of US goods and energy products by $200 billion over 2017 levels, (2) a Chinese pledge to change its business regulations, which often push US firms to surrender technology and form joint ventures with local firms as the price for access to the Chinese market, and (3) an agreement by Chinese central bankers to be more open about their interventions in currency markets.[18]

The positive aspects of the agreement, from a US perspective, are that there are specific quantitative targets for increasing Chinese purchases of US goods and energy. It is also important to get China on record indicating that it will quit coercing American firms into giving up their technology to gain entry to the Chinese market. Transparency in its currency market sales and purchases is useful for understanding Chinese monetary policy, but the real question is whether the information will be available in a timely and accurate manner. Similarly, China has made many previous pledges to open its economy but has rarely followed through on those commitments. Many economists thus see the Phase I Agreement as going beyond past negotiations but still not having enforceable penalties if it is not complied with.

Moreover, now that the COVID-19 pandemic is leading to a major contraction of economic activity across the globe, the Chinese government is likely to claim it cannot be expected to fulfill its commitments because the entire macroeconomic environment has changed since January 2020. For example, if Chinese citizens are not allowed to travel to the US for health reasons, it will be much harder to negotiate any complex trade deals, especially if new firms, new individuals, and new terms are involved.

Decoupling and Reconfiguring Supply Chains

It came as a shock to the American public, during the COVID-19 crisis, to learn that most of the antibiotics used in the US are fabricated in China. US researchers did the original research, identified the ingredients, tested their effectiveness, and determined the dosages required for different circumstances. But the final preparation of the capsules and pills is now mostly done in China. Some policy makers in China have also suggested that Beijing might limit the export of certain antibiotics if there were shortages inside China. Americans have thus realized that, despite having developed these medicines, control of manufacturing in China might mean that adequate supplies in the US are not guaranteed.[19] Similar issues have arisen regarding Chinese supplies of computers, electronic parts, and semiconductors.

The possibility of supply interruptions has made both businessmen and policy makers newly sensitive to China's power over the US market. Basically, there are two ways to remedy the situation: (1) having government guarantee the purchase of a fixed amount of key items that are made in the US so that companies can justify the higher cost of producing here, or (2) establishing and constantly updating stockpiles of essential items. Domestic manufacturing is, in many ways, preferable because it maintains the expertise and domestic supply lines to keep the US ready to surge production if necessary. Nevertheless, protected domestic manufacturing is often, in the long-run, more expensive. We can anticipate significant debates on this topic in the coming years.

On their own, private firms will also have to decide whether they want to retain their current heavy reliance on China as a location for supply chains. Obviously, China was selected as a location for manufacturing because of its good infrastructure, reasonable wages, and low taxation. Moreover, once established there, a foreign firm could use its presence and contacts to attempt to sell into the local market. However, if political factors are going to interrupt the movement of product, the current process of "decoupling" from China will accelerate.[20]

Global Order Issues

For most of the period between the beginning of Deng Xiaoping's reforms (in 1979) and today, American policy makers have assumed that China would gradually adapt to Western norms in the international economic and security realms. This has partially happened in economic policy, but it is increasingly clear that China intends to preserve major mercantilistic features of its economy and that Beijing plans on having its own zone of influence in defense and security policy.[21]

The COVID-19 pandemic has highlighted the contrast between Western and Chinese styles of handling crises and gives us a perspective on how different the two spheres of influence are. Chinese decision making is highly centralized, authoritarian and secretive, while Western styles are more open and collaborative.

It is not preordained, but it is now highly likely that China will not, in the foreseeable future, fully open its economy as Western governments had hoped. In addition, it now appears that China will establish a separate sphere of influence that directly challenges the security environment created by the US after the Second World War. We may therefore be at a stage in international development where the economic and security systems that China favors diverge sharply from Western preferences. The COVID-19 crisis may thus provide a prism through which deep structural differences are made apparent.[22]

If so, then the West needs to recognize that heightened rather than reduced competition may be the norm in both the economic and security arenas. Hence, trying to convince China to follow Western standards and offering incentives for Beijing to do so may be a wasted effort. The West does not need to continue its accommodation to China, but it does need to accept that the vision of a unified, liberal global order is not attainable at present.

A divided world is thus the most likely outcome. We now turn to the final question: will China be strong enough and skillful enough to impose its vision on the rest of the world?

Will China Be Able to Implement Its Grand Strategy?

There are three key arenas where China will need to excel and eclipse the US if it is to become the preeminent global leader: (1) economic performance, (2) military capability, and (3) instilling confidence in potential allies.

Economic performance is the area where China is most likely to succeed. For four decades China has maintained an impressive economic growth rate. Despite a rapidly aging population, a bureaucratic state-owned enterprise sector, and mounting debt, China has been able to overcome many obstacles, including the 2008–09 global recession.

The engine for the transformation of the Chinese economy has been the foreign sector. Soaring exports have been a source of foreign exchange and, along with foreign direct investment, have enabled the purchase of up-to-date technology. Additionally, low tariffs on imported raw materials and intermediate goods have been a stimulus to low-cost production. Those factors, combined with moderate wages and good transport infrastructure have made China a very attractive location for manufacturing. This has made it possible for China to move, in one generation, from obscurity to being the world's largest manufactured goods exporting state.

The leadership in Beijing has recognized that it cannot rely indefinitely on foreign investment and trade to power its economy. In response, it has made major efforts to shift growth away from manufacturing and foreign markets toward the service sector and domestic sources of growth. Nevertheless, state-owned enterprises are still the source of employment for millions of citizens and are the safety net for job placement of Communist Party family members. A rapid reduction of the foreign sector or of state-owned enterprises thus poses dangers for China's leadership.

The most conspicuous uncertainty in the economic picture is how far "decoupling" will go. Over the past few years, China has already faced a gradual loss of interest from foreign investors because of its rising wages, but the trauma of the COVID-19 crisis will certainly accelerate the movement out of many firms. The Japanese government has set up a $2.2 billion fund to help its corporations shift operations out of China, and President Trump's economic advisor, Lawrence Kudlow, has urged that the US pay moving costs for companies willing to shift operations out of China back to the US.[23]

Decoupling is an expensive and time-consuming process, so it may take several years for the actual corporate moves to take place. However, if companies are willing to consider moving out of China, then it is reasonable to expect that new inflows of foreign direct investment will be affected soon, as well.[24] Nevertheless, China's overall economic scene is still impressive. The skill levels of the workforce are high, savings rates are high, and productivity and GDP are still forecast to rise even with a global recession underway.

Military and technological superiority are essential for China to achieve global leadership. Five years ago, it would have appeared fanciful to talk about China eclipsing the US in military technology and power projection. It is still not likely to happen anytime soon. But the idea is no longer just conjecture. In the past decade, China has made enormous strides in military and high-end technological development.[25]

China now has equal capabilities or has surpassed the US in artificial intelligence, super-computing, quantum computing, and Fifth Generation telecommunications technology. Moreover, Beijing is now willing to intervene militarily in disputes, like those in the South China Sea, which it tended to avoid in the period of Deng Xiaoping's leadership.[26] In addition, China is now willing to set up overseas bases in locations like Cambodia and Djibouti, which it eschewed a decade ago.[27]

The combination of technical prowess and willingness to project power mean that China is already in a position to challenge the US in certain parts of the globe. If these trends continue, China could doubtless challenge the US in a growing number of continents. Yet to be a true global leader, China would need to have committed allies in vital locations around the world. We thus now turn to the issue of how likely it is that China can develop a reliable set of allies.

The key element in creating allies is instilling confidence.[28] The BRI has been an enormous step forward for China. Though, obviously, the loans and grants made through the BRI are meant to benefit China, the program has also created vital infrastructure in the recipient countries. From the standpoint of China's global stature, the BRI has been critical because it shows that Beijing has an overarching plan for its global role.

The BRI links China with countries in every continent at the construction stage, through commitments of future investment, and finally through the trade that is likely to result. Therefore, if one assesses China's conception of the BRI itself and the related funding operations in the New Bank and the Asian Infrastructure Investment Bank, one would have to see it as an impressive achievement.[29]

The problem for China's global ambitions is that Beijing has nothing comparable in the security realm to match the BRI in the economic arena. For the first sixty years of its existence, China proclaimed that it would not station troops overseas and that it would not be a hegemonic power. Now it has begun the process of setting up overseas military outposts and clearly exerts dominant influence over many of its closest neighbors.

China has some major decisions ahead. What will Beijing do when the NATO forces leave Afghanistan? What will Chinese authorities do with the hundreds of thousands of Uighurs currently detained in Xinjiang? Will China continue to expand its influence in Pakistan? Would China support Pakistan in a confrontation with India? Will China be able to keep up its current close relationship with Russia if there are differences between Beijing and Moscow over Central Asia?

There are two intangible but significant issues that will affect China's ability to form alliances in its pursuit of global leadership: (1) the extent to which Beijing can inspire trust in other states, and (2) whether there are enough countries that share China's values to form a strong network of allies.[30]

China has been remarkably effective at promoting the "Beijing Model" of economic development. It has stressed that centrally directed, authoritarian political rule can work with market-oriented economies. Many leaders in other states, however, wonder whether China truly intends to let its allies pursue their own objectives or if the Beijing Model is just an excuse for imposing its will on allies. This is where trust and values become important. When outsiders look at the way Uighurs are treated in Xinjiang, the harsh rule in Tibet, and the frequent threats from the People's Liberation Army against Taiwan, they are uncertain about Beijing's intentions. If China were to adopt a less harsh style of rule in Xinjiang and Tibet and be less truculent toward Taiwan, it might more easily gain allies abroad. But if it took a softer stance, Beijing might also face more vigorous separatist movements.

The People's Republic of China has an extraordinary record in economic and technical development. These are both essential elements in its aspiration for global leadership. What we don't know is whether China can maintain its momentum if it can no longer rely on exports to spur growth and it has less access to Western technology as decoupling proceeds. Finally, we also don't know whether Beijing can adjust its governing style to attract and hold important allies.

* * *

In sum, China's current grand strategy depends on three conditions: (1) rapid and steady economic growth, (2) avoidance of any major internal political upheavals, and (3) no effective military balancing by a coalition of outside powers (notably the US, Japan, India, and Australia). A coalition to counterbalance China is not very likely but substantially slowing economic growth and internal political unrest are certainly very possible. Thus, the Chinese juggernaut is a daunting enterprise in the making, but by no means certain to be fully developed by the time of the one-hundredth anniversary of the founding of the People's Republic of China in 1949.

Also, if it can be proved that the Chinese government was directly or indirectly responsible for the spread of the COVID-19 virus, it will be years or possibly decades before other states will trust its word. Under these circumstances, it would be virtually impossible for China to build the kind of alliance system necessary to be the dominant global power. China is already an Asian regional power. Beijing's global aspirations, however, depend on the simultaneous success of its economic, technological, and diplomatic ventures.

NOTES

1   Singapore is a middle-income country, so it isn't likely to be swayed by offers of BRI funds.

2   From its independence in 1947 until roughly 2000, India was unquestionably the dominant power in South Asia. China's link to Pakistan was an annoyance to India, but all the other South Asian states have shown deference to New Delhi.

3 Benkler, *The Wealth of Networks*.

4 Condliffe, "Tik Tok's Troubles Start with Its Success."

5 "China's Huawei Sees 480 Million Households Worldwide Will Gain 5G Access by 2025."

6 Segal, "When China Rules the Web." For example, the UK government has selected Huawei to construct part of its 5G network. This decision has caused considerable friction between the US and UK. At the time of this drafting, there is discussion in the UK about dropping that Huawei contract because of China's handling of the coronavirus issue.

7 Lee, *AI Superpowers*.

8 Meng, "US Technology Chief."

9 Holstein, *The New Art of War*.

10 Auslin, "De-Mystifying Sino-US Decoupling."

11 Broadman, "Forced US-China Decoupling Poses Large Threats."

12 For a comprehensive summary of these Chinese government efforts, see Diamond and Schell, *China's Influence and American Interests*.

13 For a chronology of the steps the Chinese government took in responding to the crisis, see Thiessen, "China Should be Legally Liable for the Pandemic Damage It Has Done."

14 Myers, "China Created a Fail-Safe System to Track Contagions. It Failed."

15 Hamid, "China Is Avoiding Blame by Trolling the World."

16 Li and McElveen, "Mask Diplomacy."

17 China has a long history of epidemics. See Peckham, "Past Pandemics Exposed China's Weaknesses." Major epidemics have included bubonic plague in 1894, pneumonic plague in 1910, cholera and meningitis in 1951, HIV in the 1990s; SARS in 2002–03, and H1N1 in 2009.

18 Eavis, Rappeport, and Swanson, "What Is in (and Not in) the Deal."

19 Farrell and Newman, "Will the Coronavirus End Globalization as We Know It?"

20 Decoupling is not just an issue between the US and China. For example, the European Union faces a fundamental challenge to its cohesion when states like Germany prohibit (as they did recently) the export of medical equipment to Italy and Spain—despite EU rules to the contrary.

21 Lipson, "How the Wuhan Virus Will Change the World Order."

22 Openness about ideas and protection of intellectual property are areas where Western and Chinese views fundamentally differ. See Benner, "US Charges ~Chinese Military Officers in 2017 Equifax Hacking."

23 Wang and Qin, "As Coronavirus Fades in China, Nationalism and Xenophobia Flare."

24 Michta, "The Long Hard Road to Decoupling from China."

25 China has just released "China Standard 2035," a fifteen-year blueprint for the standards of the country's technological development. This supplements "Made in China 2025" and is meant to create standards for 5G products, the internet of things, cloud computing, big data, and artificial intelligence.

26 Burns and Lee, "US Defense Chief Slams China as Rising Threat to World Order."
27 Beech, "A Jungle Airstrip Stirs Suspicions about China's Plans for Cambodia."
28 China's "allies" fit into two broad categories: (1) those where there are formal ties like Friendship Treaties, and (2) countries that informally cooperate on such matters as UN voting. Although China has long claimed it will not have overseas bases or be a "hegemonic power," it is spending over $500 million each on its "facilities" in Gwadar, Pakistan, and Djibouti.
29 Of course, the BRI has its critics, who claim its lending terms are too stringent and that some of the construction is poorly done. Yet no country is required to participate and many of the recipient countries have no plausible chance of borrowing comparable amounts from either commercial or development banks.
30 A Pew Research Center poll of American views in 2020 found that 66 percent of US residents have a negative view of China. That is a 20 percent increase in unfavorable ratings for China since comparable polling was done in 2017. See Devlin, Silver and Huang, "US Views of China Increasingly Negative amid Coronavirus Outbreak."

BIBLIOGRAPHY

Auslin, Michael R. "De-Mystifying Sino-US Decoupling." *Strategyika*, no. 59, Hoover Institution, Stanford University. July 11, 2019. www.hoover.org.

Beech, Hannah. "A Jungle Airstrip Stirs Suspicions about China's Plans for Cambodia." *New York Times*, December 22, 2019. www.nytimes.com.

Benkler, Yochai. *The Wealth of Networks*. New Haven, CT: Yale University Press, 2006.

Benner, Katie. "US Charges Chinese Military Officers in 2017 Equifax Hacking." *New York Times*, February 10, 2020. www.nytimes.com.

Broadman, Harry G. "Forced US-China Decoupling Poses Large Threats." *Forbes*, September 30, 2019. www.forbes.com.

Burns, Robert, and Matthew Lee. "US Defense Chief Slams China as Rising Threat to World Order." Associated Press. February 15, 2020. https://apnews.com.

"China's Huawei Sees 480 Million Households Worldwide Will Gain 5G Access by 2025: Executive." Reuters. October 29, 2019. www.reuters.com.

Condliffe, Jamie. "Tik Tok's Troubles Start with Its Success." *New York Times*, November 11, 2019.

Devlin, Kat, Laura Silver, and Christine Huang. "US Views of China Increasingly Negative amid Coronavirus Outbreak." Pew Research Center, April 22, 2020. www.pewresearch.org.

Diamond, Larry, and Orville Schell, eds. *China's Influence and American Interests: Promoting Constructive Vigilance*. New York: Hoover Institution and the Asia Society, 2018.

Eavis, Peter, Alan Rappeport, and Ana Swanson. "What Is in (and Not in) the Deal." *New York Times*, January 15, 2020. www.nytimes.com.

Farrell, Henry, and Abraham Newman. "Will the Coronavirus End Globalization as We Know It?" *Foreign Affairs*, March 16, 2020. www.foreignaffairs.com.

Hamid, Shadi. "China Is Avoiding Blame by Trolling the World." *Atlantic*, March 19, 2020. www.theatlantic.com.

Holstein, William. *The New Art of War: China's Deep Strategy inside the United States*. Dering, New York: Brick Tower Press, 2019.

Lee, Kai Fu. *AI Superpowers: China, Silicon Valley, and the New World Order*. New York: Houghton Mifflin, 2018.

Li, Cheng and Ryan McElveen. "Mask Diplomacy: Coronavirus Upended Generations of China-Japan Antagonism." *China-US Focus*, March 10, 2020. www.chinausfocus. com.

Lipson, Charles. "How the Wuhan Virus Will Change the World Order." Real Clear Politics. April 8, 2020. www.realclearpolitics.com.

Meng, Jing. "US Technology Chief: China Is Threatening America's Lead in the Global AI Race." *South China Morning Post*, September 11, 2019. www.scmp.com.

Michta, Andrew A. "The Long Hard Road to Decoupling from China." *American Interest*, April 12, 2020. www.the-american-interest.com.

Myers, Steven Lee. "China Created a Fail-Safe System to Track Contagions. It Failed." *New York Times*, March 29, 2020. www.nytimes.com.

Peckham, Robert. "Past Pandemics Exposed China's Weaknesses." *Foreign Affairs*, March 27, 2020. www.foreignaffairs.com.

Segal, Adam. "When China Rules the Web." *Foreign Affairs* 97, no. 5 (September/ October 2018): 10–18.

Thiessen, Marc A. "China Should be Legally Liable for the Pandemic Damage It Has Done." *Washington Post*, April 10, 2020. www.washingtonpost.com.

Wang, Vivian, and Amy Qin. "As Coronavirus Fades in China, Nationalism and Xenophobia Flare." *New York Times*, April 16, 2020. www.nytimes.com.

ACKNOWLEDGMENTS

Special thanks go to Ilene Kalish of NYU Press, who gave us most helpful counsel as this project developed. We are also particularly grateful to Zheng He, who provided superb research assistance and suggestions on the manuscript throughout the project. The following people also made insightful suggestions: Carter Booth, Jennifer Carpenter, Jerome Cohen, Richard Katz, Winston Lord, Joydeep Mukherji, and Kim Schoenholtz. Moreover, skillful research assistance was provided by Weiyue Chen, Jasmine Lee, Xing Liu, Dongbo Wang, and Kaibo Wang. Finally, thanks go to the NYU Center on US-China Relations for its support of this project.

APPENDIX

Major Stated Chinese National Goals

1. Two Centenary Goals (September 12, 1997)
    Build a modern, socialist society by 2021 (the one-hundredth anniversary
        of the founding of the Chinese Communist Party)
    Build an advanced and harmonious society by 2049 (the one-hundredth
        anniversary of the founding of the People's Republic of China)
2. Four-Pronged Comprehensive Strategy (December 14, 2015)
    Build a moderately prosperous society
    Deepen Reform
    Advance law-based governance
    Strengthen party discipline
3. Silk Road Economic Belt (September 2013)
    Belt & Road Initiative (October 2013)
4. Made in China 2025 Strategy (March 5, 2015)
5. "National Defense in the New Era" white paper (July 2019)
6. Education Modernization 2035 Plan (February 23, 2019)
7. Internet Plus Plan (July 4, 2015)
8. National Cyber-Security Strategy (December 27, 2016)
9. Rural Revitalization Strategy (October 18, 2017)

ABOUT THE EDITOR

DAVID B. H. DENOON is Professor of Politics and Economics at New York University and Director of the NYU Center on US-China Relations. He has served in the federal government in three positions: Program Economist for USAID in Jakarta, Vice President of the US Export-Import Bank, and Deputy Assistant Secretary of Defense. Professor Denoon is a member of the Council on Foreign Relations, the National Committee on US-China Relations, the Asia Society, and the US-Indonesia Society. He is Chairman of the Editorial Advisory Board of Great Decisions. He is the author and editor of nine books, including *Real Reciprocity—Balancing US Economic and Security Policy in the Pacific Basin*. He has five recent books: a monograph titled *The Economic and Strategic Rise of China and India*, an edited volume, *China: Contemporary Political, Economic, and International Affairs* (NYU Press), and he is also editor and contributor to a three-volume series: *China and the US: The Future of Central Asia* (Vol I, 2015), *Southeast Asia* (Vol II, 2017) and *Latin America* (Vol III, 2017).

ABOUT THE CONTRIBUTORS

PAUL BRACKEN is Professor at the Department of Political Science of Yale University. He focuses on global competition and the strategic application of technology in business and defense. He is a consultant to private equity funds, accounting, and insurance companies as well as several arms of the US government. He has led games on the future of European asset management, US financial services re-regulation, and strategies of technological competition with China. A member of the Council on Foreign Relations, he serves on the Chief of Naval Operations Executive Panel, and co-chairs the Board of Advisors of the US Naval War College and the Naval Postgraduate School. His books include *The Second Nuclear Age: Strategy, Danger, and the New Power Politics* (2012), *Managing Strategic Surprise: Lessons from Risk Management and Risk Assessment* (2005), and *Fire in the East: The Rise of Asian Military Power and the Second Nuclear Age* (1999).

RALPH A. COSSA is former president and Worldwide Support for Development-Handa Chair at the Pacific Forum. Cossa is a member of the ASEAN Regional Forum Experts and Eminent Persons Group. He is a founding member of the multinational track-two Council for Security Cooperation in the Asia Pacific (CSCAP). He co-chairs the CSCAP study group aimed at halting the proliferation of weapons of mass destruction in the Asia-Pacific and is the executive director of the US CSCAP Member Committee (USCSCAP). He serves on the Board of the Council on US-Korean Security Studies and the National Committee on US-China Relations (NY). His publications include *The United States and the Asia-Pacific Region: Security Strategy for the Obama Administration* (Washington DC: Center for a New American Security, 2009); "US-Japan Relations: What Should Washington Do?" in *America's Role in Asia: Recommendations for US Policy from Both Sides of the Pacific* (San Francisco: Asia Foundation, 2008); and *An East Asian Community and the United States*, Ralph A. Cossa and Akihiko Tanaka, eds. (Washington, DC: CSIS Press, 2007).

ANDREW C. KUCHINS is president of the American University of Central Asia in Bishkek, Kyrgyzstan. From 2007 to 2015 he was Director of the Russia and Eurasian Program at the Center for Strategic and International Studies in Washington, DC, and from 2000 through 2007 he also held a series of positions with the Carnegie Endowment for International Peace. His recent scholarship has been devoted to issues including US-Russia relations, Russia's Asia strategy, and the role of energy in the Russian Far East. His recent publications include "Perspective: What's to Follow the Demise of the US-Russian 'Reset'" (*Current History*, October 2012); "The End of the 'Reset'" (*Foreign Affairs*, March 2012); "Russian Foreign Policy: Continuity in Change," coauthored with Igor Zevelev (*Washington Quarterly*, Winter 2012); "Laying the Groundwork for Afghanistan's New Silk Road" (*Foreign Affairs*, December 2011); and "Putin's Return and Washington's Reset With Russia" (*Foreign Affairs*, September 2011).

HE LI is a Professor of Political Science at Merrimack College, Massachusetts. He has written widely in his field, with articles in leading scholarly journals and three books to his credit, and he is the series editor of the Modern Chinese Thinkers series. Dr. Li has also been a Fulbright Scholar in Taiwan (2004) and China (2015) and the recipient of major research grants and fellowships from organizations including the Ford Foundation, the Henry Luce Foundation, the Tinker Foundation, and the Chiang Ching-Kuo Foundation for International Scholarly Exchange. Professor Li's most recent publications include "China's Rise in Latin America: Myths and Realities" (in *China, The United States and the Future of Latin America*, ed. David Denoon, 2017), "Chinese Discourse on Constitutionalism and Its Impact on Reforms" (*Journal of Chinese Political Science*, 2017), and "The Chinese Model of Development and Its Implications" (*World Journal of Social Science Research*, 2015).

ANN MARIE MURPHY joined the School of Diplomacy and International Relations at Seton Hall University as Assistant Professor in 2004.

Prior to joining Seton Hall University, she taught at Columbia University and Barnard College. Concurrent with her appointment at the School of Diplomacy and International Relations, Dr. Murphy is a Senior Research Scholar at the Weatherhead East Asian Institute, Columbia University and an Associate Fellow of the Asia Society. At Columbia University, Dr. Murphy chairs the University Seminar on Contemporary Southeast Asia. She has also been a visiting scholar at the Centre for Strategic and International Studies, Jakarta, Indonesia, and the Institute for Security and International Studies, Bangkok, Thailand. Dr. Murphy's research interests include international relations in Asia, political development in Southeast Asia, US foreign policy toward Southeast Asia, and the rise of transnational issues such as climate change and global health. With the support of a grant from the Smith Richardson Foundation, she is currently researching and writing a book on the impact of democratization on Indonesian foreign policy.

GULSHAN SACHDEVA is Jean Monnet Chair and Director, Europe Area Studies Program, School of International Studies at Jawaharlal Nehru University (JNU), New Delhi. He is also Editor-in-Chief of International Studies. He headed the ADB and the Asia Foundation projects at the Afghanistan Ministry of Foreign Affairs in Kabul (2006–10). Earlier he was Chairperson, Centre for European Studies and Director Energy Studies Program at JNU. His research interests include the European Union, Eurasian integration, Afghanistan, development cooperation, and energy security. He was Indian Council for Cultural Relations (ICCR) Chair on Contemporary India at the University of Leuven; and Visiting Professor at the University of Warsaw, University of Trento, University of Antwerp, Corvinus University of Budapest, and Mykolas Romers University, Vilnius. His recent publications include *India in a Reconnecting Eurasia* (Washington: CSIS, 2016) and *Evaluation of the EU-India Strategic Partnership and the Potential for its Revitalization* (Brussels: European Parliament, 2015).

ROBERT SUTTER is Professor of Practice of International Affairs at the Elliott School of George Washington University beginning in 2011. He also serves as the school's Director, Program of Bachelor of Arts in International Affairs. A PhD graduate in History and East Asian Languages from Harvard University, Sutter taught full time for ten years at Georgetown University's School of Foreign Service and part-time for thirty years at Georgetown, George Washington, Johns Hopkins Universities, and the University of Virginia. His most recent books are: *Foreign Relations of the PRC: The Legacies and Constraints of China's International Politics since 1949* (Rowman & Littlefield 2018); *US-China Relations: Perilous Past, Uncertain Present* (Rowman & Littlefield 2018); *Chinese Foreign Relations: Power and Policy since the Cold War* (Rowman & Littlefield 2016); *The United States and Asia; Regional Dynamics and 21st Century Relations* (Rowman & Littlefield 2015).

JOSHUA W. WALKER was recently named president of the Japan Society in the United States. He got his BA from the University of Richmond, an MA in international relations from Yale University, and a PhD from Princeton University in Politics and Public Policy. Formerly he was the Global Head of Strategic Initiatives and Japan, Office of the President at Eurasia Group. He has actively expanded Eurasia Group's global events and new business offerings, including leading the company's first-ever geopolitical summit in Japan. Joshua had more than two decades of international business experience before becoming the founding dean of the APCO Institute and senior vice president of global programs at APCO Worldwide. Before joining the private sector, he worked in numerous roles at various US government agencies, including the State Department and the Defense Department. He was also a Transatlantic Fellow at the German Marshall Fund of the United States and taught leadership and the American presidency at George Mason University.

ZHIQUN ZHU is Professor of Political Science and International Relations at Bucknell University. He is Bucknell's inaugural director of the China Institute (2013–17) and MacArthur Chair in East Asian politics (2008–14). Dr. Zhu's teaching and research interests include Chinese politics and foreign policy, East Asian political economy, and US-China relations. He is the author and editor of over ten books, including *Understanding East Asia's Economic "Miracles"* (Association for Asian Studies, 2016); *China's New Diplomacy: Rationale, Strategies and Significance* (Ashgate, 2013); *New Dynamics in East Asian Politics: Security, Political Economy, and Society* (Continuum International, 2012); and

US-China Relations in the 21st Century: Power Transition and Peace (Routledge, 2005). Professor Zhu has received several research fellowships and grants, including two POSCO fellowships at the East-West Center in Hawaii, a Korea Foundation/Freeman Foundation grant to do research in Korea, two visiting fellowships at the East Asian Institute of National University of Singapore, a visiting professorship at Doshisha University in Japan, and a research grant from the American Political Science Association.

INDEX

Page numbers in *italics* indicate Tables.

www.ingramcontent.com/pod-product-compliance
Lightning Source LLC
Chambersburg PA
CBHW020247030426
42336CB00010B/659